Of Games and God

Of Games and God

A Christian Exploration of Video Games

KEVIN SCHUT

Foreword by
QUENTIN J. SCHULTZE

BrazosPress

a division of Baker Publishing Group
Grand Rapids, Michigan

© 2013 by Kevin Schut

Published by Brazos Press
a division of Baker Publishing Group
P.O. Box 6287, Grand Rapids, MI 49516-6287
www.brazospress.com

Printed in the United States of America

Library of Congress Cataloging-in-Publication Data is on file at the Library of Congress, Washington, DC.

ISBN 978-1-58743-325-2

Scripture quotations marked NIV are from the Holy Bible, New International Version®. NIV®. Copyright © 1973, 1978, 1984, 2011 by Biblica, Inc.™ Used by permission of Zondervan. All rights reserved worldwide. www.zondervan.com

Scripture quotations marked NKJV are from the New King James Version. Copyright © 1982 by Thomas Nelson, Inc. Used by permission. All rights reserved.

The internet addresses, email addresses, and phone numbers in this book are accurate at the time of publication. They are provided as a resource. Baker Publishing Group does not endorse them or vouch for their content or permanence.

13   14   15   16   17   18   19   7   6   5   4   3   2   1

For Kristin

You are a part of everything I write

***

Contents

Foreword

In today's era of smart phones and dumb users, the term "angry birds" quickly became associated with a mini-gaming application—an "app." The app captured players around the globe who, because of boredom, curiosity, or peer persuasion, digitally transferred a few dollars to a cyberstore to join the angry-birding fold.

Meanwhile, young software developers from Seattle to Jakarta tried to create the next big game that would temporarily saturate the expanding gaming-app marketplace. Programmers played with technology in hopes of creating a paying technology.

Perhaps nothing is more natural for human beings than play. When I was a young boy growing up in Chicago, on some muggy and boring summer days my neighborhood peers and I seemed to exhaust every method of generating fun. Then one of us would ask one of the most important questions about life, "Whaddaya wanna do?" That question was all it took to get us back to play. Most of us were Roman Catholics, and we would then respond together, like a Gregorian chant, "Sit in the shade and go pooh pooh."

No matter how many summer days we resorted to that ritual, it always worked. We laughed together. For a few moments, we re-created the verbal playground of childhood delight. We didn't need a theology of creation or recreation to embellish let alone justify our scatological humor. We never wondered if Adam and Eve played in their yard. Play for us was the most natural thing in the world—much more heavenly than school. Play was right and fitting, the way the world was supposed to be. The devil was in the agony of July boredom.

Play seems to be so basic to the way we're created that it pops up in all human activities. In fact, we intentionally or unintentionally invent ritualistic forms of play that lend a kind of liturgical quality to everyday life. Just as we delight in worship, we delight in gaming. We don't worship the game or its creators. But we discover pleasure by participating in the playful rituals that others have created for us to enjoy—even if they make a few dollars off of us along the way.

I create play for myself while studying and writing at home. Outside my home office is a hanging bird feeder framed by a casement window. Constant visual motion occurs on the other side of the window. It's like a looping video image. Goldfinches and house finches playfully push each other around to get access to the seed while chickadees dart in and out of the playing field without joining the ongoing mischief. The birds never stop jockeying around, nosing each other, squawking and peeping while grabbing, cracking open, and scarfing down safflower seeds.

I let the birds play until I get bored. Then I might let loose with a red tailed hawk call from the app on my phone. The next time I might tap lightly on the window pane—just enough to cause them to cock their heads and listen up. But most of the time I just chat with them. I ask them to get creative, to attempt a novel ornithological game for the pleasure of their human observer.

And occasionally it works. One scruffy male house finch will climb up the cylindrical meshing on the outside of the feeder and let himself down on the inside, right on top of the seed that's being dispensed underneath him to his feathered neighbors. He knows I will not stand for it; like one of Pavlov's subjects, I always come over to the window and clap my hands to scare the scruffy scoundrel out of there before he drops white bombs on his friends' vittles. "What's with this clown?" I mutter to myself out loud, shaking my head. And he probably wonders what's with me. So the play goes on, back and forth, until I'm no longer sure who's in charge of the game. I'm caught up in the flow of my entertaining bird-human ritual.

I think my neighborhood friends and I had it right on those summer days, playing at playing without excessive worry, absent the nasty conflicts that divide human beings around the world. There is something so fitting about playful delight that God commanded the ancient Hebrews to rediscover it every week on the Sabbath. Today, as a more cynical human being—what seems to count for a mature adult—I yearn for those leisurely yet adventurous days under the elm leaves in our tiny backyards.

In this fine book, Professor Kevin Schut has kept his Christian, scholarly head about him while simultaneously letting the joy of play speak to us. He rightly tells us, without preaching, that gaming at its best is a form of play and needs no justification. Play is as important as work in our lives. Those of us who can't play a game are also humorless people who take ourselves too seriously.

Those of us who see others having a good time and feel like they should instead be laboring in the vineyard of paid employment, or studying Scripture, are sad souls who need an extra measure of unmerited grace to seduce us back into the luxurious yards of our more innocent youth. Often we're too quick to reject too much of one good thing and to embrace too much of a different good thing. Work is essential as stewardship of creation, but so is play. Play can help us to flourish as emotionally healthy people. Sabbath keeping and play are intimately related. When we rob our lives of play we game God's system.

One measure of play in our era is how thoroughly technological so much of even our good gaming is becoming. Young and old alike are increasingly defining gaming as a kind of manufactured, standardized form of play whose rules are dictated by distant programmers and regulated through computer networks. That's not all bad. Regardless of how technological a game is, someone has to set the rules.

I want rules for my games, just as I need some liturgical order in my worship. And in both cases I want rules that make me feel good about what I'm doing. I don't like outsiders gaming me—unless I appreciate the way they set up the rules. So it is that each of us tends to prefer some games and some rules over others. There is a considerable measure of personal taste in what we like. *Of Games and God* helps us understand how Christians sometimes use their personal preferences about high-tech gaming to criticize others about their play.

Jean Shepherd, who wrote the screenplay for *A Christmas Story*—now the most popular holiday-season movie—once told me that holy wars start at the local church-league baseball games. Many Christians' strong feelings about which games are appropriate to play sound like the fiery rhetoric over appropriate worship music. Professor Schut instead offers balance and moderation in his well-informed assessments of digital gaming. He's charitable toward all sides even as he holds up the possibility that there is more "liturgical" good in gaming than is dreamt of in our philosophizing about it.

I don't need high-tech games to be delighted. But is that because of my generation? Am I missing new avenues of delight just because the rules of the game are foreign to me? Am I turned off by stereotypes about electronic gaming, especially the notion that the high-tech rules lack proper decorum? Or am I scared of the possibility that high-tech gaming, compared with the simpler board games I grew up with, might better allow players to write the rules along the way? Is that too much like Pentecostal liturgy for me? I feel that by regularly playing Scrabble I have affirmed my Presbyterian sensibilities. Is there an older Presbyterian who doesn't play Scrabble? Where are the Lutherans and Methodists on the high-tech gaming issue? Missional church folks? Read *Of Games and God* and then speak up!

Of Games and God shows us the relationships among faith, gaming, and technology. It challenges us to consider how much our positive and negative views of gaming are analogous to our opinions about faith. The book accepts the likely possibility that God has even more delight ready for us to enjoy in video gaming. But it reveals that gaming is implicitly like worship liturgy. After reading this book someone will probably write a doctoral dissertation titled, "Worshiping Outside the Xbox: Liturgical Styles in Secular Computer Gaming."

Professor Schut discerningly explores the developing world of computer and video gaming, in which the players can freely create and enjoy fictional worlds. To some people, such virtual worlds are scary. If my children were young I would probably be leery myself. But then I recall the fact that we did similar things with low-tech means in my day. We grabbed junk from backyards and created our own little circuses and carnivals. We used the technologies of our hands and feet, coupled with our God-given communication abilities, to fabricate our own tiny universes of fun. Then we acted out our roles within our contrived universes.

Of course gaming can be serious business; it can be worldview oriented, a matter of intra-game life and death. Our games can reflect some of our deepest desires for good and bad for ourselves and others. They can play on our existing stereotypes and help us to convince ourselves that caring for our neighbors is not as vitally important as ridding ourselves of neighbors we don't like. There is on-screen, realistic fighting and abject violence. There are the video games that seem like training modules for children to learn how to run remote-controlled killing machines.

A few years ago I asked Professor Schut to demonstrate some cutting-edge computer-gaming software in my seminary class at Regent College in

Vancouver, British Columbia. The class was made up of graduate students from nearly every continent and represented a wide range of ages. Even the techno-savvy students were amazed at some of the games we previewed. Professor Schut demonstrated games that challenged and delighted us.

He taught me to be more open-minded about the high-tech gaming frontier. I needed that for the sake of my own teaching. Calvinist professors like me are not known for being the most fun-loving creatures in the classroom. Now when my own students start talking about computer games in those preciously revealing moments before I call a class to attention, I listen in and learn about the games they're playing.

I know wonderfully gifted college professors who employ gaming to teach some of the most important truths about human nature, social institutions, and human decision making. I know teachers who successfully use games to teach students how to think and to expand their imaginations. I yearn to be better at that, to know how to more fully engage the imaginations of my students in the process of learning so that they might not just know the course material, but may more fully see themselves as imaginative and responsible players in God's own creation.

I admit that I bothered Professor Schut for a number of years until he finally agreed to write this book. Having surveyed the landscape of books on the topic, I felt that a book like this simply had to be written. I knew he was the one to write it. *Of Games and God* shows on every page that mind-engaging, heart-opening gaming can bring us healthy delight and help us to be more faithful stewards of God's neighborhood. Thanks to God for giving us a playground for gaming. Thanks to Professor Schut for showing us the possibilities as well as the potential pitfalls in the expanding world of electronic gaming.

—Quentin J. Schultze, author and Arthur H. DeKruyter Chair in the department of Communication Arts and Sciences at Calvin College

Preface

Just like a good video game, I have faced a few significant challenges while writing this book. Challenge #1: compact time and space. There are too many things to talk about. Readers who are gamers are going to wonder how I could do an entire book without really talking about Nintendo's *Zelda* games or *Madden NFL* or whatever. I try to at least dip my toe in the most popular **worlds**, but I have gaps in my experiences as a gamer. (NOTE: When you see a **bolded** word in the text, look for a definition of it, as used in the video game universe, in the glossary that begins on page 199.) Likewise, topics are missing and others are only barely addressed. I could do an entire book on race, class, gender, and sexuality in video games, or many chapters on the kinds of religious perspectives video games encode. I'm missing important academic perspectives—there are books I haven't read and articles I've forgotten to cite.

Challenge #2: I'm writing for a lot of different people. Some of my readers will be **hardcore** gamers who will find much of my explanation to be tedious and obvious. Others will be video-game novices, who might think I'm assuming too much or going too fast. I have tried my best to strike a balance, but I know it won't always work.

Challenge #3: conversations about video games have a "best before" date, and anything that arrives in print is going to be stale the minute it's picked up. The video-game world moves quickly, and some of the games I cite heavily will look ancient to gamers even when this book is new, let alone after it is two years old. I have tried to deal with this by mentioning game *series* where possible, as their relevant features tend to stay the same from sequel to sequel. I have also tried to draw on examples from all over video-game history so that the book has a fairly long time line.

All this is to say that if readers think I've neglected an important game or topic, have not gone deep enough, or have made arguments that are obsolete, they're probably right. And I hope this doesn't matter too much. In the end, I hope the reader will forgive these shortcomings because this book is not intended to be the final word: I have designed it to be a conversation starter. Carefully researched and written Christian commentary on video games is really just starting to get going in earnest, mostly on blogs and online magazines—*Halos and Avatars* was the first book-length treatment of video games from a Christian perspective, and is the only one I know of at the time of writing this book. There's so much more to say, and I look forward to others improving what I've written here.

Enough instructions. Press "Start" to begin.

Acknowledgments

I have a T-shirt that says "I never finish anyth"

I wore it a lot while I was writing this book, as a challenge to myself. I've never done anything like this before, and I'm deeply grateful that God has provided me the opportunity and means to do it. While writing is a highly individualistic activity, it can't happen without a huge amount of support, and I want to recognize a few of the people most directly responsible for helping me finish.

First, I owe much to the communities where I live and work: the city of Abbotsford, Trinity Christian Reformed Church, and especially my colleagues at Trinity Western University. The latter have been models of good scholarship, great encouragers, wise advisers, and good friends—especially my coworkers in the Department of Media + Communication and the School of the Arts, Media + Culture. And thanks to my administrators for granting me a sabbatical in the fall of 2011; it made this book happen. It's great to work in such a stimulating and supportive environment!

I am deeply grateful for games and gamers. My thanks to Sid Meier, to BioWare and Bethesda and Blizzard, to Jenova Chen and Gary Grigsby, to Telltale Games, Interplay, Epyx, Cyan Worlds, Riot Games, LucasArts, and so many more for entertaining, inspiring, and provoking me, and for giving me such an interesting line of work. I'm also thankful for the Vanguard gaming group in Abbotsford, my friends in Edmonton, my friends from Calvin College, and my siblings and parents, who've gamed with me all my life. A special thanks to the gamers who responded to my survey and to the game makers who did their interviews with me—you guys rock!

I have had incredible help in writing this book. The people at Brazos, including Robert Hosack and Lisa Ann Cockrel, have been awesome. I've also had a bunch of readers giving me great feedback at every step of this process. Former students Keharn Yawnghwe and Mark McIntosh, my friend James Bentum, my former pastor Jim Dekker, and my mom, Jessie Schut, have all given me incredible feedback on both the content and the writing. My friend Mike Terbeek is one of the sharpest people I know, and his extensive comments have made this a better book. My former student Janelle Weibelzahl was my unofficial editor, working on my book proposal for course credits, but then continuing to give me great feedback after she graduated.

This is a work of scholarship, and so I owe a great debt to all the teachers and professors I've had who taught me what I know about reading, writing, and thinking. I still remember lessons I received in the Edmonton Christian school system, writing tips from my profs at Calvin College, and the best role models for cultural scholarship at the University of Iowa. One person in particular, however, deserves special mention. Dr. Quentin Schultze, my prof at Calvin and peerless mentor of so many students, has continued to guide and encourage me in my career. He suggested I go into Communication Studies as an academic field, has encouraged me in my scholarship, first suggested I write this book, helped me prepare the proposal, and then essentially acted as my agent. I can't repay that—I only hope I can be half as good a prof for my students. This is what building the kingdom of God is about.

Of course, there's nobody in this world I love and cherish more than my family. My siblings, siblings-in-law, parents, and parents-in-law are nothing but supportive. My daughters—Karina, Geneva, and Aerin—are my gifts from God, and their love gives me the joy that animates my work. My wife and best friend, Kristin, has known me all my life, and I can't even begin to count the ways that she makes it possible for me to do anything. I love her more than any other person.

Finally, to God be the glory. The great message of Jesus's gospel is that all that is offered to him is accepted as beautiful, no matter how flawed it is. Have this book, Lord.

Finding Balance in an Unbalanced Discussion

Starting a Journey

Reality is mundane, completely devoid of swashbuckling and derring-do.

The boy starts his journey in a dimly-lit room, oblivious of his surroundings. The sole object of significance is the little beige box with the dark brown keyboard, connected to a loud, clacking cube that eagerly devours a big floppy disk.

```
LOAD "*" , 8, 1 _
```

The machine launches the world into slow motion. After an endless wait, the silhouette of a ship with full sails against a moonlit sky appears. Pasted on top in giant letters: "Pirates!" The boy plunges in.

The black-and-white fifteen-inch TV screen is home to the Caribbean, a world of Spanish, French, Dutch, and English merchants, governors, forts, duels, and—of course—buried treasure. The boy daringly storms

1

the battlements of Cartagena, chases the Spanish Treasure Fleet, searches for hints of his long-lost family, earns promotions from governors, and builds an estate for the inevitable retirement from years of adventuring.

Two hours turn into years in this magical land, but the boy must depart. He will return many times, however, to the sandy shores of Curacao; later to the war-torn skies of 1940s Europe; later still to the depths of ancient history, the endless expanses of starry skies, and mythical castles in fantastic lands. The journey still continues.

Sid Meier's Pirates! first released in 1987. The player is a privateer in the Caribbean, and engages in ship-to-ship combat, sword fighting, treasure hunting, and land battles.

Confessions of a Gamer in a Christian Community

This book is about helping the Christian community find a balanced approach to computer and video games—and also, I hope, a little about helping people outside the Christian community understand some of the issues relating to faith and games. But in the interest of being open, I should let readers know where I'm coming from: the warm and sometimes smothering embrace of gaming culture. Yes, I'm a lifelong gamer; the boy playing *Sid Meier's Pirates!* in the story above was me.

I played chess and *Monopoly* growing up, and when my family bought our first Commodore 64 home computer (the machine described above), my eyes were opened to a whole new world of games. I've blasted spiders in *Centipede* and spent hundreds of hours sailing the Caribbean waters in all three versions of *Sid Meier's Pirates!* College homework hours were sucked up by the collectible card game *Magic: The Gathering*, weekly Thursday night tabletop war games with seventy-page rule books written in nine-point font, and Sunday night role-playing sessions. *Settlers of Catan* and the German board-game scene are my new obsession. And towering above them all is the world-history strategy-simulator *Civilization* (Sid Meier owes me at least a month or two of my life back).

My graduate-studies professor told us in our first class that we should study what we love. It took me only a few minutes to embark on a career of studying computer games. I've often joked with friends that my field of study is really just an excuse to play games and get paid for it. Except that it's not really a joke (ask my long-suffering wife).

I say all this so readers understand where I'm coming from. A big part of me would like nothing more than to stand up and zing off a loud-and-proud defense of gaming. And I suspect that this bias is going to leak through all over the place. I've tried very hard to stay balanced, but if I lean in a direction, it's to praise games.

There's another part to this story, however, and that's what underlies my motivation in this book. Since I was a teenager, I've had to struggle with reconciling this big part of my life—my love of games—with the *biggest* part of my life: my Christian faith. I was raised in a community that believed God was the Creator and Ruler of all things, and that God matters in everything we do. But for many years, God didn't seem to have much of an opinion about games—at least, nobody in the church said much about *Monopoly* or chess. Sure, I knew lots of Christians who *played* games, but nobody ever connected that with God. Not like work or education or art.

When I *did* finally start to hear Christian commentary on any kind of game, it was almost always a complaint or an attack. Just like heavy metal music and horror movies, **role-playing games** (**RPGs**) flirted with satanic spirits. And just like TV, computer games sucked time away from wholesome things like physical activity and homework. Of course, as with many Christian teens, that didn't stop me from playing. It just made me feel vaguely defensive and guilty about something I enjoyed. But as I grew older and my faith grew more sophisticated, I started to engage the idea of games as good or bad—or, more precisely, what games were good and bad at doing. It's an internal struggle that continues to this day.

What This Book Is About

This book is my attempt to work out the relationship between Christian faith and games. I am *not* writing a review book on specific games; anything like that would soon be hopelessly outdated. I respect people who take the time to write guides, but what we really need is a way to think about God, faith, video games, and gaming culture. If we can learn to think critically, we can be our own guides.

Video games are a blind spot for many Christians, but they shouldn't be. In terms of money alone, the game industry is huge—not quite the size of the global film industry, but in the same multibillion dollar neighborhood.[1] More important, video games are a major catalyst for changes in the way we think and relate to one another. We need to talk about them seriously and think about them carefully. This book is written to help Christians do that thinking, but not to do the thinking *for* them.

Loving and Hating Games

There is no shortage of thinking and debating about games. Ever since they became a major cultural force in the late 1970s and early 1980s, video games have received both praise and condemnation.

The Game Enthusiasts

Gamers, whether Christian or not, are enthusiastic about their pastime. They rave about video games online, badger reluctant houseguests with "you gotta see this!" and spend many hours a week playing. Ask gamers why they love games so much and they'll be ready with a passionate set of justifications—sometimes even if they're *not* asked.

The heart of games, enthusiasts argue, is that nebulous buzzword *interactivity*. Of course, *everything's* interactive these days—our TVs, our cars, our crackling bowls of cereal. What gamers mean by it is that when we get involved with games, we do stuff that *changes* the game.[2] In other words, we're not just sitting back and finding out if Harry Potter wins the Quidditch match; we're making him do it ourselves (or not, depending on our skill).

Not only are games interactive, but—second overused term alert!— they're also *immersive*. Video games suck the player in. When a player gets into a game, the sense of focus and the rhythm of play create an intense experience some theorists describe as *flow*.[3] Good books or movies can immerse us in fictional worlds, but with a good game, it doesn't just feel like we're looking in—it feels like we're *there*. (More on this in chapter 5.)

Game fans also talk a lot about the social aspects of games. This may come as a surprise for nongamers. The long-held stereotype of the computer gamer is a solitary teenaged boy hunched in front of a flickering screen in his parents' basement. But gamers today are a diverse, vibrant community, and most games invite some kind of social connection. Many gamers, in fact, insist there's something special about friendships formed over games.[4] (More on this in chapter 9.)

Some gamers also note the ability of games to exercise the human desire for fantasy.[5] While game fans of all sorts mention this, the Christian game community has a special connection between the appeal of the fantastic and the writings of C. S. Lewis and J. R. R. Tolkien. As we'll explore in chapter 5, these authors argued that fantasy gives us a deeper appreciation of reality, and games are fantasy builders par excellence.

Other Christians describe games as potential avenues for the betterment of the human condition. Specifically, they argue games are good for teaching uplifting things—such as improving character, morality, and biblical knowledge—and even evangelism.[6] (We'll mostly talk about this in chapter 7, but also touch on it in chapters 2, 4, and 9.)

Finally, people are increasingly realizing the artistic and creative potential of games.[7] While this is not a dominant theme in Christian gamer discourse, there's a natural connection. If Christians really want to argue that God loves expressions of creativity and beauty, then it makes sense to celebrate games just as much as sculpture, music, and novels. (This is partly what chapter 8 is about.)

The Game Critics

Of course, if we hear anything from the Christian community about games, it's typically the bad stuff. Game critics, whether Christian or not, range from full-out anti-game crusaders to mildly concerned parents, so it's important to note that people deliver the following lines of argument with differing levels of vehemence.

Game critics commonly note objectionable content as a major concern.[8] Until recently, most top-selling games featured some type of violence, a trend continued today by the *Halo*, *Grand Theft Auto*, and *Call of Duty* series. While this emphasis on guns, gore, and explosions is shifting as the game industry starts concentrating increasingly on mass audiences (we'll discuss this in more detail in chapter 4), in some cases, the shift has led to new emphasis on an old concern: sex. Some critics attack *The Sims* series for permitting homosexual relationships[9] and point to titles like the 2003 *Dead or Alive: Extreme Beach Volleyball*, with its bikini-clad, impossibly pneumatic beach volleyball players, to show that the industry has brought the exploitation of women to new lows (discussed in chapter 6).

Another major issue for game critics (discussed in chapter 5) is the growing specter of game addiction. The very immersive quality that game fans love is the trap that can keep them in the game for longer than is healthy. It's one thing when the occasional session lasts a few hours. It's another thing again when employees don't show up for work and friends go AWOL because they won't stop playing *World of Warcraft*. Game addiction isn't a clinical term, but many anecdotes and studies clearly demonstrate a link between games and addictive behavior.[10]

A uniquely Christian complaint about games involves spiritual issues. The RPG *Dungeons and Dragons* hit mainstream infamy in the early 1980s, in part because a series of groups publicly linked it with witchcraft and demon-possession.[11] Some Christians made similar claims with the enormously popular *Pokemon* game and its associated television shows and merchandise.[12] Critics argue that games like this contain sorcerous elements and unholy symbols that encourage the corruption of players. Although the degree of furor surrounding these specific games has died down, many Christians still have a lingering distrust of games featuring magic (discussed in chapter 3).

While these worries grab the lion's share of the airtime given to game critiques, they are not the only complaints people make. Many critics, for example, complain games are physically unhealthy and tied to laziness. Games are linked with a wide range of antisocial tendencies, including, but not limited to, disrespect for parental authority, an unhealthy fascination with control, a tendency to view other people as means to an end, and a poor appreciation of the consequences of actions.[13]

Loving and Hating New Media Is Nothing New

What's particularly interesting about this back-and-forth conversation is that it's not new, even though video games themselves are a relatively recent arrival. All this has happened before, and all this will happen again.

Fearing New Technology and Popular Culture

Video games are not understood by the present generation of adults. They are new; they make an enormous appeal to children; and they present ideas and situations that parents may not like. Consequently, when parents think of the welfare of their children who are exposed to these compelling situations, they wonder about the effects of the games upon the ideals and behavior of their children. Do the games really influence children in any direction? Are their conduct, ideals and attitudes affected by the games? Are the parts which are objectionable to adults understood by children, or at least by very young children? Do children eventually become sophisticated and grow superior to games? Are the emotions of children harmfully excited? In short, just what effect do video games have upon children of different ages?[14]

I'm guessing most of us have heard something like this before. But what's interesting about this quotation is that it wasn't actually written about video games—I simply replaced the words *film* and *pictures* with *video games* and *games*. It was written in 1933. We might get the impression that when we hear complaints about sex, swearing, and violence in games or the internet that these are relatively recent concerns. In fact, such worries belong to an established tradition. Our culture has a history of worrying about our culture.

One root of this collective hand-wringing is a long-running fear of popular culture. According to many historians, the rise of the nineteenth-century urbanized, industrial masses and mass media (such as phonographs, film, and radio) freaked out the traditional social elite. They transferred some of the fear into critiques of crass popular culture: first vaudeville theater and "penny dreadful" novels; and later popular film, radio, and the "vast wasteland" of TV.[15] This is why "popular culture" and (especially) "mass culture" have become derogatory terms, used to describe the tawdry, stupid, and formulaic entertainment made for millions of boneheaded, slobbering consumers.

Academics also got in on the alarmism. The frightening experience of effective propaganda in the early twentieth century, the growing demand from marketers on how to do effective propaganda, and the worrying of moral leaders about the corruption of youth led a variety of serious scholars to scientifically chart the impact of newspaper, radio, and television.[16] The field of media effects has, since the 1930s, attempted to precisely map and explain how watching the hapless coyote drop boulders on his own head while chasing the road runner makes young James want to hit his sister. The findings have been enormously complex and have consistently shown the public are often influenced but never brainwashed by mass media; of course, an anxious public untrained in social science methodology can certainly read many of the findings as thoroughly alarming.

On top of all this, there is a long history in the West of suspicion or outright hostility to new technology. Back in antiquity, Plato had Socrates complain about the dangers of writing.[17] The Luddites of the Industrial Revolution objected to the modernization of the textile industry by destroying new machinery that eliminated their jobs. Throughout the twentieth century, a whole series of critics have urged Western culture to fight against the instrumental logic of technology. Neil Postman, for example, decried the unthinking acceptance of all new machines and tools, worrying that we would lose the wisdom of tradition and the perspective of history.[18]

When we put this all together—the fear of popular culture, the academic suspicion of the effects of media, and the backlash that new technology incurs—it's hardly surprising that as video games have started to make it big they have attracted a crowd of naysayers. Strike one: video games are extremely popular. Strike two: many gamers change the way they live because of their entertainment patterns. And strike three: video games are new technologies. It may be a bit surprising, however, to find that while attacks on games fit a long-term pattern, so does the praise of games.

Worshiping New Technology

In their important essay "The Mythos of the Electronic Revolution," James Carey and John Quirk argue that new technology has always had a near-religious fascination for Americans.[19] First the railroad, then the telegraph, then the telephone, then the radio, and so on: all touted as the great fixers of all that ails us, promising a bright and better future. The theme of technological utopianism is strong in Western culture in general.[20]

Historically, there are a couple of major sources for this onward-and-upward narrative. The first is the entrepreneurs who see technological revolution as their ticket to financial success. These inventors have often been risk takers with big visions whose dreams take the form of the film-based camera, or the wireless telegraph, or television.[21] While such innovators may honestly believe in helping humanity, they—and their bank balance—have an obvious stake in the success of whatever technology they are promoting. So there is a long history of technology industries and inventors explicitly arguing to the public—via advertising and other channels of communication—that their products will lead to a better, happier world.

Another strand of techno-utopianism has less interest in the financial success of technology and more in its idealistic potential.[22] These are the visionaries who either look to inventions as a simple solution to some terrible problem (genetically modified food will end world hunger!) or are simply in love with the newest, sleekest, bestest toy ever. Today's green energy enthusiasts stand at the front of a long line of problem solvers, such as the promoters of domestic appliances (which actually created more, not less, work for stay-at-home wives[23]) or the idealists who thought televisions would solve dysfunctional family relationships.[24] Today's toy-loving early adopters of the newest iPhone likewise echo the crowds at late nineteenth- and early twentieth-century expositions in Philadelphia, Chicago, Buffalo, and St. Louis who saw electrical lighting as sublime.[25]

And We Care Because . . . ?

Both the fearing and the worshiping camps, taken at face value, have really bad track records. No technology has managed to fix family dysfunctions or eliminate hunger and injustice. Neither has any technology turned the population into gibbering idiots (despite elitist proclamations to the contrary) or destroyed the world (although nuclear and biological weapons certainly have the capability). While these things might still happen, the historical pattern is pretty clear: neither side has been entirely correct.

So when people talk about how awful television is or how wonderful electric cars are, they are usually doing more than that. They are locating our cultural fears and hopes in something that may not truly be the root of those hopes and fears.[26] Technology, in other words, is a useful screen upon which we can project our fondest wishes and deepest nightmares. The same applies to video games. The ongoing nature of the optimist/pessimist discussion doesn't negate the concerns over video games or invalidate the enthusiasm of gamers. Rather, it indicates that the vehemence behind the public debates are probably not *entirely* due to the games themselves. Are games, then, just a stand-in for movies, comic books, or novels? Certainly not, as we'll see in the next chapter. Games have unique characteristics that deserve critique and development. But I'm convinced that part of the argument about games is really about culture and technology in general.

This suggests that a wise consideration of video games avoids blanket praise or condemnation of them. But there is another approach we'd be wise to avoid: that of not questioning at all. For every passionate evangelist and prophet of doom, there are ten people that either don't care or don't bother to think it through. History washes over most people, who are too busy getting their next paycheck, managing families, and having fun to stop and realize what is happening to them. This is reasonable—we live in the moment-to-moment, and big-picture thoughts are, well, big picture.

But our moment-to-moment existence is shaped by a lot of the big stuff. Life before and after the introduction of an important new technology such as the automobile or cell phone is often profoundly different, but typically, after an initial burst of interest, people stop paying much attention to it, even though the effects don't go away. How many of us think very often about how profoundly weird the relatively low-tech telephone is (speaking with a disembodied voice from thousands of miles away!) or how it shapes the way we live? The video game is likewise changing our world. I don't think we should give it mute acceptance—we need to engage the attacks and praises carefully and consciously.

Finding a Balance and Finding a Place for Faith

This much my scholarly study has taught me: video games are caught up in an ongoing discussion of utopianism, dystopianism, and apathy. But let's get back to the project we set up at the beginning—that of connecting faith with games. Where should Christians stand in this ongoing debate? The more I read and speak with other followers of Jesus, the more I realize there is no one answer to that question. So what follows is my understanding of the impact my faith should have. It's not an idiosyncratic vision, a truth created *ex nihilo* by and for myself. Rather, it's my understanding of what greater and wiser leaders have argued.[27]

Engaging Culture

Some Christians, when confronted with a filthy world, want to pull back or force clean it. Don't touch video games because they're of the devil, or, if we *must* go there, purify out all the sex, drugs, and laser guns. While such responses are perhaps appropriate at times, I believe both the monastic and the sanitizing response are at best incomplete: when taken to extremes, they assume that we can somehow escape what's wrong with the world, that we can go somewhere or do something that isn't tainted with sin.

The narrative of the Bible and the Christian tradition argues that *everything* is partly messed up, from hallowed cathedral walls to the cleanest Christian romance novel to wholesome potluck dinners to a newborn infant. It's all corrupted to some degree—all I have to do is look at myself to know this is true. While we are still alive, there is no such thing as complete escape from evil. Besides, Jesus argues it's not the stuff outside of us that makes us broken, it is our own hearts, our selfishness, our weaknesses.[28] People can surround themselves with *Dora the Explorer* (or better yet, *VeggieTales*) and still be rotten misanthropes.

The Jesus I see in the Gospels lived *in* this messed-up world. Jesus sometimes took a break on a mountaintop, and he certainly didn't lace his speech with profanities, but he hung out with the bad boys and girls. He planted God's kingdom where people needed it most. That wouldn't have worked if he was a hermit. Video games are my part of my culture. If I'm Jesus's follower, that's where I go.[29]

Understanding Culture

But this is still a potentially negative view: as a paragon of purity, I'm called to shine forth light into the muck-infested swamps of the video-game world. (As a gamer, this scenario sounds eerily familiar.) As comforting as such condescension might be, however, it's ultimately wrong. My poor self-discipline, know-it-all attitude, and self-indulgent behavior make me a lousy paladin. And Christians like me don't fix the world by inserting so-called Christian content (more on this in chapter 8). Take a moment to think about watching a good movie, reading a good book, or playing a good game. The stuff that makes it good usually has nothing to do with the number of explicit references to Jesus.

We can find God and traces of God in the most unexpected back alleys of the very real Lagos and the virtual Liberty City. Just as the biblical narrative and Christian traditions argue that all creation has been tainted, so all of it was created good by a good Creator God. There's more to game playing as a Christian than putting up with the so-called ignorant heathens—there are great things to learn, even from people who, for whatever reason, wouldn't want to ever be associated with Jesus. I don't want to be an unquestioning game fanboy, of course. I feel that Christian understanding means careful critique—just not *self-righteous* critique.[30]

Transforming Culture

It's good to get involved with culture, and it's good to be humble while doing so, but that's not the whole story. Jesus didn't just go with the flow. He recognized that people are hurt and busy hurting others. So as a healer, he made things better. He found grasping, insensitive Matthew and Zacchaeus and turned them into philanthropists. He lifted prostitutes out of a life of abuse. He found headstrong thickheads and made them into model leaders.

Jesus proclaimed the kingdom of God. And he called his followers to likewise transform the world around them, not as superior, know-it-all, do-gooders, but as humble people ready to love, listen, and play games alongside everyone else. A lot of stuff in this world is arguably good or bad, but many things are just plain awful: hate, selfishness, neglect, cruelty, and the like. We are supposed to do more than just watch; we are to plant love, whether it be in our everyday world or that of *World of Warcraft*.[31]

Exploring the Video Game One Facet at a Time

To sum up: the cultural debate about video games is a part of a long discussion about the nature and value of technology. I believe my call as a Christian is to engage video games and their surrounding culture, gain critical understanding of them, and help transform them. This book is mostly about the second step—gaining critical understanding.

Each chapter of this book develops a different angle of the cultural phenomenon of video games. Chapter 2 is the necessary first step. Before we start talking about games and culture, we need to talk about video games themselves. We'll briefly explore the unique characteristics of the **medium** and the gaming situation. This will help us avoid common mistakes critics make when discussing games.

Chapter 3 tackles the religious and spiritual issues surrounding games. What does it mean to be Christian and play games? Can games be Christian? Can they accommodate *any* religion? Can spirit live in the machine?

In chapter 4, we'll consider how games have become closely tied to the culture of destruction. We will look at the debate surrounding violence and media effects and what a Christian response might include. We'll also talk about the ethics of playing a game: Is it okay to do bad stuff in an imaginary game world?

Chapter 5 explores the double-edged sword of escapism. Many game critics consider addiction the number one issue facing gaming culture today. Yet a significant body of Christian thought suggests the powers of fantasy that games wield are an important, positive part of what it means to be human.

Chapter 6 examines gender and games. The representations of men and women (and boys and girls) in computer and video games have been extremely limited in the traditional market, and the exploitation of sexuality is very common. The last five or ten years, however, have seen some significant shifts in how games portray gender, changes that we need to consider critically from a Christian point of view.

Recently, several commentators have promoted games for educational purposes, which is chapter 7's topic. To evaluate these claims, we need to talk about the common critiques of digital media and the body of theory known as media ecology.

Chapter 8 is a consideration of the computer and video-game industries. Specifically, we'll look at how the Christian faith impacts and *should* impact game making. After reviewing where the industry stands and the problems that critics typically pin on it, the chapter will share the opinions of Christians who make games for a living—in both explicitly Christian companies and mainstream ones.

Chapter 9 breaks the gamer out of solitary confinement in a parents' basement. The old stereotype of the solo gamer is justifiably fading, as video games are the center of all kinds of communities and a new way of socializing. To get a good understanding of what game communities are all about, we'll hear from Christian gamers who belong to a variety of gaming groups.

Throughout all of these topics, I want to paint a picture of a balanced Christian approach to games. In Philippians 1:10, the apostle Paul prays that followers of Christ will be able to practice discernment. That's what this book is all about. Whether we're playing games, supervising game players, considering games as a teaching tool, or making games, I believe we need to exercise wisdom informed by the nature of reality and the faith that God gives us. I hope the subsequent chapters illuminate what that means in practice.

2

How to Understand
a Video Game

How I Got Confused about the Purpose
of Video Games

One of my college roommates unintentionally booked up many hours of my life when he bought the then-cutting-edge Super Nintendo Entertainment System. What made it so dangerous (for the completion of homework) was the combat tournament game *Street Fighter II* (see the game image on p. 16). Our friends would regularly gather around the screen to challenge each other in cartoony pugilism. Usually we'd choose one of the campy characters—Zangief the massive Soviet wrestler, Blanka the Brazilian monster, Chun-Li the Chinese martial-arts babe—and fight duels. But I also took on the Super Nintendo itself in a series of player-vs.-computer battles. I stink at action games, and since saving games wasn't possible, I found it infuriatingly difficult.

I only managed to win the whole game with Blanka. I recall the sense of satisfaction at having triumphed over M. Bison, the ferocious final opponent, and the anticipation I felt during the reward narrative at the end. How would the game top off this monumental achievement? As it turns out: with a very poor-quality bit of storytelling. I got a badly written, poorly animated, ridiculously short cinematic sequence about some hackneyed reunion with Blanka's mother—where did *that* come from? I remember feeling a little disappointed.

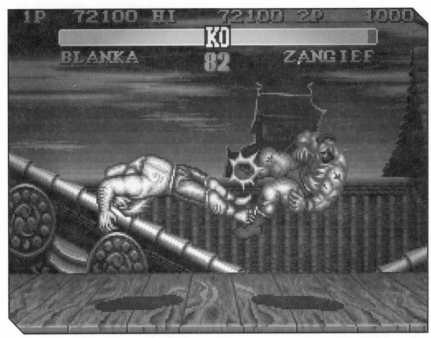

Blanka kicks Zangief in *Street Fighter II*. The action is great, and that's really all this title is about.

In retrospect, I don't know what I was expecting. Video games had already been around for almost thirty years at that point, and the vast majority of them had bad stories, if they had any at all. It hasn't really changed all that much. Released nearly twenty years after the version I played in college, *Street Fighter IV* carries on the tradition of bad storytelling with apparent glee. Some prominent games have well-developed narratives, like the *Uncharted* game series or the *Fallout* games, and game makers are continually improving their storytelling abilities. But most video games are full of shallow characters, trite settings, and predictable plot developments. And here's the thing that I should have realized then that I do now: it doesn't really matter.

Video games aren't movies. They aren't novels. Sure, they share some elements—characters, settings, plots—but they aren't the same. *Street Fighter II* wasn't really a drama or even an action flick. I played it for the *game*, not for the story, which isn't possible with a Hollywood blockbuster, romance paperback, or radio play. The narrative *feel* of the game is always important, but often the plot isn't.

The problem is, because video games *do* share many characteristics with those other media, people keep trying to talk about them in the same way—especially if they just watch others play instead of playing themselves. People who don't get gaming are liable to think about video games as movies with joysticks—and some gamers might even think that way. But that doesn't cut it. So if we're going to talk about games intelligently, we have to figure out what they *are*. This chapter is a first step toward establishing what video games are and how we should think about them.

What Exactly Is a Game?

What do we associate the term "video game" with? **Fighting games** like *Street Fighter*? **Casual puzzle games** like *Angry Birds*? Conquer-the-world **strategy games** like *Civilization*? We could picture a **console** attached to a TV or an internet-based game on a cell phone. We don't have room here to discuss the many genres and forms of video games,[1] but it's clear we're dealing with extremely diverse cultural artifacts. So what ties them all together? This is a somewhat stickier question than it initially appears. We actually have two questions: What is a game, and what is a video game?

The second question is a bit simpler, so let's start there: a video game is a computer-run game meant to be played on a video screen. This seems obvious, but in fact computer processors can run more than just screen-based games. For example, it is possible to play games with nothing but sound.[2] It would theoretically be possible to play digital games that rely only on the sense of touch as well—the experimental *PainStation* game uses a video screen, but physically punishes losing players with small electrical shocks, rubber whips on the arm, and extreme hot and cold points on the hands. Some live-action games (often called "location-based games" or "urban games") involve communication and coordination via the miniature digital screens of cell phones or GPS devices, but the main activity is running down streets and doing physical chasing. In other words, some computer games are not *video* games.

To be honest, I'd prefer to use the term "*digital* game," which would encompass all games involving some kind of computer processing. But this isn't how most people talk about video games. Besides, the vast majority of computerized games *do* involve some kind of screen, so we'll stick with "video games" for this book.

Defining "games" is a much tougher job. What do board games, **first-person shooters, adventure games,** and **sports games** have in common? Twentieth-century philosopher Ludwig Wittgenstein argued that no one feature belongs to *all* the things we call games.[3] That hasn't stopped intellectuals from trying to formulate an overarching description, however. My favorite definition is that of game-design theorists Katie Salen and Eric Zimmerman: "A game is a system in which players engage in an artificial conflict, defined by rules, that results in a quantifiable outcome."[4] Let's unpack that.

All games involve some kind of made-up struggle—a conflict that is artificial because we make it and agree to enter into it. We're never *forced* into a game of chess, and even if we were, the rules have force only because we agree to them; otherwise, what's to stop us from simply grabbing the other player's king and declaring checkmate?

It's not just a question of artificial conflict, however: when we watch an action flick, the hero is busy fighting off contrived bad guys, but it's not a game (at least, not for viewers; we could, of course, watch a film that shows people playing a game). No, it becomes a game when we *participate* in the artificial conflict. Games need players—not viewers—who actually manipulate the game in some way.

And what guides this artificial conflict between players? A system of rules. It is possible to have artificial conflict that is relatively random and not very gamelike, as when my daughters argue about who's the princess and who's the puppy in their free-form make-believe sessions. Their arguments and mechanisms for resolution are pretty fluid. But when we play chess, the goal of the game is highly defined (get the other player's king piece into checkmate), the order of actions is invariable (first one player gets a move, then the other), and what we can do with each game piece is set in advance (the bishop, for example, can only move in diagonal lines). These rules interlock—they all apply together, and as such, they form a *system*. This is a big difference between free-form play and a game. Note also that the rules define an *outcome*—they dictate the results of our actions and a win condition (if there is one). In the case of chess, the outcome is one player putting the other in checkmate, thus causing one to win and the other to lose.

Let's think this through with the simplest video game: *Pong.* In this classic, two people control electronic tennis paddles on a screen. A ball bounces between these paddles, and if a player misses the ball, his or her opponent scores a point. The player with the most points wins. Extremely simple. Is there conflict? Yes. The players are competing over who has the most points. Is it artificial conflict? Yes. Whatever depressed existentialists might argue, life doesn't consist of people stuck in a box banging a square ball back and forth. Does it require players? Yes—if nobody turns the control knobs then nothing happens. Does it run according to a system of rules? Yes. The ball behaves in a consistent manner, as do the paddles and the scoring—and all of these rules work together simultaneously. Is there a quantifiable outcome? Yes. It's not a matter of judgment, personal taste, or opinion: according to the rules, one person wins and the other loses.

With something as complex as games, it's pretty much impossible to come up with an airtight definition. Some people would point out that this way of defining games overemphasizes games with clear win/loss conditions (like chess or *Pong*); many video games today, like Will Wright's *The Sims*, are **sandbox games**—open-ended experiences where players set their own goals. Others might argue that the division between artificial and real conflict is pretty fluid: poker, for example, can have serious real-world consequences. People could also make the case that while a game requires players, those players don't have to be human. Computers can play games via artificial intelligence.

These are all fair points, but I think we've still got a solid definition, and it's important for understanding the following discussion. Games are systems of rules that players enter into in order to interact with one another (even if some of those players are computers). Video games are games run by computers and displayed on video screens.

How to Read a Video Game (Or, A Game Is *Not* a Movie with a Joystick)

Why spend so much time hashing out a definition for video games? The big point is that a video game is not a movie with a game controller. Both movies and video games are multimedia communication tools, but they have different purposes and communicate in very different ways. Ditto video games and novels: there are similarities, but they're essentially different. If we try to read them the same way, we'll fundamentally misunderstand one of them. *The Lord of the Rings* the book is not the movie is not the game.

So how *do* we "read" video games properly? To answer that question, we need to address three different issues. First, we'll consider the distinctive structure of the video-game medium. Second, we'll go into more detail about how and what video games communicate. Finally, we'll take a brief look at an issue we'll revisit throughout the book: the difference between players and viewers.

What Kind of Medium Is the Video Game?

The video game is a *medium*: a set of tools we use to communicate (and if the notion of games communicating seems problematic, don't worry—we'll get to that in a second). When we talk about media (plural of medium), we can define them very broadly (e.g., the radio medium, the print medium) or somewhat more narrowly (e.g., the medium of the novel vs. the medium of the comic book). Either way, we use a medium to communicate. *What* we communicate is the content. For example: a radio talk show session (content) uses microphones, broadcast towers, and the radio station's staff (medium). In other words, for the purposes of this discussion, the medium and the message are two different things.[5] So what are the distinct characteristics of the video-game medium?

Because video games are a computerized medium, they are emulation machines: computers can play the role of other media. Like photos or film, games can use still pictures or moving visual images: an icon of a hand, the lush landscape of *World of Warcraft*, a raging demon in *Doom*. Like movies, games can use sound, either as part of the imaginary game world (such as the boom of an explosion in *Call of Duty: Modern Warfare 3*) or as a tool for creating emotional atmospheres (such as the historically themed background music of *Civilization 4*). And just like books and TV shows, games can use words, either as printed text or as spoken dialogue, like the extensive conversations of the *Final Fantasy* games or *Dragon Age*. But these apparent similarities often mask the unique structure of video games and their distinctive way of communicating.

Take storytelling, for instance. As I discovered with *Street Fighter II*, game stories are typically inferior when judged by familiar narrative criteria. Good films, television series, and novels have rich characters, relatively complicated or otherwise interesting plots, profound themes, and emotional power. Only a few games score well on *any* of those standards. And yet video games can be very engrossing—even their cliché-ridden narratives can grab the player. Video games are redefining what we expect from stories.[6]

Why? One of the big differences between other media and video games is that video games are participatory machines.[7] By some definitions of the word, we *do* interact with movies—we have to think through them to make sense of them, especially if we're looking for subtle stuff. But nothing the average viewer does is going to change the actual movie. The same goes for a novel. With games, however, the player *must* get involved or nothing happens. And what the player does changes the passage of the game. Even the most limited games allow the player to fail, meaning the game won't progress until the player gets good enough.[8]

Think of this in terms of game stories. What happens is up to us, the players. We don't have *complete* freedom: the story is prescribed in many games (often as noninteractive **cut scene** mini-movies) plus we're restricted by the rules. But if we're playing the catlike space creature Ratchet in *Ratchet & Clank: Tools of Destruction*, nothing happens until we start moving him. And when we do, if we make poor choices, he dies, and we have to start the level over again. What we do as players changes what happens on the screen. Contrast this with a movie: about the only decision point that affects the unfolding of the story is when to press "play," "pause," and "stop."

Note that a game is more than just a string of cut scenes with simple decision points. The *Choose Your Own Adventure* novels are like this, composed of little bits of prescribed narrative, each of which end with a choice for the reader as to which bit comes next—turn to this page or that.[9] Although similar in appearance, such things are fundamentally different from games. The choices of the *Choose Your Own Adventure* reader do not change the narrative fragments. An audiovisual text with the same structure would more properly be called an "interactive movie," not a game. Remember the definition: games are made up of systems of rules. Video games are not fragments of stories connected by trivial choices (*that* would be an interactive movie): the connection between our actions and what happens on the screen are constant (or at least frequent) and immediate.

Rather, games are more like machines—like blenders, microwaves, or cars—but they're machines that use and produce language, visual symbols, and aural cues. Press "frappe" and *voilà*, we get the blades spinning fast enough to make our strawberry milkshake. Press the "2" button on our Wii wheel, and Koopa Troopa starts speeding his car around the track in *Mario Kart Wii* (see illustration on p. 22). The blender blade gets jammed and we press "off" and unplug the silly thing so we can shove a spoon in there and loosen things up. The *Mario Kart* track curves, and we tilt the wheel to the left so we stay on and don't run into the wall. The end goal is a berry milk shake or a gold cup, depending on the machine.[10]

Mario Kart Wii is a machine of interlocking bits: the track, the drivers, the power ups, the hazards—these are all things the player can interact with.

Video games are not like any old machine, however. For one thing, they can be phenomenally complicated. For another, they are computerized systems of information and culture. Janet Murray argues that games are "encyclopedic," meaning they can store a lot of data for use when we want or need it.[11] Games will often contain whole worlds or scenarios that players never engage, unlike a novel or narrative movie, which typically doesn't waste much of the information it delivers, and whose viewer or reader is also likely to see *all* the material. I spent around one hundred hours in *Fallout: New Vegas* and probably visited only half of the game's locations.

But video games are very much like books and films and television—as already noted—in the sense that they are *culture* machines. When we play *Street Fighter*, *World of Warcraft*, or *Pac-Man*, we are engaging cultural items, things that speak to our understandings of the world, of ethics and morality, of identity, and so on. In the end, then, we can say that the video game is a hybrid of older media and machines. It has connections with cinema and automobiles, books and coffeemakers. It *will* communicate, but it will *not* communicate in the same manner as our more familiar cultural forms and media.

How and What Video Games Communicate

Video games, then, are part machine, part communicator. This blend has important implications for understanding their cultural force. When scholars analyze a film, they often look for its message. What does *The Godfather* have to say to us about power and morality? With video games, it doesn't always work quite the same way.

In some senses, we could question whether games communicate at all. Typically, when we think of communication, we think of sending messages. What's the message of *Mario Kart*? That going fast gets us a gold cup? Remember, games are machines. To say that a machine has a message usually misses the point of a machine. What's the message of a microwave oven? In fact some game designers and theorists greatly dislike the notion of focusing on the communication of video games—a game isn't about *communicating* (even if that's going on); it's about *playing*.[12]

The reason we're hitting a bit of a dead end here is because we're operating with a rather limited notion of communication. Just because we can't boil down a cultural text to a single, overarching message doesn't mean we have a failure to communicate. Communication—the process of cocreating meaning—is a remarkably complicated and marvelous human activity. When we create community, identify with an idea or a person, and emote together, we are communicating, we are sharing meaning, even if we can't boil that down to a simple dump of information.[13] A complicated movie or dinnertime rituals or a cacophonous talk show or an action-packed fighting game may all lack a simple message, but they still communicate. So let's look at a few video-game tools of communication.

It was a bit deceptive to ask about the message of a microwave. In fact, the oven *does* send messages: it tells us it's two minutes until the popcorn is done. True, this is not the overall point of the machine, but it *is* constantly sending us little missives. Video games work the same way in many senses. Take *Mario Kart Wii*. We see the track zooming and see other racing cars and see obstacles and special **power-ups**, we hear the noises of the cars and the music, and we manipulate our steering wheel in response to all this, causing our cart to zoom and swerve and shoot red turtle shells. All the little objects in the games are like little messages: here's a tree, here's a bike, here's the road, when we pressed that button we zoom forward, and so on. Video games, in other words, are constantly using signs—visual, textual, and aural representations of things and ideas—to tell us what is happening in the game.[14]

It's important to note that signs communicate on more than one level. Some meanings are pretty straightforward: the tree-like image represents the presence of a tree. But signs can evoke a lot more than that. Trees can represent peacefulness, healthiness, environmentalism, or even (in the right context) a brooding menace. Often these connotations are flexible and open to debate, but nonetheless they can be exceptionally powerful. Critics often describe the 1993 hit *Doom* as having a threadbare plot, but it drips with atmosphere: the dark tunnels, echoing sounds, and sharp explosions of noise help create a feeling of horror and nervous anticipation.

We could argue that another way many games communicate is by structuring their signs in narrative patterns. We've already noted the frequently poor character of game narrative. Along with MIT media scholar Henry Jenkins, I'd argue that poor narrative doesn't mean video games can't or shouldn't have stories; it just means these will be different narratives from those of books, TV shows, and film.[15] Game stories are not meant to be watched so much as to be played with and explored. Thus the characters, settings, and even plot are (for many games, anyway) more about creating narrative atmosphere, creating narrative space that the player moves around in, and engaging players in a very active way. Clearly many big-budget video games lavish attention on their stories, and throughout this book I pay close attention to those narratives.

That, however, should not obscure the fact that stories are optional for games. Some games are completely abstract, such as *Go*, an ancient East Asian strategy board game played with a grid and many little white and black pieces. The player could, of course, project a narrative onto the game ("it's a story of black and white beetles eating each other in a struggle for insect supremacy"), but the game itself contains no truly narrative elements. It is very common for video games—especially casual games—to have only the barest of narrative elements. *Tetris*, for example, has some Russian-sounding music playing in the background and some stereotypical Russian imagery at the borders of the screen. While this evokes a Russian atmosphere, we are stretching things enormously to say that the game tells a story. Narrative patterns *can* be important for video games, but they don't *have* to be.[16]

So what communication tool do *all* games have? Worlds. By this I don't mean "planets," I mean "alternate realities." Remember, all games are systems of rules. What the game communicates to us as we play is an alternate reality, where things work differently than in everyday life. In *The Sims*, the little people have seven different needs, which are measured on bars: if, for example, the bladder indicator drops too low, the unfortunate Sim will pee on the carpet. In *Angry Birds*, the player-controlled birds are locked in eternal struggle with the wicked egg-stealing pigs, who do nothing but wait to be crushed by a rapidly-descending avian weapon. In *Civilization V*, cities can build monuments that increase their cultural output, eventually causing the civilization's borders to expand. These are all examples of different realities that games communicate. Some of these realities are pretty abstract—in the world of *Tetris*, a line of blocks disappears when they stretch from one side of the play area to the other. But even simple video games propose alternate realities.

These worlds are not just the communicative *content* of the game—they are also communication tools. This is just like stories. What can a printed book communicate? Among other things, it can deliver a story—say, one of Aesop's fables. But that story also can communicate something to us. Fables are easy examples because they're so pointed and moralistic: the grasshopper shows us that sloth is bad, the ant that hard work is good.[17] More complex stories, however, can also communicate, although in much more fluid and variable ways. *The Lord of the Rings* doesn't really have a simple hit-you-over-the-head message, but it does communicate heroism, the qualities of good and evil, the piercing quality of beauty, and so on. Video-game stories can do many of the same things.

Game worlds don't typically have simple, fable-like messages either, but in modeling a reality, they *do* tell us something. For example, in *The Sims* there is no religion—no religious expression, no deity. In *Age of Mythology*, a real-time strategy game from 2002, players use the power of religious figures from the Greek, Egyptian, or Norse pantheons to defeat their enemies. Both of these games model a kind of spirituality in their game worlds, and in the process they communicate something.[18]

In short, then, games communicate in some ways that are similar to older media: they use images, sounds, and words. They *can* use stories to communicate, although those stories are typically quite different from what we get from books, TV shows, and movies. And games always deliver alternate worlds, which usually have something to say to us. Video games are a site where we create meaning.

The Player Versus the Viewer

Given the unique nature of the video-game medium, it shouldn't surprise us that game players are not the same as readers and viewers. Much of the rest of this book will discuss exactly what it means to be a game player, so I won't get into much detail here. But since we've been talking about games communicating, I want to highlight a few key observations about players.

The first point highlights a similarity: players, like readers and viewers, are active meaning-makers. For decades, our culture has been frightened by the stereotype of the brain-dead "vidiot": the couch-bound, glassy-eyed television viewer who soaks in waves of poorly done acting, hackneyed scripts, and morally degraded behavior without questioning it. Since at least the 1970s, however, some academics have questioned such a caricature.[19] Even while engaging the cheapest, most stupid trash, we're still trying to make sense of things, trying to make connections, and often questioning or challenging what we watch. Ever yelled at a TV? That indicates thinking, interpreting, an active engagement—at assuming the TV is on. Gaming is no different. The player's mind is constantly processing and making sense of things.

Why does this matter? Quite simply, we can't judge a book by its writing alone. When meaning-makers are active, there are going to be differences of interpretation. Take politics: When a highly contentious candidate gives a speech, are all the listeners going to hear the same speech? Technically, yes. But in practice, there will be some fundamentally different connections between speaker and individual audience members. If we want to understand the communication occurring, we need to pay attention to the listeners as much as—some might say *more than*—the speaker.

All this is to say that we might *think* we know what that no-good teen-aged guy is picking up from the latest *Grand Theft Auto* or *God of War* game. But have we *talked* to him and actually listened to his understanding of his experience? I mean *really* listened—not just arguing disguised as listening. Talk to a hundred guys that age, and (especially with games that complex) I guarantee they're not all going to say the same things. The point is not that these are great games or that a teenager is going to have a healthy and mature understanding of them. The point is, until we really pay attention to the player (just as with a reader or a viewer) we're not going to get a handle on what he or she is actually understanding. Looking at the game itself is not enough to get the full picture.[20]

The second important point about the player as opposed to the viewer or reader is the player actually *impacts* a game, as we've already discussed. So not only does the player have the interpretive freedom of the reader and viewer but he or she also has the option of literally changing the substance of what's on the screen. And while the game makers do put all kinds of constraints on the player, it's pretty amazing how some players can do things the designers never intended.[21]

The upshot of all this is when we're talking about the effects of games upon players, we have to be careful about making broad, definitive statements about what's going on based on what we think about the games. It's bad enough to do this when we're talking about films or books. It's even more problematic when we're talking about the people who play with media items that are almost never the same twice in a row.

Summarizing Video Games

As we go through this book, we need to keep a few things in mind:

1. The video-game medium has the potential to communicate, and it has similarities to other media, but it's not exactly the same.

2. The tools of communication for a video game are:
   - the signs of a game: its visual images, words, and sounds, whether realistic or abstract, can communicate, both simply and with flexible but powerful connotations;
   - the narrative of a game: the game can communicate a story and that story can communicate something as well; games don't require stories, however, and the medium tends to present them in a unique way; and
   - the game world: a game communicates an alternate reality, and that alternate reality in turn can communicate things (ideas, emotions, possibilities, etc.).

3. Because video games are computerized games:
   - they can be encyclopedic—they hold and process tons of information;
   - they are interactive—games have to have players actually manipulating the game; and
   - they are systematic—games of any type are systems of rules.

4. Video-game players:
- are not passive sponges—like readers, viewers, and listeners, they are always interpreting what they are engaging; but
- unlike readers, viewers, and listeners, players get to mess around with the game—they get to *do* something that on some level affects the game and how it turns out.

Using this as a foundation, let's take a look at the intersection of faith, video games, and culture.

3

Making the
Immaterial Playable

Games, Religion, and Spirituality

The Trouble with Games, Religion, and Spirituality

A few minutes into the game *Dragon Age: Origins*, I hit a moral dilemma: I had to decide whether to protect or turn in my friend who'd been accused of being a blood mage. On the continent of Thedas, **mages** are dangerous, powerful casters of spells who draw power from their connection with the ethereal realm of the Fade, a spirit realm where demons and noble entities reside. Through the centuries, ambitious mages have caused all kinds of harm when they grasp for too much power—they frequently attract demonic attention and can become possessed abominations. Some mages also turn to the frightening blood magic, a powerful form of magic that gets its strength from living things. The Chantry, an order of monks and knights dedicated to serving the Maker (a quasi-monotheistic god of this world) and his martyred prophetess Andraste, keeps all mages under close watch. If any young mages show signs of being dangerous, they undergo the Rite of Tranquility, which severs their connection to the Fade and leaves them in an emotionless, semi-lobotomized state.

My character, a young member of the Circle of Magi, ran across Jowan, who'd been accused of dabbling in blood magic and was scheduled to undergo the Rite of Tranquility. He claimed the accusations were because of his secret (and forbidden) romance with a young priestess of the Chantry—since he'd been sneaking off, people thought he'd been playing with blood magic (see image below). He asked for help to escape the Circle so he and his lover could start a new life, free of magic. And so I faced a choice. In this world, blood magic is a serious wrong—but it wasn't at all clear that Jowan was guilty. The Rite of Tranquility is eerie—probably terrifying to my character. Inflicting this on someone for a minor offense is like executing someone for stealing a loaf of bread. Mind you, there are good reasons for barring liaisons between mages and Chantry members. And so I found myself playing a video game and engaged in a most unexpected activity: engaging religious beliefs and grappling with questions of good and evil.

Do I turn in my friend Jowan so he can be lobotomized? What is right and what is wrong?

Can God Fit in the Machine?

This is not normal for a video game. It's not that video games have nothing to do with religion, spirituality, mystery, and the supernatural. Magic is a staple element of the Fantasy genre, which includes stories or games set in worlds full of dragons, elves, wizards, warriors, Greek- or Norse-like deities, and spiritual forces like ghosts and demons. But unlike

Dragon Age, the gods of most Fantasy RPGs are rarely fleshed out in any detail, and the engagement of good and evil is surface-deep. Spirituality is typically no more than a source of power, much like nuclear generators.

But is this the way it has to be? Can we use games to talk about God, good and evil, right and wrong, love, and the immaterial world of the spirit in a healthy way? Christians have very publicly questioned whether any spiritual good can come from the video-game medium. Some fear that playing games leads players to flirt with the occult or anti-Christian ideologies and theologies. Another critique is that the medium encourages a kind of mechanization of spirituality and morality. These are serious issues that we need to examine carefully. Ultimately, however, I think the medium of video games has tremendous, if underdeveloped, spiritual potential. Video-game worlds have room for religion, faith, and spirituality to be treated in a deep and thought-provoking manner. But that won't happen if we fail to understand the character of the medium: because they are part representation and part machine, video games have unique strengths and weaknesses.

In this chapter, we're going to look at the two challenges to integrating Christian Spirituality and video games: the apparently non-Christian ideologies of many games and the mechanization of spirit. Then we're going to examine some power-ups that games employ to deepen their potential. We'll end with a balanced consideration of how to put these two sides of the coin together.

Challenge Level 1: Incompatibility with the Christian God

Occult Games?

One of the major concerns about the spirituality of video games is that it can lead players to dabble in demonic spirituality. When I was a kid, I was fascinated with the tabletop (nonvideo) RPG *Dungeons and Dragons*, but I knew that, for some reason, people disapproved of it. Later in life, I discovered that several Christians had mounted high-profile campaigns against the game in the 1980s, claiming that it was a recruiting tool for occultists, witches, and Satan worshipers and that it led to depression and suicide attempts. Perhaps the high point of the public attack was a 1982 made-for-TV movie called *Mazes and Monsters*, starring Tom Hanks, about a college student who descends into insanity because of the RPG he's playing.[1]

While critical research in the 1990s discredited the leaders of some of the more prominent campaigns, such as Patricia Pulling and her organization B.A.D.D. (Bothered About *Dungeons and Dragons*),[2] some of the arguments of this perspective remain to this day. Some critics believe that the power fantasies of RPGs make it easy for occult practitioners to recruit gamers. Another argument is that playing pretend roles can eventually lead people to adopt these roles for real. Others believe exposure to the symbols and concepts of magic and paganism are enough to confuse, corrupt, and mislead, while some see dark spiritual forces directly at work in the games. There's no question that some game artwork is very dark, drawing on horror conventions and the very well-developed European traditions of artistic representations of demons. While *Dungeons and Dragons* still gets the worst rap on this account, newer pop culture, such as the Harry Potter and *Pokemon* media empires, have received similar critiques.[3]

Non-Christian Spirituality

Even if we're not worried about seduction by evil spirits while playing games, we may question the religious and moral ideas that games model. Orthodox versions of Christian faith have very little traction in the world of video games—at least openly. This is a significant challenge for Christian spirituality in video games: regardless of the spiritual forces present, there are clearly non-Christian *ideas* about faith and spirituality.

While many genres ignore the spiritual, plenty of games express explicit religious ideas—but many of these seem incompatible with Christianity. There is, for instance, the standard polytheism of Fantasy RPGs. The Forgotten Realms world, for instance, featured in extremely popular video-game series like *Baldur's Gate* and *Neverwinter Nights*, has an incredibly intricate, crowded pantheon, peopled by entities like Bane, the malevolent god of hate, and Oghma, the goddess of wisdom. And games like this often import theologies: in the world of Forgotten Realms, as in other games, the gods and goddesses derive their power from worship—if their flock dwindles, they become weaker.

Other games model very different religious sensibilities. One commentator notes that Japanese games sometimes use overt religious names, characters, and symbols, although they tend to blend diverse traditions together.[4] *Final Fantasy VII*, for instance, has a villain named Sephiroth (a term from the Jewish Kabbalah) and a superpowered alien entity named

Jenova (not much different from "Jehovah"), and its world has a Life Stream, which sounds remarkably like the New Age idea of Gaia. We can see a similar alteration of mythology in the newer *El Shaddai*, which, according to one writer, is made by a "multi-faith team."[5] The game is based on the apocryphal *Book of Enoch*, and one of the main characters, Lucifel (clearly Lucifer pre–fall-from-heaven) talks to God on a cell phone. Another recent game, *From Dust*, puts the player in the role of the guiding spirit (the "Breath") of a Polynesian-like animist tribe, shaping islands and protecting the people from the threats of the world (see image below). There are surely more religious ideas and ideals in the vast panoply of the video-game universe; the point is that many of them do not immediately seem compatible with Christian teachings.

The player-controlled deity of *From Dust* has the ability to pick up earth, water, lava, and plants and use them to reshape the land so as to protect The People.

Antichurch Hostility

Another theological/ideological roadblock for Christians playing video games is the general hostility of many games toward religions, or perhaps more accurately, toward the church. Whether good or evil, many systems of spiritual belief are obviously fake or flaky. A typical example would be the slightly unhinged pious zealots of the Church of the Children of the Atom in the postapocalyptic world of *Fallout 3*. These are harmless but loopy, pathetic devotees who worship the power of the Atom near an unexploded nuclear bomb at the center of the appropriately named town of Megaton.

Another example is *Final Fantasy X*, the plot of which revolves around a religion that the player eventually reveals to be a false front.

Some video games also present religious people as oppressive moralists, pious hypocrites, or corrupt charlatans. In the opening cut scene to the gritty Western RPG *Red Dead Redemption*, for example, the rugged but flawed (and nonreligious) hero John Marston sits on the train overhearing a pompous pastor indoctrinating an impressionable young woman on the ultimate moral uprightness of dispossessing (so-called) injuns of their land.

Finally, another common religious theme is the partial or complete role reversal of good and evil. Game makers have long had fun with the stereotype of the over-the-top campy mastermind of destruction, such as Peter Molyneux's *Dungeon Keeper*, in which the player finds amusing ways to kill heroes. Another example is the iPhone game *Pocket God*, which allows gamers to be a malevolent deity toying with cute little Polynesian followers. Evil in these games demonstrates a character akin to a snickering little boy, rather than an archdemon hell-bent on corruption and conquest.

Some games, however, flip standard religious narratives in a more intense manner. In *Darksiders*, for instance, the player controls War, one of the four horsemen of the apocalypse who is a neutral party caught in the middle of a selfish, destructive war between the forces of heaven and hell. A similar story is *Bayonetta*, in which the player controls the title character, a witch who fights a series of angels in a quest to regain her memory. The mythology of this world is quite different from Christianity, but there are quite a few clear parallels, and there's no question that in these games, the angels are the bad guys.

Putting all of this together, we can see that many video games are not exactly the friendliest environment for orthodox Christian spirituality. When religion is actually present, it may be dark and disturbing or it might not align with Christian teachings.

Challenge Level 2: Mechanical Worlds, Simplified Religions

Those who know video games may well be wondering why I have so far avoided some of the most explicitly religious games ever made. We might, for example, point to a whole string of games by the aforementioned Peter Molyneux. Game historians typically identify his 1989 hit *Populous* as the first "god game," a high-level social simulation wherein the player literally takes the role of a god controlling the fate of nations and worlds. A decade later Molyneux created *Black and White*, a considerably more accessible and character-based game that gives the player the ability to act as a good or evil god for a primitive tribe. Another example of explicitly religious games would be Sid Meier's strategy game *Civilization IV*, which actually allows the player to discover the great world religions (seven in all: Hinduism, Buddhism, Judaism, Confucianism, Taoism, Christianity, and Islam). And the popular action-oriented *Assassin's Creed* is set in the faith-against-faith maelstrom of the Crusade-era Middle East. Wouldn't all of these games seem to demonstrate that the representation of a robust spirituality—if not a *Christian* spirituality—is at least *possible*?

I actually happen to like some of these games (especially *Civilization*), and I think there are some promising aspects to most of them, spiritually speaking, which I'll dive into a bit later. But we first need to deal with a serious religious drawback of the medium: the very form of the video game encourages mechanical, systematic, and functional representations of spirituality. A video game does not deal well with ambiguity. Even a board game must clearly define its pieces and its play space; it must also have very detailed rules. But in a board game, if there is a lack of clarity in the rules (which dictionary can we use for *Scrabble*?), players can at least come to an ad hoc agreement. A computer takes things a step further: programs tolerate zero ambiguity. If a variable or object is not precisely defined in a program, it is nonfunctional.

Much of our experience is not so quantifiable. Think about a warm summer day, with just a slight hint of a breeze and a comfortable amount of sun. There's greenery all around and the pleasant sound of moving water. We can hear just enough noise from animals and rustling plants to keep it from being somber but not enough to ruin the overall sense of peace. Mentally drink in this scenario. Now what about this can we capture mathematically, scientifically, with precision, and with a complete lack of ambiguity? We could record an image or the audio. We could take the temperature. We could describe the biological components of the ecosystem. But valuable and interesting as they are, do all these things capture the totality of the moment? Could this pile of data give me the heart of the experience?

Life is bigger than what we can describe and manage systematically. We can use definitions and simulations to *partially* represent the greatest (and most terrible) aspects of humanity. But something as powerful and amorphous as love is much more than just a set of neurochemicals mixing in our noggins (even if they are a necessary part of the experience). Likewise, video games, due to their systematic nature, have a strong tendency to miss something of the full wonder, mystery, and ambiguity of the great human experiences of religion and spirituality.[6]

Point-Based Morality: Good and Evil Have a Numerical Value

One of the first characteristics of overly systematic video games is the phenomenon of points-based morality, which, ironically, is most on display in video games that take the issues of right and wrong seriously. While many video games ignore religion and tend to give morality short shrift, some game makers have attempted to tackle the challenge. One of the earliest examples is Richard Garriott's renowned *Ultima IV*,[7] a 1985 game that attempted to move beyond the simple kill-or-be-killed mentality common to RPGs: player actions earned positive or negative points for up to eight virtues. Giving money to a beggar would earn two compassion points and three honor points, while attacking nonevil creatures would take points from compassion, honor, and justice.[8] While a few other games, such as the *Fable* series, use similarly complex interlocking scales of strength and weakness, most other games that rate good and evil have been simpler. *Fallout: New Vegas* and *Star Wars: Knights of the Old Republic II* use binary scales: every morally coded action gains good or evil points. For instance, in the *Star Wars* game, helping the selfish Czerka corporation ruin the planet Telos IV gives dark-side points, but combating them by siding with the ecologically minded Ithorians gives light-side points.

Simple or complex, all of these games have the same issue: morality is reduced to a system of points. I hope the problem here is self-evident. The reality of moral decision making outside of a game is just a tiny bit messier. How can we score wartime decisions? Should we spend some lives now in order to hopefully save some later? Execute prisoners of war in order to keep mobility and stay alive? There is no way to objectively quantify such quandaries: all options are a tremendous mix of good and evil.

In addition, such mechanics make moral choices very much a matter of extrinsic motivation. Most of the games mentioned above open and close different narrative paths and may change play style based on player decisions. In *Fable II* evil characters end up looking terrifying, and good characters look angelic. Jedi Knights in the *Knights of the Old Republic* series get different Force powers if they adopt a strong light or dark alignment. Due to the rewards or punishments, ethics become instrumental: we do the right (or wrong) things, not because they are valuable in and of themselves, but because doing these actions gets us something.

Religion as Faction

A second feature of systematic anti-mystery in video games is the reduction of religion and the ideas of good and evil to markers of faction. Everyone knows that this is, in fact, how religion often operates: if I'm on team Protestant, someone on team Catholic is my opponent, and I play to win. Likewise, followers of Forgotten Realms god Tyr might get along with followers of Torm but *not* with followers of Tiamat. Religion functions much the same as putting on a hockey jersey—and results in about as many fights.

Those of us who have living faith commitments know that belief and commitment involve more than picking a team. I'm not a Christian because choosing that path gives me a club and affiliation—although such sociological impulses are certainly a big part of my motivation, often in unhealthy ways—but because I have a relationship with a living God. I adopt Christian religious institutions and practices because that's part of following my God, not because the religion itself is the purpose for life.

More important, religion-as-faction blurs the very real distinctions among different perspectives. Good and evil are part of practically every dramatic video game, but frequently the only difference is which side wears white and which side wears black. Typically, the good side *looks* pure and has a title like "guardians of wellspring of life" while the evil side *looks* nasty, with diabolical narrative descriptions like "vicious invading brigands of doom." But they *do* exactly the same thing: conquer and destroy the other side, meaning good and evil are only cosmetically different. As one of my friends puts it: "A true Jedi uses the Force for knowledge and defense, never for attack—unless you're fighting *bad* guys." When perspectives have no real difference, it's hard to take *any* religion seriously: they're just self-interested power machines (as they are in *Darksiders*). This is easy to design and program, but it's not particularly good at getting at the heart of the experience of faith.

Quantified Spirit

A final example of the over-systematized nature of video games is the way the medium tends to quantify the spirit. Spirits are mysterious, immaterial, ambiguous, and amorphous. Depending on our perspective, spirits are ghosts, a life force, a source of authority, or strictly psychological projections—and there's no way of proving beyond a shadow of a doubt which is most correct. In movies and books, spirits are usually unpredictable forces that do not have defined effects. They can be monsters or angels, intelligent or instinctive, purely ethereal or sometimes physically present. So it is with all kinds of similar phenomena, such as magic or religious emotion.

Not so, however, in video games. We can have suitably luminous artwork, ghost warriors, and magic spells—but if they're going to make a difference in the game, they have to be turned into statistics. No ambiguity here: if something is going to *work* in a game, we need to know what it can and can't do—or at least, the computer needs to know. And even if we don't know the precise nature of the beast we're combatting in, say, *Elder Scrolls: Skyrim*, we know its *effects*. In a dramatic scene from Tolkien's *The Lord of the Rings*, the demonic and powerful undead Ringwraiths on flying mounts pursue the noble Faramir. The situation looks hopeless, when suddenly the good wizard Gandalf sallies forth and intervenes with a stab of blindingly white light that causes the Ringwraiths to shriek and quit the pursuit. Tolkien does not explain the precise mechanics of the interaction. This is *magic*—a mysterious power that none but wizards, elves, and great craftsmen know how to wield. Even Peter Jackson's cinematic representation of the event, which diminishes mystery by *showing* us the light rather than leaving it to our imagination, does not explain to the viewer how Gandalf can do what he does.[9] In *The Battle for Middle-earth* real-time strategy game based on the movie, however, we have a rather precise understanding of Gandalf's Istari Light power. We know not only what it looks like but also roughly how much damage it does, its range, and how often we can cast it.

All magic, ghosts, angels, and demons in video games are, in fact, numerically defined and effectively function as technologies, just as a gun or vehicle would. Video-game magic sheds its mystery and simply becomes a technological, killing spirit. In addition, since we typically need to know how the morality system works in order to play with it effectively, the potential exists for us to gain complete mastery of right and wrong. This is not, however, particularly in line with Christian tradition, which emphasizes the omnipotence and omniscience of God and the limitations of humans.[10]

Functionalism

What unifies all of these features of video games is that they all tend to focus on the *function* of faith and spirituality—how these things *work*. As machines, video games are systems of precisely defined elements working together according to fully defined rules. And there's nothing inherently wrong with simulations of the effects of spiritual things. Codes of morality have social effects. Religion is a sociological phenomenon that structures how people interact and how they earn and spend their treasure. Spirits and concepts of spirituality impact the way humans deal with physical reality.

The problem comes when we reduce the ambiguous, ineffable, difficult-to-understand realms of life down to *just* their observable and definable functions. Religion is more than its sociological effects. Or at least, if the Christian tradition of faith is to be believed, there's more to life than just institutions, rituals, physical matter, and electrical impulses racing around our cerebral cortexes. But a notion of reality that recognizes an immaterial omnipresent God who is beyond full human comprehension doesn't fit very easily into a video game. It's difficult enough to get our minds around how God *works*, God's effects on everyday life or the grand sweep of history, and where God's agency ends and ours begins. It's even harder to stuff the very *nature* of God into a box, especially if that box needs to be a manipulatable machine.

In short, there's more to spirit, morality, and religion than what they *do*, but what they do is exactly what the video-game medium excels at representing. One of the worst examples I've seen of this, unfortunately, is a game that tries to model Christian beliefs: the controversial real-time strategy game *Left Behind: Eternal Forces*. Based on the best-selling novel series by Tim LaHaye and Jerry Jenkins, the player controls the Christian Tribulation Force in its struggle with the antichrist's evil Global Community (read: UN) forces. Every human walking around in the game has a spirit level between 0 and 100, which determines whether a unit belongs to the evil Global Community, the redeemed Tribulation Force, or an in-between neutral. Each side has tools to raise or lower spirit values: prayer for the good guys, cursing for the bad guys. Christian spiritual warriors can use praise songs to raise the spirit levels of everyone in a certain area (the Global Community has punk rockers), but only one-on-one discussions with evangelists can bring a person across the point threshold necessary to be saved.[11]

Faith, in this game, becomes a matter of earning or losing points. It suggests that formulaic actions and behaviors can positively or negatively affect my faith. In short, spirituality and spiritual actions become technology in this video game—a far cry from a Christian faith that is built on a relationship with a living God. The religions in most video games are just like guns, footballs, and spaceships: they're power tools. I'm sure the **developers** of *Left Behind* would be the first to tell us that their game is only a partial imitation of the real experience of faith; all simulations are a simplification of reality. But this clearly illustrates the inclination of the video-game medium to systematize aspects of life that aren't mechanical.

Opening Up a Space for Spirit: The Human Positives of the Video-Game Medium

This leaves us at a pretty bleak place. When video games address religion and spirituality at all, they stand accused of teaching non-Christian ideas and mechanizing mystery. So how can we possibly argue that the medium has space for a healthy engagement of a Christian understanding of faith and spirit?

Demonic Games?

Let's start with the arguments about video games and demonic forces. The tone and character of the 1980s anti-RPG narratives was right in line with previous moral panics in American history, such as those against gangster films in the 1920s and '30s or comics in the 1950s.[12] As noted in the first chapter, some of what is going on here is likely not about the games themselves: they're just convenient screens upon which we can project other fears. We do, however, need to deal with the substance of the accusations themselves. There's superficial evidence that some video games are occult tools. Sorcery, the undead, demons, witches, and disturbing artwork are commonplace. And in a sense, gamers *do* magic when they play a spellcaster.

But games featuring these things bear little or no resemblance to real occult and New Age practices. The spells of most Fantasy RPGs are about as spiritual as actuarial tables at an insurance company. Read this description from *Dragon Age: Origins*:

Spell	Cone of Cold
Range	Short
Activation	43 [points to cast]
Cooldown	10 [seconds]
Description	The caster's hand erupts with a cone of frost, freezing targets solid unless they pass a physical resistance check, and slowing their movement otherwise. Targets frozen solid by Cone of Cold can be shattered with a critical hit. Friendly fire is possible.[13]

This is typical. No popular game I know of explains the actual process of spellcasting, just its mechanical effects. These games deal with imaginary worlds and imaginary magic—that, in fact, is the appeal.[14] The focus of most RPG players, even when playing games with (imaginary) evil characters or demonic spirits, is on each other or in-game achievement or cracking jokes—they know very well the division between the game world and the physical world.[15]

Gamers get fed up with outsiders' warnings that have little connection with the actual experience of game playing; and the worry about "satanic influences" has become a clichéd joke in game culture.[16] Game culture takes Christian hostility to games so much for granted that video-game giant EA ran a promotional campaign for its hell-themed action game *Dante's Inferno* by hiring actors to fake protest the immorality of the game in the name of Christian decency.[17]

There's virtually no evidence that video games are gateways to the occult. All we really have are the testimonies of a few people who make impossible-to-verify claims about previous involvement with occult practices. The vast majority of players who engage magic in video games have no interest in the occult, and playing these games does not typically result in personality disorders or extremely negative changes in personality.[18]

The key issue is not whether a game has magic or evil forces in it. Satan and all manner of evil behaviors appear in the Bible, and we typically don't discourage people from reading *that*. Signs and symbols aren't inherently good or evil; we need to interpret them to make them meaningful. What's key is the context in which we interpret them. Does the video game encourage cruel attitudes, hate, or anger? Does it glorify death, destruction, and suffering? Or does it show those negative attitudes and behaviors as properly harmful? Some games do, and some don't. For instance, *Dragon Age*, like many other RPGs, is full of magic and demons but allows the player to conquer the forces of evil and to live out true self-sacrifice.

To be clear, I do believe that evil is a reality, and I believe there are good and bad spirits. There are games I don't play because I believe the artwork draws too deeply on evil spirituality—a judgment based on my personal experience, context, and conviction. But I also take very seriously the affirmations in the New Testament that when Jesus is our Lord, we have protection from spiritual forces of evil.[19]

Responses to Non-Christian Ideologies

What about the challenge of non-Christian ideas and attitudes toward the church? As with the arguments about spiritual corruption, I don't think things are quite as neat and simple as the above critiques would indicate. The first reason is that many of the issues I've pointed out here are hardly limited to video games. The corrupt cleric is a staple of Western literature, going back in the Christian tradition to the Pauline Epistles and the story of Simon Magus in Acts (besides, it's often a legitimate critique!).[20] There's plenty of criticism of religion in books, movies, and TV shows, and there are lots of examinations of non-Christian perspectives. This doesn't mean video games are spiritually okay—it just means that if we're going to condemn them on the basis of representing religious ideas contrary to Christianity, then we'll have to throw out all that other media too.

Second, some game stories that seemingly promote evil don't do so as much as we might think: many narratives are only skin deep. When we look at the plots of many video games (and practically *all* our pop culture), almost all of their stories are essentially *Avatar*.[21] They are melodramas: very simple stories that feature a clearly good guy struggling to stop a clearly bad guy in a well-defined conflict.[22] Such narratives are easy to boil down: soldier of fortune with a heart of gold first betrays, then—due to the love of a woman—successfully helps an alien tribe of noble savages to fight the big bad corporation, ultimately saving the planet and becoming one with the tribe. Did I miss anything other than the floaty islands and the flying lizards?

This exact same plot is at the heart of the vast majority of video games. Peaceful tranquility reigns in the land of Hyrule but is heartlessly upset by the thoroughly evil M. Bison. The good guys seem helpless to stop the evil

Shinra corporation, but one Master Chief Petty Officer decides to take a stand against all odds. By combining the psionic energy of both Aiur and Shakuras, plus some help from best friend Clank (and the hyper-competent Elaine Marley, the love interest), the forces of good win the day.[23] Whether the good guy is super-commando Solid Snake, freelance police Sam and Max, or the witch Bayonetta, they all do about the same thing. We can call the enemy the evil sorcerer Ganondorf, the walking dead, or even the angels of heaven, but they're not really that different. So, do evil-is-good games like *Darksiders* or *Bayonetta* really challenge the ideals and values associated with *true* Christianity?

In fact, apparently non-Christian religious perspectives in video games are very often in tune with Christian ideas and values; at the very least, they are frequently thought-provoking rather than aggressively anti-Christian. This was certainly my experience playing *Dragon Age: Origins*. The religions of the game invoked all kinds of real-world traditions: the Old Gods seemed to be a pagan pantheon, the religion of the Maker and his martyred prophetess Andraste seemed clearly modeled on a militaristic medieval Christianity, and the Dwarves had a form of ancestor worship. It's possible to read the game as a critique of Christian churches and their frequent self-righteousness and inflexibility. It's possible to read the spiritual structure of the game world as a postmodern suggestion that all faiths are equally valid (or invalid). But it's also possible, as with all imaginary worlds, to read it as a thought experiment, a way to play with ideas and perspectives. If nothing else, the video game prompted me to think pretty carefully about the nature of my faith and how it could look to an outsider. In any case, I don't see an attack on the church (if that's what this game was really doing) as an attack on Jesus. We Christians screw up an awful lot, and it's good to acknowledge that.

Saying that video games contain ideas and perspectives contrary to Christian teaching does not make it imperative to stop playing them or to argue that there is no space in the medium for a Christian spirituality. Rather, I think we need to critically engage video games. We shouldn't run and hide from atheist, New Age, or Eastern spirituality–themed video games any more than we should run and hide from Greek mythology or the latest blockbuster movie spouting a vaguely pop-agnostic spirituality. To wall ourselves off, outside of the periodic retreat into a quiet wilderness that Jesus practiced, is to miss the point that *all* media is broken (including the explicitly Christian stuff) and that Christ called us to live *in* the world.

Breaking the System: Ways to Reintroduce Nonmechanical Life into Video Games

The potentially non-Christian ideologies of many video games should not lead us to discount the medium, but to exercise discernment while playing. It is true that the challenge of mechanized spirituality seems to suggest that this particular medium might be irredeemably hostile to religion and mystery. That does not, in my mind, however, disqualify it as a worthwhile human activity (I think it's difficult to spiritualize visits to the restroom, although I'd argue they're pretty significant), but it would certainly limit the cultural potential of the medium. So is this it? Is there no room for a healthy, nonmechanical Christian spirituality in video games? Ultimately, I think there *is* room: video games employ a series of tools and tactics to develop positive moral, religious, and spiritual aspects of the medium.

A Quick Trick: Using Random Numbers

One of the simplest, most widespread, and probably least effective tools for establishing mystery in video games is the use of random numbers. In board games, dice add an element of chance to games: in *Monopoly*, they determine whether we move two or twelve spaces. Likewise, video games use all kinds of random numbers: a sword attack will do between nine and sixteen points of damage, attacked troops have a 30 percent chance of running, this or that town is overcast only half the time, and so on.[24] Random numbers create fun but can do more than that.

We all know that much of life is unpredictable. While some pretend, for example, to have figured out how to succeed invariably in their quest to build romantic relationships, they're full of it. The ups and downs of courting mean that a game simulation of love can't be like chess, where nothing is left to chance. A love simulation needs random numbers. The player can increase chances to forge a lasting relationship in the simulation by buying flowers, learning another language, brushing up on *Star Trek* trivia, or getting a black belt in chocolateering. But in the end these are just modifiers; the game still has to roll the dice, because we can't buy love. Likewise, the movement of God in our hearts and in our world is anything but mechanical and predictable. A game tackling spiritual and religious themes could help itself by allowing for random numbers.

This tool, however, has significant limits. A video game can't have a truly random or improvised *system*—that's an oxymoron. Elements of the game system can be partly random, but if it's going to be a game instead of a giant computer crash, it needs to have a set of rules. The randomness exists within a decidedly predictable framework. A game that simulates a monastery or prayer or miracles can't introduce new elements that the programmers didn't allow for. In a game, then, the unpredictability of random numbers can make for a lot of fun, but it can only suggest a tiny bit of the complex mystery of spirituality, morality, and religion.

The Representational Escape from Mechanical World: Narrative

A much more promising tool for presenting or infusing mystery and examining human experience is a video game's story. Narrative may have a complicated and controversial role in video games, but it's nevertheless a huge part of both big- and small-budget productions of all types of genres. Our familiarity with stories makes them excellent tools for addressing a wide range of human experience, including nonsystematic stuff like love and spirituality. Stories are highly emotional, can be completely unpredictable, and can ask readers and viewers to use imagination.

The narrative elements in video games, such as noninteractive cut scenes, dialogue with other characters and even the story setting can, if used correctly, de-systematize or de-mechanize the experience of a video game. This is certainly the case with *Dragon Age*. One example: I learned that the dudes in the flowing robes are mages and the ones with the full suits of armor are from the Templar Order, and that Templars keep mages in line so that they don't become abominations. The game makers _could_ have reduced these characters to little abstract pieces (like a standard chess set) and made combat a set of mathematical equations. But the narrative elements ignite our imaginations, which allows nonsystematic life to return. I don't *have* to think of my friend Jowan as a tool to get points—instead, I can think of him as a person whom I can interact with, which invokes my sense of morality. I don't mean that we confuse the game with reality (that would bring us right back to the arguments about demon possession). Rather, we are able to imaginatively enter the game's world, as we can with a book or movie, allowing us to empathize without literally becoming part of the world. It's not surprising, then, that many contributors to the book *Halos and Avatars* attach theological significance to imaginative game stories. Kevin Newgren, for example, argues that Irrational Games's critically acclaimed *Bioshock*, a strange, futuristic action game set in a dark city called Rapture, "offers an opportunity to consider and feel the consequence of redeeming a fallen place."[25] An abstract game like chess couldn't support such an analysis—without a story, few would argue it has clear messages about spirituality.

However, video-game stories have their limitations as well. First of all, to this point in video-game history, the most powerful game narratives have been fully scripted in advance, leaving the player little opportunity to radically alter the plot, which reduces the sense of interactivity.[26] Second, gamers usually can ignore the narrative elements of a video game, and frequently do so, by skipping past anything that looks like a cut scene to get to the action. And finally, game narratives that don't match gameplay can create some pretty strong cognitive and emotional disconnects. When I played *Knights of the Old Republic II*, for example, I was frustrated that I had built a powerful Jedi character yet at key moments I wasn't allowed to use my skills to change the game's plot. This cheapened the power of the narrative.

The Social Escape from Mechanical World: Interaction and Interpretation

There is a final tool that game makers may invoke to bring more elements of nonmechanical interaction and thinking into the video-game experience: other people. We will talk more about this in chapter 9, but playing with real people often adds a very different element to the experience of a game. No matter how good the writing and complicated the programming, the fake computer-controlled personalities of a video game are prescribed programs that have a limited range of possible interactions with the player. Real people are generally far less predictable. This isn't to say that an artificial intelligence can't surprise us or fool us into thinking it's human, and we all know that real people can act in routine and unimaginative ways. But in the end, each human has the ability to act autonomously and imaginatively, whereas a program is limited by its code.

What this means is that all the moral and religious issues associated with humanity have the possibility of appearing in a multiplayer game. When I play the team-based, real-time, tower-defense game *League of Legends*, I find that other players can be warm and encouraging or hurtful and callous, while computer-controlled players are mute. And whenever we find real humans role playing, anything that could be part of a story could be part of the video-game experience, opening up the possibility that all the nonquantifiable aspects of faith can be explored in an imaginary world. A video game might allow players to kill and rob other players without consequence, but a human player may nonetheless decide to play an honest and upright character that simply won't do such evil.

Of course, there's possibility, and then there's reality. The gaming community is just as wonderful and flawed as any other group of humans. And while the medium certainly opens up space for social interaction that positively engages faith or spirituality or morality, that potential isn't usually tapped all that heavily in my experience. Game friendships can be wonderful, but those friendships aren't necessarily spiritual in a deep sense, and many gamers are far more focused on playing games for light, frothy fun than for tackling the deep mysteries of the universe. Don't get me wrong: I love playing with other people. I think such play is normally very healthy and builds great relationships, which are key parts of a healthy faith life. But I doubt that very much of that gaming consciously engages the spiritual and moral dimension of life for most gamers. In the end, the main point is that the social interaction opens the *potential* for such engagement, whether or not it is fully exercised.

The Joy (and Burden) of Choice

The one dimension of the video-game medium that is hard to replicate in other media is choice. The next chapter will look more closely at how in-game actions relate to the real world, but for now I want to note that a game player has a different sort of interaction with good and evil than a book reader or TV viewer does. When I read about an imaginary place or see it in a TV show, it may emotionally engage me, but I cannot change it very easily. Not so with video games.

The moral challenges a player-controlled character faces in a video game—such as my character's decision about what to do with fellow mage Jowan—are ones the player needs to decide. In noninteractive cut scenes, that need or ability to decide is temporarily suspended. But in general, video games excel at pushing the player to make choices. Of course, the player can make these choices flippantly or experimentally, but it is also possible, as it was the case for me when I was playing *Dragon Age*, that the player will engage in some serious soul searching and careful consideration. Those who haven't played a game like this might easily underestimate the power of such choice making—it can be an exercise in extreme empathy. And when players and their imaginations are heavily involved, it is quite possible to exercise faith and spirituality in a way that other media cannot match.

Responding to the Challenges: A Call to Critical Engagement of Video Games with Faith

We return now to the question I asked at the outset of the chapter: Can we use games to talk about God, good and evil, right and wrong, love, and the immaterial world of the spirit in a healthy way? I would argue that the video-game medium indeed has room for religion, morality, and spirituality. Because it is part representation and part machine, however, those things will not operate as they do in more established media such as books and movies.

Very few video games currently engage an explicitly Christian spirituality in a healthy way, but I don't think such a thing is impossible. A growing body of video games engages religion, spirituality, and morality in an interesting and challenging manner. And even when the ideas the video game espouses are problematic, they can encourage the player to grapple with important issues and perspectives. This slowly developing potential raises, I think, a couple of challenges for Christians interested in video games.

First, I think the Christian creative community is called to broaden the world of video-game spirituality. If we are to be light and salt to the world, this is a good place to do so. I don't think there is a set formula for games created by Christians, but I *do* think that our faith commitments should in some way inform the worlds and game systems we make. I keep waiting for a video game, for instance, that explores the theological concept of grace—a kind of experimental anticompetitive game.

But those of us who are unlikely to ever *make* a video game face a further challenge: we need to critically engage what we play. I've argued that we don't need to run and hide from ideas and perspectives that disagree with our own. But neither should we always play without thinking. I can't disagree with *Red Dead Redemption*'s cynical take on religion or *Fallout 3*'s marginalization of true believers unless I take notice of it and think it through. Obviously, we're fallible players and we're going to miss things. And sometimes, it's okay to just play and have fun and not worry about deep things. But as much as possible, I think God calls us to think about our entertainment and to use those thoughts to gain better understanding of our world and our relationship with God.

I confess that I'm not always pleased with the representation of religion and spirituality in video games. Many games seem to be all about destruction and suffering, as we'll discuss in the next chapter. There are some very dark places in video games, theologically speaking—places where I simply won't go as a gamer. But some of the apparently bad stuff is not necessarily wrong, and there are also some bright lights and some thought-provoking material—enough to suggest that a healthy engagement of Christian faith is possible. Before we conclude that with complete certainty, however, we need to take another look at one of the greatest demons of the medium: violence.

Games and the Culture of Destruction

Violence and Ethics in Video Games

Blasting Ourselves to Death?

Shoot or be shot. Hunt or be hunted. Kill or be killed. The *Resistance* games are set in a grim alternate history where an alien species called the Chimera is infecting and mutating the human race into a horrific race of hive-minded soldiers. All three games in the series are first-person shooters: action consists of running around a blasted world, shooting monsters and blowing up enemy installations. In *Resistance 3* (see the image on p. 52), the latest iteration of the series, the player controls a former super-soldier trying to save the last remnants of humanity from being wiped out by its ravenous and merciless enemies. The premises of this game are hardly unique. The details change, but a majority of the most famous big-budget titles in game history adopt the same kind of dog-eat-dog, shooting-oriented scenarios.

In this chapter, we'll tackle the first of two major specters attached to the cultural perception of video games: that of violence (the other is

addiction, which I will address in the next chapter). For many critics, it's
pretty cut-and-dried: video games are unacceptably violent, and playing
them leads to antisocial attitudes and behaviors. We're going to challenge
that simplistic assessment of video-game violence in several steps. First,
we need to gauge just how violent video games actually are. Then we need
to look at the body of research that the public so often associates with
questions of media violence: media-effects scholarship. After that, we'll
talk about a Christian theological perspective on media violence and how
that would apply to video games. Finally, we'll look at the connections
between the actions and experiences of a player inside and outside of a
game. In each case, we'll find that the issues are more complicated than they
may appear on the surface. There's no question that our media is awash
in violent imagery, and many video games take a culture of destruction
for granted. But what that game violence means and how we respond to
it is another thing.

The aliens never stop coming in *Resistance 3*. The player spends pretty much the
whole game shooting things (or dying).

Evaluating Games and Violence and Death

A History of Violence: Games as a Blood-Sport Arena

Video-game violence has an ancient pedigree. Many of the earliest
board games—such as chess—were simulations of war, and today's

computers are descendants of machines developed by the US military.[1] So perhaps it's not a huge shock that the first widespread computer game, *Space War*, is about two spaceships firing at each other. Plenty of early video games, such as *Pong*, were nonviolent. Exidy's arcade game *Death Race*, however, kicked off the first public outcry over game violence in 1976, as the point of it was to use a car to drive over little stick men (see image below).[2]

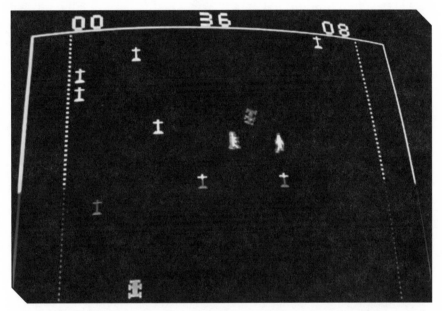

It may look primitive today, but this game was, in fact, about running over walking people. While the company later claimed these were gremlins or zombies, that wasn't the initial idea. When hit, the people turn into little crosses and make a weird, high-pitched scream.

Things took another step in the 1990s when the furor over the fighting game *Mortal Kombat* and its brutally graphic "fatality" moves led to US congressional hearings. The end result was an industry-sponsored game rating system, which today is the ESRB (Entertainment Software Rating Board).[3] Fears about video-game violence were further encouraged by the 1999 Columbine shooting; mass murderers Eric Harris and Dylan Klebold were huge fans of *Doom*, and they obsessed about the game in the writings and recordings they left behind, making explicit comparisons between the video game and their planned slaughter.[4] Today, "video games" and "violence" are virtually synonymous for many people.

Evaluating the Current Field: Are Games Really All That Violent?

So game violence is old and has gotten a lot of attention. But is video-game violence widespread, or are we perhaps unfairly singling out a few bad apples? A truly comprehensive overview is more than we can do right now, but a quick look at today's offerings shows quite a mix of violence and nonviolence.

There is no question that several video games have steadily pushed against the boundaries of taste. The premise of the 1995 game *Postal* is that the player is a deranged lunatic mowing down innocent bystanders. Developer Rockstar has made a very successful living off of controversial games such as the *Grand Theft Auto* series, which allows the player to engage in carjacking, murdering, abuse of prostitutes, and more. Extreme violence hasn't gone away in recent years. EA promoted its 2011 space-horror/zombie-survival game *Dead Space 2* with the advertising slogan "Your Mom's Gonna Hate It" and thirty-second spots showing motherly looking women reacting in shock to the incredible blood and gore of the game.[5]

Games like these, however, are notable for their excess. It's almost more important that violence has become *un*remarkable in so many best-sellers. Combat and destruction are incredibly common themes in video games. Many series, such as the many varieties of *Call of Duty*, the *Battlefield* games, *Halo* and its sequels, zombie games like *Resident Evil* or *Left 4 Dead*, and the *Fallout* games are drenched in fighting, yet they simply don't warrant much attention in the popular press and don't spark mass protest, as *Grand Theft Auto III* or *Mortal Kombat* did.

In the last decade, however, there has been a sea change in video gaming, a huge growth in the production of nonviolent games. Breakthrough title *The Sims* (in 2000) suggested to the industry that there might actually be a substantial market for games that had no shooting, sports, or car racing. The Nintendo Wii (released in 2006) further cemented the notion of a market for accessible nonviolent games, as did the rise of smartphones and ubiquitous gaming. A mass of paying customers are interested in quick, light, easy, and nonviolent video games.

While sports games, such as EA's *FIFA* (soccer) series, and racing games, such as the *Gran Turismo* games, have long been popular and aren't terribly bloody, there's a far greater variety of nonviolence today, as many of the biggest selling video games are safe and cute. Charts are likely to feature titles such as the latest versions of *Just Dance*, a physical dance series, and *The Sims*, a virtual dollhouse. The eight-hundred-pound gorilla of the industry is as likely to be the Facebook-based city-construction simulator *CityVille* as it is the latest entry in the destructive *Call of Duty* franchise. The popular press writes about hot-selling iPhone games such as doodling game *Draw Something*, cute puzzler *Cut the Rope*, and the delightful bouncing-bird game *Tiny Wings*. The violent games are still big business, but nongamers might be surprised to find how easy it would be today to play games all day long and never have to decapitate or shoot anyone.

This chapter is going to focus on the games that *are* violent, partly because they get the negative attention and partly to determine if that negative attention is fair. That means we'll be talking almost exclusively about the shooting and war games, but we need to be aware that they are *not* the sum total of gaming experience—just a prominent subset.

Do Violent Games Make Us Violent? (The Question of Effects)

The School Shooters and the Science of Media Effects

The Columbine massacre thrust video-game culture into an uncomfortable spotlight from which it has never really been able to retreat. Tragic, incomprehensible events like mass shootings prompt searches for answers, and violent video games are an easy target for blame. Every shooting since that fateful day has sparked investigations into the media use of the perpetrators. Sometimes the search turns up video-game play, as in the case of Anders Breivik, the Norwegian fanatic who shot sixty-nine people on July 22, 2011; he claimed he had played many video games and even used the popular *Modern Warfare 2* to train for the atrocity.[6] Sometimes there is little or no apparent connection to video games: Seung-Hui Cho, who committed the 2007 Virginia Tech massacre, apparently didn't play games much, if at all, as a university student.[7] But violent video games almost always get a mention.

Is this fair? I can state with certainty the general consensus within the gaming community: only ignorant outsiders would think that playing a game could cause such horrific actions. People don't shoot other people because of *Doom* or kill and rob prostitutes because of *Grand Theft Auto*. But are gamers fooling themselves? Obviously not everyone who goes crazy with a gun in virtual space does the same in real life. But if video games don't automatically program people to be mass murderers, is it still possible that media violence encourages gamers to be more violent than they otherwise would be?

The discipline of media effects examines this question. We're going to spend a few paragraphs looking over media-effects research because it is a substantial body of scholarship and because it is tremendously important to the public discourse on the issues of violence and media use. But we are not going to find easy answers here—this is complicated stuff and highly contested. Ultimately, we will turn elsewhere for answers.

Media-Effects Research

Media-effects scholars research psychological and sociological science to measure and predict how media use affects the way we think. Researchers try to isolate the impact of TV or video games from other factors of behavior. Political media-effects research, for example, could measure the opinions of a randomly selected group of voters before and after watching a negative ad to determine its effects. Many scholars in this tradition base their work on Albert Bandura's Social Learning theory, which was partly based on experiments that noted that children were more likely to attack punchable "Bobo dolls" after watching films of adults playing aggressively than children watching peaceful play. The basic argument is that we learn how to behave by observing and mimicking other people.[8] Some media-effects scholars believe that research has indisputably proven Social Learning theory and has demonstrated that watching violent media leads to short-term rises in aggression.[9] Evidence of long-term effects from violent media is harder to find, although George Gerbner's cultivation theory, based on decades of research, argues that people who watch a lot of TV tend to see the world as a scarier and meaner place than those who watch moderate amounts.[10] Nobody argues that media violence is the *only*—or even the most significant—factor in the way someone behaves, but many academics are convinced that good scholarship demonstrates that violent media texts encourage increased aggression.

Another group of scholars question these findings. They point out that human behavior in the artificial setting of a media-effects research laboratory is probably different from behavior *outside* a lab. A second problem is "publication bias": dramatic research results have greater appeal to scholarly journals and are far more likely to get published than studies that have *no* results, skewing our picture of reality. Another critique is that the definition of "media violence" varies across many studies and is often too simplistic or broad: Is the limb-rending thrill of *Gladiator* really in the same category as a cartoon anvil landing on someone's head? Most cuttingly, critics argue that believers in the effects of media violence have lost their objectivity and become political partisans rather than seriously questioning orthodoxies such as Bandura's studies. In the world of social science, where objectivity is the necessary prerequisite for *all* work, this is going for the jugular.[11] Popular authors, such as Gerard Jones in his 2002 book *Killing Monsters*, go a step further and argue that aggression, fear, and anger are going to be part of growing up, so allowing kids to engage media violence is *good*. Violent games are a better way for them to deal with negative emotions than bottling it up inside of them: "It's when people are most anxious about real violence that they most want to see it in make-believe."[12]

However, Jones's work rests largely on anecdotes—stories that are engaging but could have multiple explanations—and the scientifically unproven "catharsis hypothesis," which says that people use imaginary violence as a kind of safety valve to defuse real-world stress and tension. His lack of social-science credibility highlights another difficulty of the media-violence debate. We are actually dealing here with two conversations that often connect but ultimately remain distinct: the scholarly conversation and the public conversation. Media-effects researchers speak to one another in a dense, highly technical jargon that is necessary for them to practice their complicated craft. However, this conversation is very hard for outsiders to fully understand, and so the discussion on media violence *outside* scholarly circles is somewhat distinct, largely relying on impossible-to-prove common sense and borrowing from the academic literature when convenient. The problem is, when the nonscientific public sees results linking violent media with increased aggression, it can easily read this as: "watching violent movies makes us hurt others," when in reality the results are more complicated than that. And of course, most researchers believe in the importance of their research, so they often try to get involved in the public debate. Yet in doing so, they must translate their work into common-sense language and concepts, and this process often leads to exaggerations or simplifications of very nuanced research.

To this point, I have hardly addressed video games themselves, but the discourse about violence in video games largely follows the patterns established in the 1930s. One group of scholars is quite convinced that numerous studies show that playing violent video games creates short-term increases in aggression. Others argue that not even that limited position is verifiable with certainty.[13] The first group then responds that the critics are paid off by the video-game industry, are bad scholars, and so on.[14] From an outsider's perspective, the tone of the discussions sometimes feels quite personal, like a schoolyard fight with a lot of jargon about mathematical analysis thrown in.

Should Effects Research Be the Measuring Stick for Video Games?

So what *can* we take from all this? Well, I think it's fair to argue that there is probably *some* consistency of behavior inside and outside research labs, and enough evidence exists to suggest that exposure to violent media can lead to short-term increases in aggression. To be honest, this just makes sense. Violence is exciting. It would take a strong conscious effort *not* to get pumped up (either positively or negatively) by seeing swordfights, explosions, and shootings. I noticed this recently when I was playing *Red Dead Redemption*. There were a few intense sequences in which I had to mow down enemies with a Gatling gun, leaving my heart pounding and my hands almost squeezing the controller apart. It also makes sense to me that *unthinkingly* exposing ourselves to (or participating in) a constant stream of violent video games would shape the way we look at the world.

But there's the rub: we can and do consciously and thoughtfully engage our media, at least to some extent. Media-effects research might measure some weak, society-wide attitudes, but it can't guarantee the psychological and sociological effects of any given game on any given individual. Besides, increased aggression doesn't necessarily equal violent behavior. In the United States and Canada, violent crime rates have been falling or staying the same since they peaked in the early 1990s.[15] Could they have been even lower if there were fewer violent video games? Hard to say—but I rather doubt it.

Humans are tremendously complex beings. That doesn't mean we can't scientifically study human behavior. But it does mean that the more we find out about people, the more we realize how little we know. Also, playing video games is a meaning-making activity. As soon as we get into meaning making, truly systematic analysis becomes extremely difficult. Here's a simple example: for one person, the knife evokes the fear of an attack, and for the next, the joy of cooking. So does the image of the knife suggest violence or tastiness? Video-game worlds are phenomenally complex, requiring a lot of interpretation.

It's going to be a long time—if ever—before we get definitive proof about the psychological and social effects of violent media. But even if the evidence were stronger, I don't believe that Christian ethics rest primarily on a consequentialist logic. What do I mean by that? Well, when someone argues against violent media because of its effects, that person is justifying his or her opinion by the *consequences* of using violent media. Christians teach that sinful thoughts and actions have bad consequences, but the gospel notion of right and wrong isn't based on the results of actions alone. It's based on a relationship with a living God—the ends do not justify the means in Christian thought. It's important to consider whether violent games screw people up, but I think it's the wrong question for us right now. Instead, I think we need to be asking if playing violent video games is *inherently* wrong and is clearly outside of what a healthy relationship with God should accommodate.

Is Violent Media Inherently Wrong for Christians?

A few years ago, I came across a news article about churches using *Halo 3* gaming sessions as a way to get kids to participate in youth ministries.[16] This isn't the most disturbing game out there, but it *is* primarily about shooting. Is this an example of the church selling out—using violent tools to spread the gospel? There's a long history of argument within the church about the role of violence. Early Christians were generally pacifists, but when the emperor Constantine converted to Christianity, the church became directly implicated in state-sanctioned violence.[17] Since then, Christians have had a great diversity of opinions about violence, ranging from nearly glorifying it to arguing that God will never condone or accept violence of any sort.

In *Eyes Wide Open*, Bill Romanowski nicely describes and deconstructs the American version of the almost-pro-violence side.[18] A strong tradition within American popular culture sees violence as a tool for saving what is good by eliminating evil. Take, for instance, the *Transformers* movies: earth faces extinction at the hands of the evil Decepticons, but the upright Autobots preserve our planet through clever and righteous application of explosions and robotic fistfights. Romanowski notes that American Christians sometimes adopt these themes in explicitly Christian popular art, and I would add that we often see the same thing in real life when Christians support a kind of militaristic triumphalism in American politics: let's bomb those terrorists/radicals/dictators to hell.[19]

At the other extreme is someone like Jacques Ellul, whose excellent book *Violence* is an incredible challenge that calls readers to a radical Christian faith. Ellul argues that all of society is suffused with violence: it is unavoidable in politics, in economics, and in relationships. Yet violence is wholly outside the kingdom of God: it is all bad, and it *always* results in more violence. Once started it will be impossible to stop, he believes, partly because all perpetrators of violence seek to justify their use of it. Most damningly, however, Ellul believes that violence *cannot*, under any circumstances, lead to anything good—it can lead only to more pain and suffering.[20] For Ellul, the message of the gospel is one of freedom from the *necessities* of a broken world. Clearly, violence is *required* for our governments to function, for justice to be enforced. But this is precisely because the government is enmeshed in the corruption of original sin. The message of Christ is that the world no longer has a hold on the believer. The only way to point to the kingdom of God is to live the new and better reality as wholly as possible. A true follower of Christ may occasionally make mistakes by working within a violent system, and may be forgiven those mistakes, but we should never be under the illusion that the application of violence is God-approved.[21]

Somewhere in between the extreme of Christian militarism and radical Christian antiviolence are many flavors of more reluctant approval of violence in select cases. My favorite cultural representatives of this in-between perspective are the fictional writings of C. S. Lewis and J. R. R. Tolkien. Both men fought in the trenches for the British army during World War I. The fiction of both men emphasizes struggle between good and evil, and both present violence in a complicated manner. They reject violence as inherently negative: Lewis's beautiful visions of heaven in *The Last Battle* and *The Great Divorce* are free of violence, as is Tolkien's blessed lands in *The Silmarillion*, until they are sullied by evil. Yet both authors present the use of violence as necessary at key times—and even exciting. In Lewis's novel *Perelandra*, the hero, Ransom, spends the bulk of the story arguing with the devil to prevent the corruption of a new and still-innocent Eve, only to finally reach a point where he knows talk no longer will suffice and that he must kill the beast. Tolkien's ideal is someone like Aragorn or Faramir, men of great learning, culture, and humanity who would be perfectly happy to never lift a sword, but who know that they must excel at warfare because duty and occasion require it. And clearly the literature of both British authors thrills to the ring of the sword and the colossal clash of armies, just as do the Nordic and medieval epics they studied and loved.

For better or worse, I reject both pro- and antiviolence extremes and end up in Lewis and Tolkien's camp. I think Ellul's antiviolence is compelling in light of the overall thrust of the gospel: the story of Scripture presents death and pain and suffering as the result of corruption. Glorifying any of those things should be problematic for people who call Christ their Lord. Ever since the time of Constantine, Christians have been too easily excusing the use of state violence, and, by extension, I think we too easily excuse violence in other settings.

Yet as a child of immigrants raised in the shadow of World War II, I reject Ellul's belief that all violence ever does is corrupt and ruin and breed more violence.[22] Christian pacifists writhe around on the question of how we should deal with a Hitler, and rightfully so. The arguments for dealing with this are ingenious, but ultimately I can't believe that turning the other cheek means watching as evil people oppress my neighbor—sometimes being a passive human shield isn't enough. True, as soon as we open the door to some violence, ethics and morality become very challenging, because we can't deal with absolutes anymore. But that, I believe, is the challenge of living in this world, painful as it might sometimes be. When he cleansed the temple of money changers, Jesus himself turned to violent action—once only and for reasons that are debatable, but it certainly suggests we should hold a nuanced view on the matter. I don't want to pretend that this issue is settled in my mind. I worry that I am taking the easy way out, to be frank, because the way of violence is the horrible but familiar default of this world. On balance, however, I think there's space for justifiable use of violence by Christians.

Even if we accept this position, however, we're left with a very knotty question: What is the difference between flying a plane into a building in a game and in the physical world? In other words, how, exactly, do the arguments about physical violence translate to *representations* and *virtual enactment* of violence? They are obviously not the same thing, but the nature of the difference is important. I have argued that Christians can practice violence in times of unusual need, but the apparent evil of violence has a great deal to do with the damage it causes: physical pain, ruptured relationships, the spawning of hatred. In a video game, however, decapitating an orc hurts no physical living being, even if it looks convincing. So what's the relationship between representation and the physical world?

Is It Ever Okay to Kill a Zombie? The Problem of Freedom, Interpretation, Game Morality, and Ethical Actions

While writing this chapter, I fell back into playing one of my favorite strategy games: *Tropico 3*, a simulation of running a Caribbean dictatorship during the Cold War (see illustration on p. 63). The game creates a complex nation on an idyllic island, challenging the player to build an economy from the ground up via agriculture, resource exploitation, industry, and tourism. El Presidente (the player) is responsible for wages, health care, food supply, education, housing, law enforcement, and more, and poor performance on any of these scores leads to disaffected citizens leaving, rebelling, or voting the hapless leader out of power. While all this is interesting and challenging, what *really* livens up the game is its narrative elements and flavor. The artwork is great, as is the music. Even more important are the dozens of little elements that play off the stereotype of the "banana republic." For instance, El Presidente has the option of setting work levels to either "sweatshop," described as a "standard 14-hour work day full of joy and merriment" or "easy-does-it," which increases job quality but decreases worker output because of a shorter day. The dictator can rig elections. Radio and television broadcasts can be set to propaganda. And more darkly, the player can establish secret police that can make opponents disappear.

To those of who have grown up in free democracies, this is all good fun. The lighthearted nature of the game makes it clear that this is all intended in a joking manner. The trouble is, for anyone who has ever lived through the horror of a dictatorship, the banana republic is no laughing matter. Prominent game scholar Gonzalo Frasca, who hails from Uruguay, a country with a troubled political history, has called *Tropico* "nothing short of disgusting,"[23] and can we blame him? It's easy for North Americans to think a small-scale autocracy in a developing nation is no big deal, but corruption and political murder is awful for the people affected. At the same time, isn't it possible that Frasca is overreacting? It's a *game*, after all.

This gets to the heart of the problem: Is it okay to do wrong in a video game?[24] In the previous chapter, I talked about games with good and evil in them. What I didn't focus on then is that most of them allow us to play *either* moral path. *Tropico* does not force the player to be a bloodthirsty despot: I can play a democratic reformer who raises the quality of life for the impoverished (which, in fact, is what I almost always do). This kind of choice is true of most strategic god games, and it's also frequently the case with so-called **open-world games.** *Fallout: New Vegas*, for example, allows us to take the route of the paragon or murderous sociopath. Of course, even the "good" paths in such games typically involve liberal doses of violence. So is an action that is wrong outside a game wrong inside a game? What does *role playing* mean, ethically and morally speaking?

In *Tropico 3*, the player is a Caribbean dictator, managing the politics and economy of a small island nation.

Unsurprisingly, a wide variety of perspectives exist on the relationship between in-game and out-of-game thought and action. Some believe that games are special spaces where the normal rules don't apply—an excellent place for us to work through ethical decision making. Others argue that this is mistaken—we can see all kinds of connections between games and the real world, even if those connections are hard to map and predict.

Playing in the Magic Circle

One group of game scholars and intellectuals argue that games are places where the normal rules don't apply, and that we have to consider in-game actions as completely different from out-of-game actions. In his classic study of games, *Homo Ludens*, Dutch scholar Johan Huizinga argues that games occur within a "magic circle."[25] While the players are within a game, the normal rules of society function differently, and actions within it can operate according to fundamentally different principles (i.e., the game's rules).

Think about how chess players act. They ruthlessly kill each other's armies. They show no mercy or kindness. In short, they demonstrate the behaviors we associate with sociopaths and dictators. In a game, however, the destructive drive to win is completely acceptable. Philosopher Bernard Suits, in his delightful book *The Grasshopper*,[26] argues that this situation is in place because games constitute an agreement to follow highly artificial rules. In fact, games are highly inefficient. Suits notes that it would be much easier to get a golf ball in the hole simply by walking up to it and dropping it in. The unnecessary requirement of using clubs, however, makes it a game. In short, "playing a game is the voluntary attempt to overcome unnecessary obstacles."[27] The upshot of this is that we don't hold players to the same standards in a game that we would in real life—we have agreed in advance that we will *not* act as if it were real life. If I stab my opponent in the back while playing *Call of Duty*, there are no grounds for murder charges; nobody was really killed, everyone knew from the beginning that we were playing a game, and this is what happens in those games.[28]

Thus, some commentators argue, a game is a safe space to try things, to experiment with ethics and morality.[29] At every point in the game, we are faced with choices that can have a powerful impact on the game world, for good or for ill. But no matter how many virtual armies I beat, no matter how many enemies I mow down, no matter how badly I screw up, not a single physical person gets hurt. I am operating in a different space with different rules. It's exactly like the kid in the sandbox kicking over fragile cities and plastic army men. However, unlike the physical playground, video games can support complex enough worlds that we get to see some of the digital consequences of our digital actions.

A game—like a novel or a movie—*can* tell us what is right and wrong and force us to do right. But some scholars argue that the best games let the kid kick over the sandcastle. The decision making of video games, they argue, is a great moral and ethical positive for the medium—even if we make so-called evil choices—because we learn different points of view and have to think them through.[30] A study that interviewed players of video RPGs video games suggested that even violent video games can get players to engage moral and ethical issues—the more consequential the decisions in the game, the more likely the players are to engage in critical ethical reasoning.[31] This was certainly evident to me in *Dragon Age*, as I noted in the last chapter: I had to deal with religious and moral perspectives that were alien to me and then figure out how that applied to my characters. It was an exercise in moral or ethical imagination.

Poking Holes in the Magic Circle

A number of scholars, however, are starting to poke holes in the concept of the magic circle.[32] Common sense and common experience suggest that there are plenty of connections between what happens in a game and outside of a game. Anyone who has played *Settlers of Catan* with a spouse or significant other, for example, knows that a particularly nasty, cutthroat play can have implications for that day's kissing quota. And why would gamers put such a high value on realism in games if there is no connection between game actions and actions outside of a game? In fact, it is impossible for games to make any sense (and thus be playable) unless they use language or meaningful sounds and images, all of which derive meaning from life outside the game.

Several scholars dislike contrasting games with "real life," which is why I've tried to avoid using that distinction in this book. The virtual worlds of **Massively Multiplayer Online games** (**MMOs**) are worth billions of dollars, and actions taken in them generate real money; obviously the game has some level of reality.[33] And it's not as if we totally forget who we are once we start playing games. As one scholar puts it:

> We cannot say that games are magic circles, where the ordinary rules of life do not apply. Of course they apply, but in addition to, in competition with, other rules and in relation to multiple contexts, across varying cultures, and into different groups, legal situations, and homes.[34]

Some players identify very strongly with their avatars, the digital characters who represent them in the game. One small study, for example, found that when participants played *The Sims 2*, their play style mirrored important parts of their own psychology (e.g., players who were very conscientious were more likely to want their Sims to have a clean house).[35] In addition, many video games are places of real social interaction. Games such as the online–combat-strategy game *League of Legends* are full of people playing together while typing messages to each other or talking on voice chat. Such interaction is rarely deep stuff, but it *is* real conversation between real people. All this means that, in a sense, games *are* real life just as much as the world of finance or literature or education.

On the face of it, this would suggest that we cannot argue that game violence is not real and totally disconnected from our out-of-game life. But while it makes sense to argue that games definitely have a connection to life outside of games, the exact nature of that connection is not straightforward. Part of the complication is exactly how players think about their avatars. In *The Sims 2*, a few players go against the grain and use the game as an excuse to do everything they *wouldn't* do outside of the game.[36] Other studies confirm that while players definitely identify with their avatars, *how* they identify varies greatly—in fact, many players will create multiple avatars in the same game so as to try out different identities.[37]

Another complication arises from what we've already touched on in chapter 2 and earlier this chapter: a game has different levels of meaning and experience, such as narrative and gameplay. *Sid Meier's Pirates!* has frequent cartoony swordfights, and the victory cut scene shows the defeated captain jumping into the water or being swept overboard—there's no graphic representation of death in *this* game's story. In contrast, in *Fallout: New Vegas* we get to blast apart feral ghouls in slow motion, which is quite a narrative contrast. In terms of gameplay, however, they are identical: after a contest, the defeated entity ceases to exist. So if the player connects the game to what we typically call "real life," what exactly does he or she connect with: the game's narrative or its gameplay?

The best scholarship I've read on this suggests that any interpretation or understanding of a game is highly culturally situated; that is, how we understand the game has everything to do with where we come from, who we know, how we're playing, and so on. One study, for example, took the infamous *Grand Theft Auto: San Andreas* and talked to teens of different races and classes—unsurprisingly, the researchers found a wide range of opinions on what the game meant.[38]

Not only is our cultural context important, but some scholars argue that we are able to engage the same game on multiple levels of understanding. Sociologist Gary Alan Fine, who spent a lot of time hanging out with role-playing gamers in the early 1980s, argued that players used multiple "frames"—perspectives or ways of looking at the world—to understand games. On one level, they thought of themselves as adventurers in an imaginary world. At the same time, they thought of themselves as game players, conscious that they were engaged in a fiction. And at an even higher level, they saw themselves as ordinary, everyday human beings. Fine saw over and over again that players could rapidly switch from one frame to another while in the middle of the game.[39]

The point of all this is that the experience of a game is a complicated thing. I suspect many of us have had the experience of playing a board game and carrying on an unrelated conversation at the same time. On one level, the game is a game, but at the same time, it is a social site—a kind of chat room. I can attest that the same sort of mental splitting happens when playing a video game, even if I'm playing solo. One part of my mind is figuring out what Boadicea, the mage of Ferelden, is feeling and thinking, another part is strategizing how to beat game challenges so I can get to the next cut scene, and a further part is busy analyzing how to turn playing *Dragon Age: Origins* into a promotion to full professor. Any gamer is similarly likely to have multiple connection points with the video game. In short, if we're looking for a nice straight line between shooting dangerous robots in a digital futurescape and behavior at the office, we're very unlikely to find it.

Conclusion: To Shoot or Not to Shoot

So what have we determined at this point? First, that media effects can't give us an unequivocal answer about how engaging violent media affects us, at least beyond a debatable short-term rise in aggressive attitudes in a laboratory setting. So I've argued that because of this—and really because of the Christian worldview—we need to base our discussion on something other than consequences. Right should be done for the sake of our relationship with God. Second, there is tenuous scriptural support for Christians to practice limited applications of violence (in real life), but there really isn't much room for the glorification of violence. Third, the actions we take *in* video games connect with the life we live *outside* of video games, but not in any simple way: video games are also special spaces where normal rules don't apply in the same way they do outside. Up to this point in the chapter, I've really been asking questions and letting other people speak, but I have to take a stand here and decide whether or not I can shoot another person in *Red Dead Redemption*. So, taking all the stuff we've just discussed, here's what *I* think.

Game Violence Is Not Real Violence

Ending a digital life is not the same as ending a physical one, and apparent pain is not the same as experienced pain. We get so bogged down in the debate about violent media that it is easy to forget this fact. It may be reasonable to argue that splattering innards across a digital landscape is in poor taste or even morally revolting. But it is not reasonable to equate pressing the "X" button with pulling a real trigger attached to a real gun that maims and kills physical, living human beings.

The only reasonable fear linking physical and digital violence is that digital actions could encourage antisocial physical actions. But that concern attributes too much power to the video game. *Players* need to make sense of the game and they need to process those meanings, or the game does nothing. When gamers go violent in the physical world there's almost certainly something else going on there. Millions of gamers play violent games, and most do not engage in seriously violent actions. Destructive games are certainly arousing, but to be honest, even chess can have that effect: competition of any kind can get our blood boiling.

In fact, it may be surprising to nongamers, but the most visceral, graphic images can start to become a little irrelevant to gamers. The first time a player encounters a game, the graphics and sound can really grab the player's attention. After a while, however, as the player repeats actions, the narrative fades and the mind shifts its focus to the gameplay—the ghoul ceases to be a rotting, raving undead monster and becomes simply a roadblock or a point-scoring opportunity. We might call this desensitization, but for some gamers at least, it is *not* a lust for destruction: eventually, some gamers start treating the representation of violence as the fiction that it is.[40]

The main point is that game violence is not real violence. That doesn't make violent video games *right*, but it does mean we can't apply the ethical and moral standards relating to physical violence in any simple way.

Stories and Games Need Conflict

I also believe that most art—whether it be visual art, storytelling, games, or whatever—needs conflict. I don't know what life was like before the fall of Adam and Eve, and I'm not sure what the renewed creation will be like. Maybe perfection means the absence of conflict. But in the broken world that we presently occupy, struggle is part of existence. A story or game without conflict isn't much of a story, because it has limited connection with our own experience. It's not an accident that the story of God's people—the sacred narrative at the heart of the Christian faith—is full of conflict (some of it quite brutal). We need to work through that conflict in our stories and in our games.

It is true that not all conflict has to be violent. Many excellent, tense video games are all about running, jumping, dodging, and so on, but not killing or destroying, including classics like *Pac-Man* or abstract music-based racing games like *Audiosurf* or *Rhythm Racer*. It is also true that conflict does not *have* to be gory and disturbing—Mario, for example, dispatches Goombas with zero bloodshed—although whether or not that's positive is a matter of opinion. Is a bloodless swordfight of the swashbuckling *Three Musketeers* type antisocially violent, harmless fun, or blithely encouraging the idea that violence is consequence-free? No matter the standard invoked, narrative conflict *can* avoid blood and guts.

But *can* and *should* are two different things. Unquestionably gory, bloody conflict is not unquestionably wrong. The apostle Paul exhorts us in Philippians to dwell on whatever is true, noble, right, pure, lovely, admirable, excellent, and praiseworthy. This is a high standard, and on first glance, a gritty, dystopian game like *Fallout 3* might not make the cut. But if we brush off the grime, we find a gem beneath the surface—in fact, the gem might *need* the grime to really highlight its beauty. The characters of this world live in hard conditions, but their humanity (both good and bad) shines through. They struggle with survival, have goals and dreams, commit crimes, forgive, and sacrifice for the greater good. As with the troubling stories of Israel's sinfulness in the book of Judges, sometimes the light shines most brightly in the darkness. Much of the struggle we face in the physical world *is* awful, and many of the monsters of our minds and culture are brutal. To put it another way: clean and clever *VeggieTales* is great, but not every production needs to be *VeggieTales*.

Video games are particularly good at allowing us to *play* with conflict—to test it and tease it and see it from multiple points of view. I don't think that being able to play through evil is an invariably positive experience, but at the same time, I agree that having a trial space for imagination gives us an opportunity to grow. To put it in more concrete terms: being able to stray from the righteous path in *Tropico* makes my Tropican democracy all that more impressive; if I had no choice, there would be no moral growth for me. Here's a nongame parallel: I think few Christians would critique C. S. Lewis for writing the deeply insightful *Screwtape Letters*, but to do so, the author had to imaginatively think like a demon.

Caution against Empty Violence

As is so often the case, it is very easy to take justifications in directions that end up in a very wrong place. This has certainly been the case with the seductive call of violence in real life: it has historically been too easy for men with power and revolutionaries to justify killing and destruction. While media violence is different from the physical kind, I think the same problem applies. Representations of murder and mayhem should have an inherent negative value for a Christian. That doesn't mean we can never justify playing violent games—as I've just argued—but we can't come to that conclusion too easily.

Many video games deploy violence for all the wrong reasons: to provide cheap emotional thrills, to provide shock appeal, to get publicity, to satisfy bloodlust. Christians should be very cautious in approaching these games. When video-game violence is simply titillating and nothing else, it is sure to have an uneasy relationship with a faith centered on redemption, peace, and shalom.

There's No Magic Answer: Judge Media Violence Based on Context

These might seem to be half-answers: *some* violence is empty and wrong, while *some* graphic violence sets the stage for powerfully redemptive messages. Isn't this just waffling or ducking the issue? Ultimately, I don't think so. Many people who debate the rightness or wrongness of violence in video games seem to be looking for a simple standard: all video-game violence is wrong or all of it is just fine. But I believe the meaning of video-game violence and its rightness or wrongness should be judged in context. This means there is no single prescription for all games and all players.

A whole series of factors should play into any judgment of violent video games. Who is the player, and what is his or her mind-set, maturity, beliefs, and perceptiveness? Does the game in question have some apparent effects on this particular individual or community of players? It might be hard to *generalize* about the effects of games, but that doesn't mean we can't look for them carefully on a smaller scale. Just as important, what is the cultural context of the game and the player? A player from a middle-class background is going to understand *Grand Theft Auto* quite a bit differently than someone who has grown up in an impoverished inner-city neighborhood. Certain outcomes, however, will *tend* to be true across multiple contexts. It's hard for me to believe, for instance, that a steady diet of nothing but video-game violence is *not* going to shape how we see the world. And I'm not totally convinced about the value of playing violent games to "blow off some steam." But I also think that gamers often have a far more sophisticated understanding of the games they play than outsiders give them credit for.

What I believe is that for the Christian, all things are permissible, but not all things are beneficial.[41] What this means in practice is constant self-monitoring, conversation, and engagement. Do bloodthirsty games encourage me to be bloodthirsty? Am I less sympathetic to the oppressed after playing video games? Am I buying into attitudes and ideologies that I should not, attitudes that glorify destructive acts, inflicting pain, and causing death? The answer may not always be yes, and so the violent video games may be simply okay, or even possibly beneficial. But we should always be prepared to think through our game playing. Unexamined ideas, actions, beliefs, and mind-sets can impact us; conscious engagement makes a difference.

War, pain, danger, suffering, and excitement will always be part of the human condition while we still live. Many video games reflect that reality. Will we use those games to grapple with or to glorify violence?

◀ ⑤ ▶

Escape!

The Peril of Addiction and the Promise of Fantasy

Worlds Full of Danger?

In February of 2011, a Chinese man in his thirties collapsed while playing a video game at an internet cafe. He was pronounced dead at a clinic shortly thereafter. This story made headlines around the world because it wasn't just any game-playing session. He had been on his computer for three straight days with no sleep and little food, and he had spent $1,500 on online gaming in the month before his death.[1] What happened? It's what most people would call addiction. He simply couldn't stop playing.

When I speak with nongamers about video games, I can almost guarantee that two issues will pop up: the problems with violence and the specter of addiction. The latter fear is so strong that it has permeated our popular culture. The morning I started to write this chapter, my kids were watching *Martha Speaks*, a cartoon about a family with a talking dog, and lo and behold, it was all about how Martha's owner Helen becomes addicted to video games on a "Game Kid." The normally responsible young lady neglects her homework, her promises, and—worst of all—her responsibility to feed the dogs. She gets a haggard look and becomes highly irritable.[2] Only when Martha steps in can Helen snap out of it. Kid's shows aren't typically on the front line of addiction research—the fact that the producers used this story line suggests that it's pretty widespread in our culture.

This is a real issue that needs some careful discussion. There is no question that millions of people find video games engrossing, and that some of these people go off the deep end, playing games so much that they destroy their own lives. Yet at the same time, the vast majority of video gamers are just as socially well-adjusted as nongamers. What is going on here? Are games dangerous traps or do they free us from cares and concerns? To answer that question, we're going to look at two bodies of research that normally don't fit together. First, we'll investigate current scholarship on video-game addiction. Second, we'll consider what mid-twentieth-century British authors and scholars J. R. R. Tolkien and C. S. Lewis had to say about fantasy and myth. What ties these two bodies of research together is the common theme of *escape*: video games allow us to leave our primary reality and enter a secondary reality. What we'll find is that this characteristic of the medium is a double-edged sword.

Video Games and Addiction Research

Stories about Addiction

Anyone I've ever talked to who's a true gamer knows games exert a kind of mental pull. If we're in the middle of a really good session, the last thing we want to do is quit. Those of us who are *Civilization* gamers know we have to wake up for work in five hours, but, well, we could afford just *one* more turn. And if we have to stop playing for mundane things like sleep, food, work, or time with family, parts of our minds are still working on the game, anticipating getting back to it, looking up strategy guides and using spare moments to plan how to defeat those pesky Persians or French.

Clearly, many people go beyond a general reluctance to quit or a temporary obsession with a game. MMOs have had problem gamers for a long time. The stories from formerly obsessive MMO players can be sad and chilling. One writer for a video-game news website wrote an excellent feature-length piece that reads exactly like a story of substance abuse. He started playing the MMO *EverQuest* as consolation after a breakup with the love of his life and essentially lost the next year or two of his life, ruining relationships, losing jobs, and withdrawing into himself, all because he played the game compulsively.[3] This is not an uncommon story. Websites such as On-Line Gamers Anonymous and WoW Detox (named after both *World of Warcraft*, the most popular MMO in the world with more than ten million subscribers, and drug and alcohol "detox" programs) are full of testimonies and pleas from people who struggle to stop playing.[4]

The Sims Social is all about gaining skills and upgrading consumer items, both of which go easier with an infusion of (real) cash.

In the last few years, however, the phenomenon has broadened from the relatively niche culture of MMO games to the mass culture of **social games**. The biggest games on Facebook dwarf *World of Warcraft*, counting their player populations by tens of millions: games like *CityVille*, *The Sims Social*, and *FarmVille*. They charge no subscription or entry fees, instead making their money off of optional purchases of decorative or gameplay items. *The Sims Social* (see illustration above), for instance, constantly invites the player to spend money on items that help the player level up or on cool furniture and decorations that aren't available for those who play for free. Stories have emerged of compulsive or excessive gaming, often by people who never would have touched a game console or an MMO. For example, one player interviewed for a feature on *FarmVille* claimed she played from 10:00 am to midnight every day.[5] We can see further evidence of unhealthy play in the economics of these games: they are wildly profitable even though over 90 percent of their players play for free.[6] How? A tiny percentage of the gamers are "whales" who spend over $1,000 per year on virtual tractors, furniture, and other collectibles. "Super whales" exceed $5,000 per year, with a few documented cases of spending in excess of $25,000 (and rumors suggest some spend more than $100,000).[7] Isn't this evidence of compulsive behavior? Who in their right mind would unload thousands of dollars a year on colored digital hay bales?

Mental Tricks of Addiction

Actually, some researchers aren't at all surprised by this kind of behavior. They have been pointing out for years that, much like gambling, video games are perfectly structured to foster addictive behavior. Most video games are just like "Skinner boxes," the cages for rats that behaviorist psychologist B. F. Skinner used to research how our brains compel us to act. In his experiments, rats that pushed a lever got a food reward. Experiments with "reward schedules," the pace at which the food appeared, produced fascinating results. Rats receiving food at fixed intervals of time—say, every three minutes—didn't really learn any desired behavior, because they were getting what they wanted regardless of what they did. A "fixed ratio schedule," under which the rat would get a reward for a set number of actions meant rats pushed the pedal more, but not too often, as they knew they could get pellets whenever they wanted. What made them frantic was a "random reward schedule": pedal pushing would still give food, but only after an unpredictable number of pushes. Since the rats didn't know when exactly the reward was coming, they worked harder.[8]

Game designers have been consciously applying these principles to video games for at least a decade, and unconsciously for a lot longer than that. Practically all games feature some kind of reward for a player. The reward of *Tetris* comes when we fit the piece into exactly the right spot, and all the lines of blocks disappear, shifting everything down. In RPGs like *Neverwinter Nights* or *Diablo 3*, defeated opponents drop loot such as money, weapons, potions, or armor. In *FarmVille*, harvesting crops gives money. Many games, however, encourage compulsive reward hunting by the way these rewards are doled out. Most games give plenty of easy rewards at the beginning—victories aren't challenging and gold is plentiful. As the game goes on, however, rewards become less frequent and less predictable. Players have to invest ever-greater amounts of time to achieve what they want to get.[9]

Another psychological phenomenon that many game researchers have talked about is "flow." Psychologist Mihály Csíkszentmihályi notes that people can achieve a special psychological state of intense concentration and pleasure when doing activities that are challenging yet feasible, have clear goals, and give clear feedback.[10] While he observes this flow state in all kinds of human behavior, today's video games are well engineered for this kind of outcome: they tend to start easily, give players clear and feasible goals, provide increasing challenge, and let the player know exactly how he or she is doing. When I started *League of Legends*, for example, the computer-powered opponents were none too hard, and when I graduated to playing against other humans, the ranking system put me in matches with people just as inexperienced as I was, meaning the challenge was interesting but didn't usually get out of hand. In addition, while playing the game, I was constantly aware of what I had to do and how well I was doing at it via animations, clocks, and scores. These are all elements of a recipe to create a kind of psychological high.[11] Another commonly used game term that has similar connotations to flow is "immersiveness," which is the idea that when players dive in (immerse themselves) in the attractive alternate realities of video games, they partly lose touch with physical reality.[12]

Some discussions of addiction include the concept of "tolerance," the idea that a substance (like drugs) or activity (pathological gambling) that produces a high eventually gives diminishing returns, meaning the user steadily needs more of it to produce the same effect.[13] Video games are perfectly built for this kind of one-upmanship. RPG designers know that a +1 broadsword might be okay when we're just starting the game, but by halfway through, we'd better be getting a +10 two-handed Sword of Smiting or we're outta there. Not coincidentally, this feature of video games also plays into our tendency to act like pack rats and to be greedy. We like to hoard things—to pick them up, admire them, and then put them away and forget about them, except when we want to compare them with others' things.[14] This is a big part of social gaming. Some of the most popular games, like *FarmVille*, involve virtually nothing else except collecting.[15] We always need more stuff.

When the features of the game fail to keep people attached, peer pressure often keeps them from leaving. As we'll discuss in chapter 9, many (perhaps most) of the most popular video games today are highly social.

The social games on Facebook are obvious examples, filled with constant invitations to share with friends or to invite them to join. But MMOs are even more intensely social. Most players join a guild—a kind of team or club that adventures together—and the relationships formed in these groups can be very strong. Guilds lean on members to participate as fully as possible, because missing warriors on a game mission can equal failure. Of course, that means that if players try to step away from the game or moderate their play, their friends pressure them to come back.[16]

The compulsion-encouraging psychological characteristics of video games are front ended by very easy entry. Free-to-play games usually don't push too hard for players to make purchases—nobody makes us buy a nice stereo system in *The Sims Social*. But once we're there, all of the other enticements kick in, and it's simple to purchase something if we ever care enough. Easy to start, harder to quit.

The Problems with the Case for Addiction

It sure looks as though video games are ideal addiction-building machines, that they have an inherent tendency to suck gamers into another world and keep them there (longer than they should). What appears obvious, however, is not quite as simple as it seems. It turns out that the idea of video-game addiction is a contested idea. Nobody denies the reality of unhealthy game playing, but many critics argue that calling video games "addictive" is seriously problematic.

The first problem is that of definition: what, exactly, qualifies as video-game addiction? Studies on the topic typically adapt tools to measure other kinds of addiction, such as gambling. But, some psychologists point out, substance abuse directly affects neurochemistry, and a primary purpose for gambling is to make money—neither of which typically applies to video games.[17] One recent study suggests an overlap between addiction to games and other psychological disorders: it found that an antidepressant drug reduced video-game addicts' desire to play *StarCraft II*.[18] It will take some time to tease out exactly what's unique and not unique about compulsively playing video games.

There's a more fundamental problem, however. How do we distinguish between healthy play of video games and harmful play? The amount of time spent playing is a surprisingly problematic standard, as some heavy-playing gamers seem to be otherwise psychologically stable: they are able to maintain relationships, keep jobs, and generally report being happy. In her *Newsweek* interview, the fourteen-hour-per-day *FarmVille* player, for example, claimed to be managing quite fine, and reported that her husband was even supportive of her play habits.[19] We may take such claims with a healthy dose of salt, but psychologists are right to be cautious here since we are in the midst of a cultural shift in media use. Most gamers play far less than that *FarmVille* fanatic, yet many people see even moderate play as suspicious. I highly doubt if many of us would be particularly alarmed if someone we knew were reading for twenty to thirty hours a week (three or four hours a day). But if someone replaced all twenty or thirty hours of reading with video-game play, many would be tempted to call that behavior an addiction. There may be concerns about games' impact on literacy, but in terms of media use, the gamer and the reader are about the same—so, no, time use by itself cannot be a measure of addiction, at least not in any simple way.[20] Psychologists have invoked other standards than length of play, of course, including things like "salience," by which they mean the amount of a person's thoughts the video game takes up. But even these other standards are contested. To date, nobody has been able to satisfactorily define video-game addiction: major medical associations such as the AMA and the psychologist's guide DSM-IV have not certified video-game addiction as an official mental disorder or disease.[21]

Even if psychologists were to establish such a list of problem behaviors that we could call "addiction," how could we identify the cause? This is not splitting hairs: if we don't know what the cause is, can we really blame video games? If we can't blame the games themselves, then removing the games would not solve any problems. Anything can attract compulsive behavior, the argument goes, if there is an underlying and unaddressed problem. If someone is deeply unhappy about something—a failed or failing relationship, a deep dissatisfaction with work and career, feelings of inadequacy, and so on—video games certainly can serve as a kind of coping mechanism. Video games become a form of escape from the festering problems. But stamp collecting or dog shows or even reading (gasp!) could fill the same need. Certainly this is the opinion of game journalist Mike Fahey, who argues that *Everquest* did not involuntarily suck him in:

> I hid. I ran from my problems, hiding away in a virtual fantasy world instead of confronting the issues that might have been easily resolved if I had addressed them directly. As far as I am concerned, the only thing Sony Online Entertainment [maker of *Everquest*] is guilty of is creating a damn good hiding place.[22]

There are also big-picture critiques of the concept of video-game addiction. For example, some argue game addiction is a convenient scapegoat to help us deal with the rapid and sometimes frightening cultural shift to an era of instantaneous global communication. As we've already seen, new technologies are screens onto which we project our hopes and fears.[23] The problem, goes the argument, is twofold. First, the idea of video-game addiction rests on technological determinism—the idea that our machines control our destinies. This is a deeply unpopular notion with many intellectuals, partly because it greatly oversimplifies the way humans work, and partly because it shuts off any possibility for us to change anything. Technologies really do not operate by themselves: we invented the pen and paper, and we are the ones who decide what to do with these creations. Often when we shrug our shoulders and say, "Meh. Can't stop technology," we are abdicating our responsibility to make the world better. And this, goes the critique, is exactly what's happening when we call video games addictive. Instead of blaming the machine, we should be working to fix underlying problems.

The other big-picture problem with the idea of video-game addiction is that it unfairly singles out the new technology. This is something I can attest to. As a public speaker on new technologies, I get an earful about the ills of video games—and other digital devices too. But I almost never have anyone complain about the problems of reading or furniture. We have become accustomed to these ancient technologies, but I can guarantee that humanity became something different after the invention of the chair. All technology has an impact on how we live—and here I'm taking a stance of "soft technological determinism," arguing that while our inventions don't control us, they *do* influence what we can and can't do and what is easier and more difficult to do. What many critics of video games—and those worried about video-game addiction in particular—miss is that technologies we take for granted also have problems. Since none of us were around to see the changes that the printing press wrought on culture, we don't normally realize that it is just as unnatural as digital technology. It *is* true that we've had more time to figure out the foibles, but in many cases, our very values for judging a technology are impacted by that technology; that is, we judge books by the standards of a post-book culture.

In fact, I would argue that reading can be just as much a cause of addictive behavior as video games. I have largely stopped reading pop fiction novels because I can't put them down. My wife can attest that the last few times I picked up a new Harry Potter book, I was essentially gone for two or three days. While I have a tendency to play video games longer than I intend, I don't go off the deep end with them as I do with a book I'm really enjoying. However, since our culture is familiar with literacy and video games are newcomers, we are likely to single out the new medium's problems in a disproportionate fashion.

So Are Video Games Addictive or Not?

So what do we do with these apparently contradictory sets of arguments? Perhaps the most important question to start with is: can people become addicted to video games? I think the answer is a qualified yes. It seems undeniable that there are people who play compulsively, who can't stop even when their excessive play results in all kinds of damage to themselves and to others around them that they love. There are too many stories and too many studies describing game addiction to argue that it is impossible. I think psychologists are wise to be careful about defining the condition—it would be very easy to draw the net too wide and cause unnecessary fear and criticism of games and game players. I also believe that a temporary obsession with a video game is okay: it's a very light form of that infatuation we feel when we first fall in love and friends get sick of us constantly mooning over our new object of affection. God built us to enjoy life. But we can obsess so much that the activity—be it playing video games or stamp collecting—is no longer fun and hurts those around us. I like the way one blogger puts it: "Addiction is not about what you *do*, but what you *don't do* because of the replacement of the addictive behavior."[24] When playing a video game takes away other activities—or takes away the *enjoyment* of other activities—then we've got a problem. The fact that we don't currently have an official medical diagnosis for such behavior doesn't mean the mental illness doesn't exist.

I'll take one step further and say that I think that we can attach *some* blame to video games themselves: many are deeply attractive to escape to. I do *not* think we are helpless to resist all the psychological cues discussed over the previous pages. I think we can feel a pull and decide to reject it—I do it all the time, and I'm sure most people do. We are not unconscious machines. But the pull of games makes them more likely to encourage compulsive behavior than many other things. People escape into addictions to hide from unresolved problems, and video games are better at facilitating that escape than other things. To put it another way, playing video games is more likely to be addictive than, say, cleaning the cat litter.

That said, here are a few caveats. First, video games are *far* from being inevitably addictive. One study I found pegged a gaming population's addiction rate at 12 percent of a game community, but I haven't seen anything else that high, and it's possible that even figures of 5 percent are likely to be quite inflated, due to the problematic definitions of addiction we discussed.[25] The vast majority of players do not develop addictions, in other words. A second point is that not all video games are the same. While game designers talk about trying to make their games "addictive" (by which they typically mean "compelling," in the same way a good book or movie is),[26] not all of them are terribly successful. Bad games, in other words, are less likely to be addictive.

More important, there are so many different *kinds* of games that their psychological effect simply can't be identical. *The Sims Social* on Facebook constantly bombards the player with requests to share gifts and announcements of accomplishments. There's no such pestering when playing *Red Dead Redemption*. Clearly, the games have different kinds of social pull. Some games are more consciously manipulative than others. Social-game-maker Zynga (maker of *FarmVille* and *CityVille*) has a machinelike system of researchers constantly testing to find the most effective sales pitches and items in their games,[27] but we shouldn't tar all game makers with the same brush. With some exceptions, the games that require ongoing investments from players—either in the form of subscription fees or in-game purchases—are going to try harder to rope people into compulsive play.

And finally, each player is different and more or less susceptible to different kinds of cues. Evidence suggests, for example, that social games and MMOs tend to have the most problem gamers. However, these genres hold little sway with me. *FarmVille*'s harvesting, for example, was so tedious that I quit playing it very quickly. Every MMO I've ever tried seems to require so much time to really enjoy that I almost immediately felt overwhelmed and quit. Obviously, the psychological pull of those games doesn't push my mental buttons. But put me in front of a good turn-based strategy game and I'm in trouble. A couple of Christmases ago I discovered the low-tech World War II simulator *Gary Grigsby's A World at War: A World Divided*, and it cost me a *lot* of sleep. Its niche status, however, indicates that most gamers do not hear the same siren-song emanating from it that I do.

It seems to me, then, that the most important key to avoiding unhealthy escape is to deal with the psychological issues that we're facing in the rest of our lives. First, we're unlikely to fall into addiction if we're feeling well-adjusted in general. And second, I think we need to be self-aware of how we interact with *particular* games and game genres. If turn-based strategy is our potential poison, we need to be careful with it. And if it's first-person shooters, then the same goes for that—set limits and stay accountable.

Proper Escape: Video Games and Fantasy

To this point, we've been making a primarily negative argument: video games maybe aren't as bad as some have made them out to be. Most of us won't get addicted, especially if we're careful. That's like saying potato chips won't kill us if eaten in moderation. Perfectly true, but does that mean we *should* eat them? Even if video games aren't crack cocaine, they're still escapist, right? They're empty calories. Is there anything *positive* to take from this flight from reality?

I think there is. And, oddly enough, to support my position I am drawing on the ideas of J. R. R. Tolkien and C. S. Lewis, two authors who, if they were around today, would probably *not* appreciate video games. Both of them were deeply in love with print and had very little positive to say about theater (Tolkien was that rare English literary scholar who didn't much like Shakespeare) or film—I can't imagine that they would be very pleased with the Xbox.[28] But both of them made passionate Christian defenses of fantasy, storytelling, and myth, and their own fiction (especially Tolkien's) pointed unintentionally to a style of communication that video games are particularly well suited for. Namely, video games are excellent tools for creating the secondary worlds that Lewis and Tolkien thought were so important.

Secondary Worlds: Getting in Tune with a Deeper Reality

Tolkien's *The Lord of the Rings* is an odd book in so many ways. It is hugely popular, one of the best-selling books of the twentieth century. It has spawned comic books, RPGs, video games, and major motion pictures. Yet literary critics tend to dislike it—with important exceptions, of course, including W. H. Auden. Perhaps this split is not surprising: like anything with a strong flavor, tasters will tend to love or hate it. And this novel has many unique features.

The dialogue is highly stylized, so archaic that much of it had to be rewritten for Peter Jackson's epic blockbusters.[29] The characters often come off as highly stereotyped stock characters, and many—especially villainous creatures like orcs—are really archetypes more than individuals. Compared to other fiction, the book's pacing is atypical, to say the least: many commentators have remarked that the Council of Elrond scene in *The Fellowship of the Ring* is ridiculously long, considering that *nothing happens* (other than people talking). Tolkien also writes so much description of his world—its geography, ecology, history, and so on—that vast swaths of his book read more like an encyclopedia than a novel. I have a better idea of the layout of the walls at Helm's Deep than I do the famous (real world) walls of Carcassonne. And then there's the odd style of writing. As essayist Andrew Rilstone puts it, Tolkien "adopts a very suggestive style of description: hinting and implying and building up impressions, rather than offering solid, objective detail." Thus, as Rilstone notes, the book never describes ents as walking trees—instead they are simply *like* trees.[30]

All of these characteristics can be weaknesses for some readers. Yet very few books of fiction have inspired a more fervent following—or sold as many copies, for that matter. I have been absolutely captivated by Tolkien's work since I first read *The Lord of the Rings* in fifth grade, even though I probably only followed about half of it and spent an enormous amount of time flipping back and forth between the text and the map at the back. Other than the Bible, there's no book I've read more often (including *The Hitchhiker's Guide to the Galaxy*!); all told, I've probably read *The Lord of the Rings* over twenty times and can nearly recite parts of it from memory.

Part of me realizes that its prose in any other context would seem stilted. I objectively note that large portions of the book are strangely devoid of action. But I have always been a man of maps and encyclopedias (I love you, Wikipedia!), oddly fascinated by *National Geographic*, history books, diagrams of great battles, and documentaries of other lands in other times. And this is precisely what Tolkien provides—and more important, what he *means* to provide.

Tolkien lays out his ideas in a wonderful essay called "On Fairy-Stories" (he often substitutes the more familiar term "fantasy" for "fairy stories"). Just like God, he argues, humans construct worlds. The imaginary places we build in story and song are necessarily of less substance than the primary world we live in, but our secondary worlds, argues Tolkien, are essential to being human. "Fantasy remains a human right: we make in our measure and in our derivative mode, because we are made: and not only made, but made in the image and likeness of a Maker."[31] He also argues that the most powerful secondary worlds are those with a convincing internal consistency, which explains why he spent so much time describing the calendars, languages, and forests of Middle-earth, and why it feels, as Rilstone puts it, that "the story—the epic quest story and war story told from the point of view of four Hobbits—is not really what the book is about."[32]

And why, precisely, is this creation of secondary worlds so important? One answer Tolkien gives is that at least some stories that visit these other places give us the opportunity to relive the "eucatastrophe," a word of his own creation that means "the joy of a happy ending." When, against all odds, Gollum seizes the ring from Frodo and plunges into the Crack of Doom and ends the reign of Sauron, when Darth Vader throws Emperor Palpatine to his doom, when Aslan slays the White Witch, the story in some respects relives the greatest happy ending of all: the resurrection of the Christ, a hope when all hope seemed dead.[33]

C. S. Lewis talks about myth a great deal in his essays, and he says much the same thing as Tolkien, although in a bit more general sense. The secondary worlds of myths echo and build off of our primary world. When we create these stories, these other realities, we do not diminish everyday life but rather enhance it, as he says in his review of Tolkien's masterwork:

> The value of the myth is that it takes all the things we know and restores to them the rich significance which has been hidden by the "veil of familiarity." The child enjoys his cold meat (otherwise dull to him) by pretending it is buffalo, just killed with his own bow and arrow. And the child is wise. The real meat comes back to him more savoury for having been dipped in a story; you might say that only then is it the real meat. If you are tired of the real landscape, look at it in a mirror. By putting bread, gold, horse, apple, or the very roads into a myth, we do not retreat from reality: we rediscover it. As long as the story lingers in our mind, the real things are more themselves. [*The Lord of the Rings*] applies the treatment not only to bread or apple but to good and evil, to our endless perils, our anguish, and our joys. By dipping them in myth we see them more clearly.[34]

In his essay on fairy stories, Tolkien calls this "recovery" or "regaining of a clear view." The power of fantasy is to free the treasure trove of experiences we take for granted and have forgotten about, to "open your hoard and let all the locked things fly away like cage-birds. The gems all turn into flowers or flames, and you will be warned that all you had (or knew) was dangerous and potent, not really effectively chained, free and wild; no more yours than they were you."[35]

What should be clear from this is that Tolkien and Lewis did not see escape from the primary world as a bad thing. To create other worlds is not the same thing as trying to avoid real life. Tolkien argues:

> [Fantasy] certainly does not destroy or even insult Reason; and it does not either blunt the appetite for, nor obscure the perception of, scientific veracity. On the contrary. The keener and the clearer is the reason, the better fantasy will it make. . . . For creative Fantasy is founded upon the hard recognition that things are so in the world as it appears under the sun; on a recognition of fact, but not a slavery to it. . . . If men really could not distinguish between frogs and men, fairy-stories about frog-kings would not have arisen.[36]

Is fantasy, then, a form of escape? If so, it's not an antisocial kind. In responding to the accusation that fantasy irresponsibly pulls us away from reality, Tolkien asks:

> Why should a man be scorned, if, finding himself in prison, he tries to get out and go home? Or if, when he cannot do so, he thinks and talks about other topics than jailers and prison-walls? The world outside has not become less real because the prisoner cannot see it. In using Escape in this way the critics have chosen the wrong word, and what is more, they are confusing, not always by sincere error, the Escape of the Prisoner with the Flight of the Deserter.[37]

The primary world, in other words, is full of darkness, and is even more full of a dulling of the senses that leave our existences drab and mundane; escaping to a secondary world doesn't at all mean leaving the primary one, it just helps us focus on it again in a new way.

Video Games, Secondary Worlds, and "Spatial Storytelling"

So what does this have to do with video games? As I mentioned before, neither Lewis nor Tolkien were particularly interested in nonprint media. Lewis felt that film was invariably about action, making it a poor medium for the creation of secondary worlds.[38] Tolkien disliked theater's attempt to make tangible what should remain imaginary, and he also thought that it overemphasized character development and underemphasized *world* development: "very little about trees as trees can be got into a play."[39]

Needless to say, the frenetic action of most video games and the televisual storytelling sensibilities that video games typically adopt do not fit neatly with their theories.

For all my hero worship, however, here is where I need to part ways with the masters and turn their arguments in a direction that they probably wouldn't have liked. Even in their own historical context, I don't believe they do proper justice to nonprint media. They are certainly right to note that different media have different strengths and weaknesses. But that's not the same thing as saying that fantasy and myth have no place in nonwritten media. Stage and cinema don't have all the magic of print, but they have their own magics. And this is true of video games as well.

In fact, video games are in some ways almost *better* tools for some of what Tolkien attempted in his own fiction (and to a lesser extent, Lewis as well). Renowned media scholar Henry Jenkins describes Tolkien's work as "spatial storytelling." Jenkins argues that a literary tradition exists of works—such as *The Lord of the Rings* and Frank Baum's books about the land of Oz—that focus much more on the nature of the world than on plot or character, something that we've already noted was a major concern of Lewis and Tolkien.[40] Lewis himself makes a distinction between stories that focus on *action* (which he associates with film) and stories that present a deeper quality. He prefers stories where the very nature of the space, character, and emotion matters more than its ability to heighten tension: pirates and giants are not just convenient devices to produce thrills; they are important because of their pirate-y or giant-ish character. In other words, Lewis emphasizes stories where the world itself matters.[41]

The reason this is important is Jenkins's argument that the novel was a fairly inefficient tool for delivering such narratives.[42] Novels are really much better for plot and character development. Novels are typically sequential— one word after the next, one sentence following the other, one paragraph leading to the next, and so on—but exploration is far less so. When we investigate, we first peek around one corner and then the next. We pick up the mystery box and shake it, go ask someone about it, and come back again. In a printed story, we can go only where the author directly leads us, meaning that extensive exploration requires a plot as enormous and wandering as, well, *The Lord of the Rings*.[43]

This is where video games excel, however, as Jenkins points out. As I noted in chapter 2, games often have terrible narratives by traditional standards—they jump around, they rely on stock characters, and they're often very poorly paced. But they're very good at providing spaces pregnant with narrative possibility. When I travel through the blasted postapocalyptic landscape of *Fallout: New Vegas*, most of my narrative experience is the world itself—its muted gray tones, its darkened sky, its blasted detritus of a pre–nuclear-war society scattered helter-skelter everywhere. I can follow the stories the game developers have provided for me, but I can just as easily wander, watch, and listen. I can randomly shoot at a Nuka-Cola bottle to see what happens, to learn the physics of this world. I can drink radiated water and pure water just to see what happens to my body. I never get to the point of confusing that reality with the primary world I live in, but it's coherent, whole, and as vivid as the world of any novel I've read.

And, lest we get the impression that video games only present worlds that are grim and dark (although there are a disproportionately high number of these), we can see the same kind of thing in the short PlayStation 3 game *Flower*. This is an absolutely nonviolent, gorgeous game that is loads of fun to play. A description won't do it justice, but the gist is that the player is (or controls) a flower petal that whooshes over fields, canyons, and hillsides, restoring health and beauty to anything it touches. This is a placid, pleasant world, suffused with a quiet glow, and is relatively risk-free (minus some electric wires that can shock a bit), a world of wind, grass, moonlit haystacks, and vibrant flowers. The same is true of the hauntingly beautiful and melancholy *Journey*, by the same company that made *Flower*. And *Myst* did much the same thing back in the 1990s (see image on p. 89).

These video games provide the secondary worlds Tolkien waxes eloquent about. They are not wholly superior to the realities conjured by a book: one of the most powerful properties of print is that it necessarily evokes the imagination. Because a novel will typically have only words (maybe a few pictures but, outside of children's books, not many), the reader must imagine whatever is being described. The cognitive and emotional investment we make in such imagined worlds can be very powerful. In video games, the world is, in a sense, external to us, because it already exists and we can see it. This is also a feature of film: what before was imagined has now become somewhat tangible. So I agree to some extent with Lewis and Tolkien's critiques of film and theater (and by extension, games). There is certainly some loss here, which is why I hope our culture never gives up on reading fiction, even while movies and games steadily become more important.[44]

But there is something uniquely powerful about exploring the secondary world of a video game, something not present in other media. The difference is hard to explain in print—it's much easier to experience—but I'll give it a shot. I think the unique feature is *tangibility*. For one thing, when we play a game, we can see and hear the world, just as we can in a film. More important, the audiovisual environment of the game is—at least to some degree—interactive. When we shoot an opponent, he or she gets hurt; when we give our dog a treat, he barks with joy; when we start the spaceship, it takes us soaring into the air.

The famous dock of *Myst*, where the game begins (this image is from *RealMyst*, a re-done version of the original).

A video game *changes* our imaginative involvement with secondary worlds, but I don't think it *eliminates* it. What we see and hear in the imaginary space of the game become the building blocks for our imagination. We shift to an explorer's imagination, questing to see what is around the next bend, what is in the building, what is behind the door, what kind of creatures live in the land. We invoke the machinist's and the scientist's imagination: what happens when we push the big red button, rearrange the jewels, click on the painting in the library, or put the duck on Guybrush's head? And at the end of the day, when we have returned from Azeroth, the DC Wasteland, the town of Armadillo, the struggle of World War II, or the placeless space of *Bejeweled*, we come back from a place that has substance, an alternate reality where our imagination can grow. It's not the same sort of substance as that of our primary world, but it has the kind of coherence and solidity of a good secondary world, as Tolkien describes it.

Evaluating Escape

There's no question in my mind that video games can be doors out of this world and into other ones. It seems to me that such escape can lead to renewal, or it can lead to death. We live in an imperfect world ripe with echoes of the perfection it could have had and could still have. Sometimes we need to leave for a while to get away from it, and sometimes we need to leave for a while to rediscover a way to see the beauties of existence that have been obscured by the day-to-day muck.

When we do it right, we can bring fresh eyes to all of the human experience by playing video games: intelligence, sacrifice, corruption, love, and beauty. We can find purified and powerful experiences in game worlds—even in rather abstract games, but especially in rich, narratively detailed settings. When we do it wrong, we use these spaces to hide from what we fear and hate in our everyday lives. There is power here. The trick is to learn how to escape without deserting, as Tolkien puts it.

There is one final issue worth discussing here. Say we all agree that video games can be a powerful form of escape. Even if done right, so that we avoid the specter of addiction, aren't we essentially being selfish here? Isn't this the typical Western approach, where everything is all about fun, even while the world around us struggles with war, starvation, and worse? Are we fiddling while Rome burns?

I turn again to C. S. Lewis, who prepared a remarkable sermon at the beginning of World War II titled "None Other Gods: Culture in War Time" that perfectly addresses this issue. Addressing a church full of Oxford scholars, he looked at the looming conflict and its likely horrors and asked the very reasonable question: "why should we—indeed how can we—continue to take an interest in these placid occupations [scholarship, that is] when the lives of our friends and the liberties of Europe are in the balance?"[45] While he obviously wrote in more perilous times (at least for people in developed nations), we might just as well ask: How can we play in a world full of suffering?

Lewis's answer: culture does not and should not stop because of the pressing concerns of survival. God made us to be more than survival machines. As Lewis puts it, it is worthy for a person to learn to save drowning people, to train for it, and even for that person to sacrifice his or her own life for that of another. "But if anyone devoted himself to life-saving in the sense of giving it his total attention—so that he thought and spoke of nothing else and demanded the cessation of all other human activities until everyone had learned to swim—he would be a monomaniac."[46] Our culture is part of what God made us for and part of what makes us beautiful, and it would be as impossible to repress it as it would be to stop breathing. Humans, argues Lewis, "propound mathematical theorems in beleaguered cities, conduct metaphysical arguments in condemned cells, make jokes on scaffolds, discuss the last new poem while advancing to the walls of Quebec, and comb their hair at Themopylae. This is not *panache*: it is our nature."[47] And while Lewis focuses on the pursuit of learning and beauty (which I think could be called "art"), the argument definitely applies to other parts of our humanity, such as the capacity to play in imaginary places as dark as a nuclear wasteland and as cute as a virtual farm.

The doorway to other worlds is open. Adventurers *will* take up the double-edged sword of escape. The question is, will they come back and share their treasure with the rest of us?

◀ ⑥ ▶

Real Men, Real Women,
Unreal Games

Barbarian Babes

The chain-mail bikini is very revealing. In Fantasy RPG artwork, a shapely woman warrior stereotypically wears her armor like a beer commercial model. She either leaves her glorious torso exposed to the slashing swords of enemies—as does the princess Amelie in the misnamed *King's Bounty: Armored Princess* (see the unavoidable image on p. 94)—or wears a skintight, suffocating suit of armor. These outfits show more than skin: in Fantasy RPGs, women are put there *by* the boys and *for* the boys.

The first year of grad school taught me I did *not* want to study gender: gender studies is a political minefield. So I tried to avoid it. The problem is, games *bleed* gender issues—lingerie-clad barbarians are only the tip of the iceberg. Playing video games forced me to consider masculinity and games. I grew up in a family that valued gender equality: I learned to cook, clean, and share in domestic (traditionally feminine) responsibilities. As an übernerd with mediocre athletic skills, I was hardly a paragon of virile cowboy masculinity, and I defensively disdained macho behavior. Yet put me in front of a computer game and I became enthralled with explosions, military campaigns, and decapitations. And I learned I'm not alone. Unathletic war gamers like me can spout some pretty choice locker-room trash talk (albeit focused on obscure references to Rokugani politics).

The princess Amelie, sporting a variation on the chain-mail bikini. A better title for this game would probably be *King's Bounty: Poorly Armored Princess*. To be fair, this really is a fun game, even if the skin shown (mostly in this game-opening image) is totally gratuitous.

Things have changed significantly in the last ten years. The good ol' boys aren't so dominant and many women play video games.[1] Newer, best-selling games are significantly more gender diverse. We're in a period of transition. An illustration: most of my male students tune in and female students tune out when I mention video games. But if I were to ask who in class plays *Rock Band* or *Angry Birds*, I might find many women raising their hands.

So what does it mean that our culture codes video games as boy toys? How is this changing? And what should we do about it? First, I'll take a look at traditional, heterosexual male-oriented video games that dominated the market circa 2000 and are still the core of video-game culture. Then we'll look at major shifts that have introduced more gender flexibility in video games. Finally, we'll evaluate all this in light of the Christian faith. While there's far more to talk about than we can cover in such a short chapter, I hope what we cover here is a good conversation starter.

Video Games and the Mediation of Gender Ideals

Sex, Gender, and Ideal Gender Roles

Before we go any further, we should consider how society deals with manhood and womanhood. What does it mean to be a man or a woman? We're partly defined gender-wise by our reproductive organs: the power of positive thinking isn't going to let a man have a baby. But biology doesn't make trucks buff and minivans maternal. So gender theorists make a distinction between *sex*, which is biological, and *gender*, which is cultural.[2]

Where do we learn our culture's take on gender? Occasionally we have clear discussions: someone labels something "girl stuff" or reads a book on recapturing "the inner man."[3] Most of the time, however, we're getting constant, unintentional, and unarticulated lessons. When we watch TV, interact with our peers, or observe our parents, we are seeing people model what it means to be a man or a woman. I personally believe that interpersonal interaction with friends, colleagues, and family shapes our thinking much more than movies, games, and the like. Nevertheless, media representations of men and women can be very powerful. Millions worldwide see the gods and goddesses of Hollywood enact gender ideals. Movie women are perfect women—princesses, hot moms, career women—and movie men are perfectly manly—buff athletes, family providers, and comedians.

These ideals aren't usually articulated in nice clear statements: people rarely say "a woman should be x, y, and z." And there's no shadowy cabal of gender programmers who make sure that all the messages we get are coordinated. We receive mixed and possibly even contradictory gender ideals—but they call to us nonetheless.

Video Games Mediating Gender Roles

Therein lies the rub. We're constantly bombarded with messages about manhood and womanhood, but we'll never embody all the ideals. That's impossible. Thus, we often need to resolve the psychological and sociological conflicts created by these clashing standards. Some theorists argue that technology or media can be sites for mediation: useful tools that help us negotiate the pressures of the different ideals.

Let's illustrate this with a look at middle-class manhood. Scholars have described at least three distinct standards prevalent in the nineteenth and twentieth centuries:

- "Respectable manliness": a Victorian-era standard for small businessmen that emphasized self-control, sober judgment, emotional restraint, and the role of protector of the family.
- "Rough masculinity": a response to the corporate domination of business in the late 1800s that emphasized strength, virility, and physical and social dominance—the kinds of things that gave men cultural power.[4]
- "Eternal boyhood": more compatible with the consumer-driven economy of the twentieth century, emphasizing fun and youth, the eternal boy was a fountain of joy, always living it up and unconcerned with what he couldn't control.[5]

This isn't a complete list, but I'd argue these ideals are still alive and well today: we still have the family man (respectable), the athlete (rough), and the comedian (eternal boy).[6]

But these values in their pure forms don't play well together. Who are we going to be at work? The team player (respectable), the aggressive bully (rough), or the clown (eternal boy)? We can flip back and forth between them, but it's pretty tough to be all three on a constant basis—even though we're constantly bombarded with all three ideals. This is where technology can play a role. Gender and communication scholar Susan Douglas argues that communication technologies such as radio can help us mediate gender.[7] Early radio amateurs, for example, found intellectual challenge in building transmitters and receivers from scratch (which appealed to the standards of respectable manliness) and fulfilled power fantasies with the newfound ability to roam the invisible airwaves across the globe (which appealed to the ideal of rough masculinity).

Gender ideals and their conflicts aren't limited to men, of course. Middle-class women are expected to be nurturers (the mother), objects of desire (the princess), and powerful, competent performers (the professional), among many other standards.[8] And we use more than technology to mediate gender conflict: vacations, education, and movies are just a few examples. I didn't pick the gender ideals above by accident, however. In their first few decades, I believe video games were gender mediation tools that functioned as playgrounds for men.

Traditional Video-Game Men: Powerful Bodies, Clever Minds

Some video gamers from the 1980s single out the ending of *Metroid* as one of the most shocking moments in console gaming.[9] After fighting through an alien landscape to kill a malevolent organism, the violent, action-oriented bounty hunter Samus Aran pulled off the space suit's helmet to reveal long, wavy hair and curvy, form-fitting clothing. Why was it so surprising that an action hero was a woman? Because jumping, blowing things up, and space exploration were completely masculine activities in the video gaming universe (never mind that many guys playing games could hardly do *any* of these things). Women have muscled in on some of this action today, but the worlds of best-selling games haven't changed all that much.

Until the twenty-first century, the game industry had a rather limited repertoire. Most big-budget productions were focused on combat, conquest, or commerce. There were plenty of important exceptions, but the money and attention flowed to shooters such as *Doom* and strategy games such as *Civilization*. This is what I call the "traditional video game" in contrast with the newer "mass-consumer games." The traditional video game made most of its money from men, and we can see a stereotypically male bias in the games themselves.[10]

Real Men Doing Man Things

While we can find infinite variations, traditional male video-game characters tend to play the role of the warrior, the wizard, or the thief. Probably the most common kind of man is the warrior: the tremendously violent Kratos of the *God of War* games (see image on p. 98), the thugs of *Grand Theft Auto*, and the barbarians or paladins of countless RPGs. The warrior is a man of physical ability, sculpted body, and powerful weaponry—a man who succeeds because he can fight. The wizard is the man who succeeds via powerful intellect, such as Mentor the mind-power superhero of *Freedom Force*, Zilean of *League of Legends* who wields time-based powers (see image on p. 98), and the stereotypical fireball-casting geek-scholar magic users. Wizards are slight of build because their power comes from their brains, not their bodies. The thief is the man who is agile, either in a physical sense, such as Mario (from the *Super Mario World* games), or in a secretive, morally flexible sense, such as the rogues and cutpurses of RPGs. Physically speaking, the thief is usually not so much muscle-bound as lean and well proportioned.

From left to right: Kratos, the brutal demigod warrior of the *God of War* games; Zilean, a stereotypical wizard from *League of Legends*; Ratchet, a warrior with a thief-like build from the many *Ratchet and Clank* games.

Many men in traditional video games mix elements from multiple roles. The catlike alien hero Ratchet—clearly coded as male—is slight and fast, like the thief, but wields massively destructive guns, a warrior characteristic (see image above). Gordon Freeman of the *Half-Life* series is a card-carrying, glasses-wearing scientist (wizard) who runs around smacking aliens with a crowbar (warrior). Nevertheless, these hybrid character types don't stray far from the themes of the three basic types of warrior, wizard, and thief.

Not only the characters in video games reflect traditional male ideals, however; the major *themes* of traditional video games also appeal to male-coded values. The theme of exploration, for example, is common to video games of all sorts. Platform games such as *Super Mario Galaxy* are all about jumping to new places and discovering their quirks, while space-themed games take us where no gamer has gone before. Another motif is that of being the hero. In the earlier stages of video-game history, this was usually assumed: the player's job was to fight the forces of evil and destruction, to be the (often literal) white knight who triumphs against the odds, the man who provides for his woman, his family, his community. *King's Quest* is an early example, and *King's Bounty: The Legend* is a more recent one. A third theme emphasized by many games—especially strategy games such as *StarCraft*—is logical thinking. And, finally, video games major on the destruction and domination of inhuman magical monsters, inhuman aliens, barely-human crooks, and dastardly super-villains. I call this the "conquistador complex": go to interesting places, meet interesting creatures, and kill them.[11]

There's nothing *inherently* male about any of this, but these themes play directly into long-standing cultural patterns. There is, for example, a literary and filmic tradition of adventure stories for boys that emphasizes exploration and heroism.[12] Western culture has long associated rationality (and thus strategic contests) with men, and emotionality with women—the latter being seen as inferior.[13] Physical power, domination, and destruction are very much coded as masculine. Women can and do appreciate and enjoy all of these themes (and some men don't), but given our cultural context (and especially that of the 1980s and '90s), it's clear traditional video games are boy toys.

Mediating Masculinity

Traditional video games are clearly excellent sites for middle-class men to negotiate the masculine gender ideals of respectable manliness, rough masculinity, and eternal boyhood. Men can be the respectable man: they can play the role of hero or überrational thinker. They can be rugged men by bashing heads, playing ripped muscular bodies, and becoming master and commander of all they see. And of course, video games are playgrounds for the eternal boy, with consequence-free actions and wide-eyed journeys through fantastic landscapes. Of course, every man is different and experiences different feelings of inadequacy (if they feel any at all). As I noted at the beginning of the chapter, I'm not very well equipped to play the role of the rough masculine man. So it's quite a rush for me (a secret relief, maybe?) to be able to blow stuff up. Other men may have different challenges: some might not care at all about a perceived lack of toughness and virile power. Or some may feel no need to act like the eternal boy. But a video game often *allows* us to play all the roles—often simultaneously—if we want.

Women in Traditional Video Games . . . Only the Buxom Need Apply?

But what about women? Just like men, they encounter numerous ideals in everyday life and in media representations. Have traditional video games typically served as mediation points for *their* gender ideals? Can they easily use the traditional video game as a tool to negotiate the complicated interplay of different standards of womanhood? A quick look seems to suggest not.

Women have typically played marginal roles in traditional video games. Even a recent scholarly survey of best-selling games on major game platforms showed that less than 15 percent of human characters that players encounter in games are female—and I suspect this ridiculously low number was probably even worse in the past.[14] Another academic project has demonstrated that visual representation of women's bodies in video games conforms to the unrealistic and unhealthy patterns we see throughout our popular media.[15] Unsurprisingly, female characters in traditional video games have remarkably limited roles.

One of the most popular representations of girls in games is the princess—the woman the player wins for completing the game. Whether it's Mario rescuing hapless Princess Peach or Dirk the Daring (of the 1983 classic *Dragon's Lair*) whisking away the simpering and scantily clad Princess Daphne,[16] the video-game princess has two main characteristics: she's as attractive as the pixels can make her and she's helpless. A less common role is the temptress—the dangerous woman, who, like the sorceress Circe in Homer's *Odyssey*, has a kind of sexual magnetism that she leverages for destruction and domination (implicitly of men). Examples would be the adventure game *Lure of the Temptress* or the horror game *Parasite Eve*, both from the 1990s. These sexual dangers threaten a male-dominated social order with their aggressiveness.

A few video-game characters in traditional video games, though not explicitly coded as female, are more feminine. For example, practically all RPGs feature healers, who, although they aren't always women, specialize in fixing, not destroying. In addition, there is a fairly well-established tradition within traditional video games of cartoony gender-neutral characters, like Q*bert. Japanese video games especially have a highly developed tradition of cuteness in their artwork and game themes. Ironically, however, even cute and abstract art can be coded as male. There's nothing masculine about a yellow circle with a missing wedge, for example, but somehow Pac-Man is male. It's the pink bow of stunningly popular Ms. Pac-Man that indicates she's feminine—apparently male yellow discs don't accessorize, or at least they didn't in the 1980s.

So on the rare occasion they appear at all, women in traditional video games typically don't take roles associated with much power (minus a few exceptions like Ms. Pac-Man) unless they are a threat. Again, this is consistent with what we'd expect to see in a video game that is particularly useful and interesting to middle-class men.

Growing Up (Girl) Gamer[17]

I was born in the 8-bit era. My mother released me shortly before the debut of the Nintendo Entertainment System (NES), and *Super Mario Bros.* came on the scene just in time for my first birthday. It didn't take me long to realize our fates were intertwined.

I've since learned that my attraction to video games is somewhat uncharacteristic of my gender. I was given every chance to be socialized into my biologically inherited role—with Barbies, dresses, and pink décor in abundance—but I simply found games far more interesting.

So what kinds of games does this "girl gamer" play? While I've enjoyed an array of genres and titles, a few stand out as thematic: platformer games such as *Super Mario World*, adventure-puzzle games such as the *Zelda* series, and RPGs such as *Chrono Trigger*. At times my preferences did distinguish me somewhat from the mainstream male gamers I grew up around: I would choose adventure, puzzle, and RPGs over first-person shooters any day.

In most of the games I played as a kid, I controlled male characters. While it never bothered me that Mario was male, it sometimes annoyed me that female characters like Princess Peach were weak, always needing to be rescued. Later games that included the option for female protagonists introduced more frustrations: how am I supposed to fend off monsters or darkspawn when my armor is either too tight to breathe, nearly nonexistent, or practically falling off? In some games, highly gendered plotlines left me internally conflicted: when Tidus and Yuna had a romantic moment in *Final Fantasy X*, I couldn't decide whether I felt awkward watching, excited for Tidus, or jealous of Yuna. Overall, though, my character's gender doesn't matter so much as how the character enables me to play the game.

I haven't encountered much external gender conflict for playing video games, aside from fighting my brother, cousins, or friends for the controller. This trend continues into my marriage, where often the biggest thing my husband and I fight over is who gets to play video games first after work.

When others discover I'm a gamer, girls are typically surprised (unless they're fellow gamers in which case they're mildly to moderately ecstatic) and guys are impressed. I've earned the label "the perfect girlfriend" from strangers for playing video games, and my husband has been told by other guys (often upon learning my other hobbies include motorcycling and snowboarding) to "save some for the rest of us."

Games and I have grown up a lot since the 8-bit era, and our paths remain intertwined. The continuing impact of games on my life is perhaps best illustrated in my recent wedding experience. After all was said and done, my new husband and I bounced out of the ceremony victoriously to the 8-bit version of the Mario Bros. theme song. If anything, video games have prepared me for this whole new world of inter-gender negotiation that marriage entails—better than a Barbie fantasy world ever could.

Janelle Weibelzahl

Gender Change: The Shifting Experiences of Men and Women in Today's Video-Game Environment

The picture painted above, however, is a bit too neat. Fantasy RPGs have always stressed gender equality in their rules (male and female characters always have the same statistics). I am also underplaying the importance of the Japanese video-game culture. In addition, some gameplay themes in traditional video games, such as puzzling or narrative play, are stereo-typically female friendly or gender neutral. Finally, the playful flexibility of videos games applies to gender. We can make a game as testosterone drenched as we want, but the player may ignore the manliness, mock it, or misunderstand it. Women who played a lot of video games in the 1980s and '90s simply got used to the masculine themes of their chosen enter-tainment (see the sidebar essay on page 101 by my former student Janelle Weibelzahl). In some cases, they embraced it, using aggressive behavior and language that was similar to the rest of the masculine culture.[18]

In any case, the traditional video game is starting to lose its clout: *The Sims*, the Nintendo Wii, music games, social networking, the App Store, and other factors have led to a boom in nontraditional kinds of games. Today's most popular stuff really messes with the old gender stereotypes. Specifically, we can see new game roles for women, new game themes that are more in tune with traditionally feminine interests, and many opportu-nities for players of all sorts to play with the idea of gender.

Different Girls on Different Playgrounds

The heroine of the 1996 game *Tomb Raider*—the impossibly curvy, acrobatic Indiana Jones stand-in Lara Croft—became an overnight global sensation. Lara puzzled her way through ancient ruins, jumped and clam-bered around dangerous caves, and shot her way out of trouble with blazing twin pistols. She was the first superstar video-game Valkyrie, or warrior woman. These characters fight as well as any man and, unsurprisingly, wear formfitting clothing to boot. They've been around in RPGs and Fantasy literature for quite some time. A good example is the famous bikini-clad Red Sonja from the Conan the Barbarian comic-book series.[19] But charac-ters such as Samus Aran of *Metroid*, Chun-Li of *Street Fighter*, and Lara made the Valkyrie a staple of gaming culture. Many of these characters are a mixed blessing for female players: women characters finally get to do something more active than being rescued, but they have to do it dressed like strippers. There are a *few* warrior women who don't resemble exotic dancers—for example, Alyx Vance of *Half-Life 2*—but the majority are clearly supposed to be eye candy for men.[20]

The 1990s also saw female game characters develop in quite a different direction: pink and cute. One clear example is the large string of Barbie games,[21] starting already in the 1980s. These varied in terms of gameplay, but they featured favorite Barbie pastimes such as shopping and dressing up. Disney also licensed a series of games focused on their princess characters, including Ariel (*The Little Mermaid*) and Belle (*Beauty and the Beast*). These kinds of video-game characters were (and are) clearly girl oriented.

Gender-neutral but cute (and thus female friendly) characters are also very common now. The last decade and a half has seen a proliferation of purposely cute avatars, like Spyro the young purple dragon and the Pokemon monsters. Japanese pop culture literally has ambassadors for cute,[22] and the wide-eyed, androgynous characters of **anime** and **manga** have become a staple of key sectors of gaming culture.

Finally, video-game characters have tended to become more and more customizable, allowing players to choose characters of any type in practically any game genre. The Wii represents players with customizable "Mii" characters that come in countless shapes and sizes. And RPGs such as *Fallout 3* and *Dragon Age* allow the player to do extremely precise edits of an avatar's appearance. While many games remain prescripted, if we look hard enough, we can find women in just about any game role available today.

New Kinds of Gaming: An Invasion of the Feminine

The kinds of gaming experiences available today are also becoming far more diverse and more commonly in tune with values our culture traditionally codes as feminine. A friend of mine once told me that when he played *Guitar Hero* with his daughters, they had different approaches. After successfully completing a song, he typically moved on to the next challenge. His girls, however, wanted to immediately spend the money from the concert on accessorizing: getting new clothes and new guitars.

This is a classic example of one of the big trends in video games today: shopping and decorating. Many games have the ability for cosmetic upgrades as in *Guitar Hero*. *The Sims*, however, is a pioneer and giant in accessorizing. The game gives the player a little person who earns cash to purchase a huge array of appliances, furniture, renovations, and so on. It is a digital dollhouse with walking, gibberish-talking dolls. An interest in decorating is hardly unique to women, as the parents of any teenage guy with rock posters on his wall can attest. But our culture traditionally sees accessorizing as a feminine activity.

Many of today's most popular games also heavily downplay the violent conflict of traditional video games. *The Sims* has no serious fighting, no killing, and no struggle to triumph (there's no win condition).[23] The booming casual game market of card and puzzle games such as *Words with Friends* or *Bejeweled*—typically not very bloody or destructive—are enormously popular on the internet and cell phones everywhere. *Wii Sports* has made nonviolent tennis and bowling simple, accessible, and lightheartedly competitive. And over all of this, the dominant visual aesthetics of mainstream video games have become ever more female friendly, shifting from jagged, dirty, and aggressive (a *masculine* aesthetic, in other words) to cute, rounded, clean, and pastel themed (considered *feminine*-friendly).[24] In short, while there are plenty of exceptions, more and more of the best-selling video games are becoming *nicer*.

Finally, many popular games today major in socializing and cooperation. Games have always been social, but the easy availability of network connections today has facilitated in-game interpersonal interaction. Many games—most notably the big MMOs such as *World of Warcraft*—are team based. The Wii, with its face-to-face playspace and large catalog of casual, accessible games, has further increased the sociability of video games. And the current hit within the game industry is the genre of social games such as *FarmVille*, which gets a lot of its appeal from its use of Facebook. Playing well with others isn't inherently feminine, but our culture expects that more from women than men.

Digital Curiosity: Gender Play in the Brave New Digital World

Today's video games are more female friendly, but they also increasingly allow for gender choice in play. One of my friends takes it as a point of pride that he always plays female characters. His joke is that if he's going to be staring at someone for that many hours, he'd rather it was a woman than a man. But his real reasoning is that what we're looking at on the screen isn't really a man or a woman at all—it's just an imaginary construction that's no more male or female than the computer's mouse or keyboard.

Video games increasingly allow gamers to play with the very concept of gender. As we've noted, role players can take on many personas, including the option of playing as a man or a woman. In fact, the games have dialogue adjusted to match the player's choice: little Sparrow in *Fable II* is either brother or sister, for example.[25] Also, countless games use gender-neutral characters: animals of undetermined gender, aliens, monsters, vehicles, and so on.

Many men play as women and many women play as men, all for their own reasons. For some, like my friend, it's kind of amusing to play against the grain. Some players are curious: they are walking a virtual mile in someone else's shoes. Certainly some gamers play with gender as an act of rebellion or defiance to social conventions. And other motivations are a little more pragmatic: some men play female characters in social games (MOGs) because some players treat the women better.[26] As the famous saying goes: on the internet, nobody knows you're a dog,[27] and that gives people license to play around with identity.

Summing It Up: It's a Time of Transition

The traditional video game typically represented gender models that were friendly to men. These games gave men a way to mediate conflicting gender ideals, but were less obviously useful for many women. However, video games aren't inevitably boy toys. There have always been offbeat and alternative video games. Players have always been able to ignore, misunderstand, or misuse the dominant representations of gender in games. And today the video-game industry is finally rushing to make games for people that don't identify with the traditional video game. Thus, games have become steadily more female friendly and gender neutral. And while this is not entirely new, today's video games are increasingly customizable and flexible, making them ideal places for players to play with the very concept of gender.

If we want an old-school, man-blows-up-enemies video game, it's not hard to find. But the landscape is changing, bringing with it incredibly diverse representations of gender and allowing for extremely varied play experiences.

A Christian Approach to Sex and Gender: Realizing Our Full Potential as Image-Bearers

Gender Standards

How is a Christian supposed to think about gender in video games? How do we judge whether a video game handles manhood and womanhood in a healthy manner? Is experimentation with gender okay? To answer these questions, many Christians turn to traditional standards of masculinity and femininity. The argument is that Scripture and Christian tradition present men and women as equally valuable to God, but that each has a distinctly different and complementary role to play.[28] This tradition-based "complementarian" position assumes that the nature of manhood is built into men, and likewise womanhood for women. Complementarians would find much of today's video-game landscape troubling: aggressive women, men playing in pastels, and everyone being able to switch genders at will.

The apparent simplicity of this position has always had some appeal for me, but I have a hard time making it work. The Bible is a remarkably diverse book. Some gender traditions are very restrictive. Even complementarians ignore Old and New Testament passages that call for stoning of adulteresses[29] or mandate head coverings and silence for women in church.[30] Other biblical traditions radically subvert gender standards of their day: Jael "outmanned" Barak in Judges when she hammered a tent peg through the skull of the enemy general Sisera,[31] and the early Christians cited women as the first witnesses of Jesus's resurrection—not a good public relations move in a highly patriarchal society.[32] This mixed bag of gender models is impossible to apply simply and completely, especially to today's video games. In practice, I think complementarians may move beyond the Bible and draw on cultural gender standards. There's nothing biblical, for instance, about the idea that a man should work and his wife should stay home with their children. Nor is it biblical to say video-game men should do the shooting and women should do the whimpering. For a Christian, tradition cannot be the *only* standard for judging gender. Tradition has a great deal to teach us—but not as a simple, unquestioned checklist of what's right and wrong.

Christian feminists typically offer the alternative standard of personal freedom. Gender, they argue, is a social construction that currently gives more power to men than women, an injustice that God hates. A feminist wants each gender to have greater freedom to choose roles and behaviors. Good examples would be the freedom for today's women to be CEOs, senators, and surgeons, as well as the freedom of today's dads to be caring and nurturing rather than stern and distant disciplinarians. By the standard of personal freedom, the grim, boys-only world of the traditional video game is far inferior to the diverse, colorful world of today's mass consumer games.

I usually hold a feminist position, but I have to admit there is a danger with using freedom as a goal. Freedom, from a Christian perspective, is a means, not an end: we can use it positively and negatively. Some restrictions are actually healthy. Women today are almost as free to be as promiscuous as men were in the past—but is this really a step forward? Men are free from the old responsibilities of providing for their families—but ask single mothers and their kids whether this is a positive development.[33] Many video games encourage players to exercise freedoms that are destructive, such as the infamous option to beat and rob prostitutes in the *Grand Theft Auto* games. Freedom is a flawed measurement for whether a change in gender representation is positive or negative. For Christians, both tradition and freedom are good things in the right contexts, but there is a higher standard.

Men and Women as Image-Bearers

I believe our standard should be the degree to which we can fulfill our roles as God's image-bearers. God is love—how well do we live this out? God is truth—do we live truthfully? God is strength and courage—do we embody these values? Whether we're talking about video-game representations of gender or real-life standards, fulfilling our human potential is more important than tradition or freedom.

For example, one of the biggest problems in traditional video games is how much they limit the capacities of both genders. Men in video games are strong, but they get their strength via destructive force and by being able to control others and themselves. In addition, masculine characters are usually devoid of responsibility for their actions.[34] The stereotypical roles of men in traditional video games have some positives, to be sure—strength, heroism, ingenuity, and curiosity are all fine characteristics. But God made men to be more than just strong providers. We also can and should be nurturers and empathizers, to pick just two stereotypically feminine characteristics.

Likewise, the full possibilities for women are absent from many video games. We've already noted that for a long time, female characters were incapable of independent action, which is hardly in tune with the Christian vision of living, acting as servants of God. Even today, though, with the plethora of active, aggressive female characters such as *Resident Evil 5*'s gun-toting Sheva Alomar, women in games are often not-so-subtly defined as servants or tools of male pleasure. The physical appearance of female characters is more important than that of men. Women are allowed to kick butt as long as they have a nice one themselves. Tight, revealing clothing is almost a must for women, unlike the more varied and frequently more functional male costumes.[35] There are many reasons for this, but one is clearly that it appeals to heterosexual men. Women are still defined, then, by their relationship with men rather than their inherent value as human beings. In addition, as study after study makes clear, many women in Western culture suffer serious psychological effects from the constant pressure to conform to mass-media standards of beauty. Women in video games can and should be more than this.[36]

In other words, men and women can and should move beyond the restrictions common to many video games. We don't have space for more extensive analysis—this is a suggestion, a sample of how to think about the video games we play and the way we engage them. The key question for me is: Does the representation of gender or the gameplay limit or enable the capacity of men and women to fulfill their roles as image-bearers of God?

I rather suspect that just like taxes, politicians, and soft drinks, the chain-mail bikini will always be with us. I'm happy to see, however, that, more and more, one outfit does not fit everyone. God has made men and women to be diverse and today's video games allow for more variety than before. Strength, tenderness, cleverness, and sociability shouldn't be limited to just half the population.

The School of Mario

The Brain, Education, and Video Games

Video games are not sinful, they're just stupid. And they're stupid in this way. Young, particularly men, and now women are joining it, they want to get on a team, be part of a kingdom, conquer a foe, and win a great, epic battle. So they do it with their thumbs and it doesn't even count. Nobody's really liberated. The Taliban is not really conquered. Women are not really freed from oppression. Generations are not really changed. It's all fake. It doesn't count.

Pastor Mark Driscoll of Mars Hill Church in Seattle[1]

Making School Cool with Games?

Is anything as big a waste of time as video games? A player pours tears, sweat, and gallons of virtual blood into something that results in little more than an unsatisfying victory cut scene—if he or she even finishes the game.[2] Could there be a less productive activity? Then why on earth would a bunch of intellectuals and educational experts today be arguing that schools should start taking video games more seriously? They don't mean to push students into the relatively low-paid career of game testing. No, this coalition of respectable academics, intelligent game developers, and wide-eyed technology boosters argues that video games are the equivalent of an exercise gym for the mind. The video-game medium, so the argument goes, engages us mentally in just the way that we *should* be engaged in a digital culture. This is a pretty significant claim, and would certainly go a long way toward redeeming the medium if it were true.

This chapter looks at these claims about the benefits of video games and also considers some critiques. First, we'll examine the complaints lodged against today's digital media environment. Then, we'll look at the new enthusiasm for video games as tools of education and social reform. We'll evaluate both of these sets of arguments with the help of media ecology theory, a body of work partly based on the work of media guru Marshall McLuhan. In the end, we'll see that video games are neither a panacea for all our ills nor a destroyer of all that is good. Rather, they bring intellectual changes that are both positive and negative, and it is our responsibility to engage the new medium wisely.

Digital Media Critics

The title of Mark Bauerlein's 2008 book is unsubtle: *The Dumbest Generation: How the Digital Age Stupefies Young Americans and Jeopardizes Our Future (Or: Don't Trust Anyone Under 30)*. It neatly summarizes his main contention. Young people today, argues Bauerlein, have squandered an incredibly rich media environment:

> The fonts of knowledge are everywhere, but the rising generation is camped in the desert, passing stories, pictures, tunes, and text back and forth, living off the thrill of peer attention. Meanwhile, their intellects refuse the cultural and civic inheritance that has made us what we are up to now.[3]

Susan Jacoby, author of *The Age of American Unreason*, likewise connects today's digital environment (along with Christian fundamentalism) with a surge of anti-intellectualism in today's American culture.[4]

Both authors point to study after study demonstrating that today's population as a whole—and young people especially—are less able than previous generations to do basic math, geography, reading, and writing. Bauerlein rolls out a host of alarming statistics:

- In a 2001 test, 52 percent of seniors in US high schools "chose Germany, Japan, or Italy over the Soviet Union as a US ally in World War II."
- A 1998 test found 59 percent of American teens couldn't name all three branches of their federal government.
- 26 out of 42 countries scored higher than the United States in a 2003 international assessment of math and science skills of fifteen-year-olds.
- A 2006 National Geographic survey of American youth found "63% of their test-takers couldn't identify Iraq on a map."[5]

These critics offer up a series of reasons for why today's media environment is to blame. The first problem is that today's screen-based media environment is relentlessly focused on entertainment. While digital media *can* make a great deal of information available, Bauerlein and Jacoby believe the constant invitation to fun means that most users today waste their intellectual potential on "infotainment" and celebrity obsessions, and thus can't develop a true appreciation for serious culture.

Today's media environment also encourages rapid shifting from one distraction to the next, so that our fragmented attention spans can only handle bite-sized pieces of information and discussion. For example, while writing this paragraph, without noticing it, I flipped away to email, several web pages, other book-related documents, and my Nintendo 3DS. Bauerlein and Jacoby would say that's typical of this environment; our media "invade, and in many instances destroy altogether, the silence . . . and the free time required for both solitary thinking and social conversation."[6]

The speed and brevity of today's media ecology, these critics argue, also contribute to a remarkable shallowness of thought in our culture. Jacoby admits that short is not always stupid, but really profound thought does require significant amounts of time and space to construct. Most people don't have the patience (and maybe even the ability) to work through long and complicated arguments—but that's precisely what a culture needs in order to be wise and mature. As a college professor, I confess that I often struggle with selecting readings for courses because I'm not certain that my students will have the mental focus to make it through difficult material that I know is worthwhile.

And this, I think, gets to the core criticism of both authors: the blinking lights and entrancing audio of our screen-based media have fatally damaged our culture's inclination and ability to read. Whether it's video games, television, or iPods, today's youth, and increasingly adults as well, have less and less time for engaging any kind of reading, and especially book-length reading. Over and over again, Bauerlein and Jacoby lament the decline of books (and, to a lesser extent, high-quality newspapers and magazines), which they see as the very foundation for *all* aspects of a healthy intellectual life.[7] Long-form reading, they argue, not only prepares the mind for serious, deep, and concentrated thought but also opens the mind to other perspectives, other worlds, other ideas. And if we're busy watching TV, browsing blogs, or playing video games, we aren't tackling books.

Educators for Games, Games for Life

Remarkably, another group of digital culture enthusiasts and education researchers proclaims that today's media environment—video games in particular—is opening new avenues of human potential.

Games for Learning

Everyone seems to be permanently in agreement that our schools are failing—and by "our" I mean every region or nation in the world. Unless we are trying to convince someone to move to or invest in our community (in which case, we have a surprisingly good educational reputation), we're busy complaining about disinterested students, overworked or lazy teachers, and falling test scores. Whether or not such critiques are fair, it's clear the demands of education have shifted in the digital age. Rather than seeing the teacher as an expert who pours knowledge into students' heads (a "sage on the stage"), education theorists want learning to be a coexploration, with the teacher as a facilitator (a "guide on the side"). The industrial economy required workers to perform their jobs almost like machines, while the best-paid jobs of the digital era are creative.[8] Literacy means more than reading and writing: it includes fluency in many different media.[9] For many educators, video games promise a way to address all of these shifts.

One thing scholars argue that video games do well is motivate players. Most students don't like difficult assignments; as a teacher, I can attest to this. Even when assigned a paper months in advance, most students tend to leave it to the week or night before it is due, not because they are malefactors who want to torture their prof with another horrid paper but because they simply don't want to do it. Yet video games, which require great dedication and mental focus to complete, can inspire marathon play sessions and dozens of hours of play per week. Some scholars argue that gamers have this intrinsic motivation because video games put the player in the position of the hero. Heroes are independent (like *Halo*'s lone gun Master Chief), their actions actually mean something (e.g., saving the universe from annihilation), and they are usually trusted and valued in some community (the princess is really counting on you, Mario!).[10] If educators can place students in situations where they play the role of the "learner hero," that might help generate intrinsic motivation similar to what gamers have to finish a game.

Others note that knowledge in video games is far more meaningful than a great deal of classroom learning. This is largely because whatever the player learns or needs to know is fully integrated into a meaningful context. Think about what we often learn in class: King John signed the Magna Carta in 1215, moss is a kind of bryophyte, the pink rocks in *Lord of the Flies* represent human flesh, the area of a circle equals pi times the radius squared, and so on. Unless we actually *use* this information in some way, it remains bits of random trivia; most non-*Jeopardy* contestants have a hard time remembering isolated facts. Gamers, however, tend to do a good job of remembering the reams of information in their games: the layout of maps, what a character's statistics mean, the goals of the current mission, and so on. That's because all of it is crucial to playing. I don't think educational game enthusiasts are quite endorsing the extreme of Sherlock Holmes, who famously didn't care whether Earth went around the sun or vice versa because it was completely irrelevant to his work—not *all* knowledge needs a direct practical application to be worth knowing! But education that makes information relevant by providing context is better than facts unconnected to any experienced reality, and video games deliver contextualized information very well.[11]

Famed game designer Will Wright (who made *SimCity*, *The Sims*, and *Spore*) argues that video games model scientific thinking in a powerful way.[12] The indie puzzle game *Crayon Physics Deluxe*, which gets the player to roll a ball across obstacles to a star by drawing items that act like objects with weight, is a great illustration of this (see image on p. 114). Gamers first must use the available information to make educated guesses about the way things should work (I can probably best get the ball by drawing a ramp from the pillar to the grass). Then they play, and playing tests their hypothesis (that doesn't work because I can't get the ramp under the ball). Finally, they readjust their hypothesis in light of the results (if I draw a hammer around the top left pivot point, it swings and bats the ball across the gap). An equally important point is that when a player fails, he or she may be *frustrated* but is much less likely to feel the crushing sense of stigma students typically attach to an F on an assignment.[13]

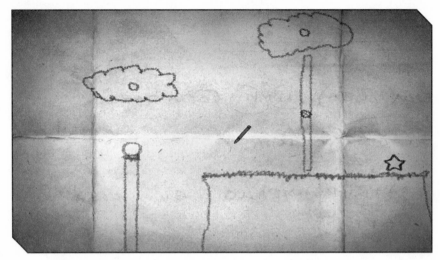

Crayon Physics Deluxe is a wonderful game for developing logical processes of thought and allows for a lot of free-form creativity to boot.

Perhaps the most powerful educational aspect of video games, however, is their ability to scale difficulty to the player, resulting in a constant, interesting challenge. Our common assumption is that people choose easy over difficult, but some commentators challenge that notion.[14] When activities are too easy, we get bored. Of course, overly difficult tasks are overwhelming. Video games have generally excelled at finding a sweet spot between too easy and too hard because they increase in difficulty according to the ability of the individual player. Most video games have levels: we can't take on the more challenging level two in *Pac-Man* until we've eaten the entire maze in level one. *Portal* and *Portal 2* are phenomenally creative first-person puzzle games that have the player move through actual testing facilities under the guidance of a demented computer, with each challenge steadily increasing in difficulty. The level system ensures that the player won't have to deal with the tougher challenges until he or she is able to handle the easier ones. Even open-world games such as *Red Dead Redemption*, which allow the player to travel anywhere on the map, subtly ramp up difficulty at an appropriate speed by strategically restricting access and limiting the difficulty of opponents. This doesn't always work perfectly: multiplayer games feature skill mismatches, and some players are quite happy to play at a very easy level because they get pleasure from something other than challenge. But games are better at pushing us than other media. This kind of individualized balance between easy and hard is extremely difficult to produce in a classroom. When teachers need to work with the whole class at the same time, the different ability levels and backgrounds of the students provide uneven responses: some kids struggle and others are bored, and the instructor *hopes* lessons will be about right for *most* of the students.

I could go on: there are reams of research, and the stack of benefits described is substantial. For a very readable and educated summary, James Paul Gee's *What Video Games Have to Teach Us about Literacy and Learning* is a great place to start.[15] The overall point of much of this literature, however, is apparently that video games are great educational tools, the exact opposite of what critics such as Bauerlein and Jacoby would have us believe. And some intellectuals and game designers would have us go even further, arguing that games are potential tools for restructuring the patterns of everyday life.

Games for Life: Alternate-Reality Games

As with Bauerlein's book, Jane McGonigal's 2011 title very effectively summarizes her position: *Reality Is Broken—Why Games Make Us Better and How They Can Change the World*. She makes the case for the value of alternate-reality games (ARGs), which she defines as "*antiescapist* game[s],"[16] games that put rules on everyday life. *Chore Wars*, for example, is a game in which players compete to clean, washing the dishes or sanitizing the bathroom for points registered on a website.

McGonigal and other ARG enthusiasts believe we can use games to socially engineer our society in a positive way. Her book is structured as a series of problems with reality and the ways in which games offer positive fixes to those problems. "Games make us part of something bigger and give epic meaning to our actions," McGonigal claims.[17] They can give us supersized, ambitious, and audacious goals to achieve. They can also make us happier, she says, citing *SuperBetter*, an ARG she created to help keep her spirits up while recovering from a concussion. Players of the game create superpowered identities for themselves, get friends and family to play the role of allies, discover enemies (i.e., the challenges of recuperation), define "power-ups" (things that give a real-life mood boost), and have a "superhero to-do list." The game helped McGonigal to focus on staying upbeat, which is a key part of concussion recovery.[18]

McGonigal also argues somewhat counterintuitively that games can be a tool to make us far more productive, as well-designed games organize life and provide clear rewards for achievements. *Chore Wars* clearly defines household tasks, values them precisely, and has a tangible reward for success. McGonigal also notes the productive power of games to pull people together for a common purpose. A prominent example is the ARG *Investigate Your MP's Expenses*, a game established in 2009 by the *Guardian* newspaper to allow British citizens to assist in wading through thousands of parliamentary expense receipts to help flag potential abuse of public money. Parliament had released the receipts under pressure and refused to organize them, but many hands made light work: motivated partly by points for successful finds, 20,000 people had investigated 170,000 receipts in the first 80 hours of the game. The game contributed to convictions and resignations of MPs. A more recent example was the use of the protein-simulation game *Foldit* to help scientists make a breakthrough in HIV research.[19] Such projects will probably become more common, suggesting that games aren't just for education: they're for living.

Do They Talk to Each Other at All?

It's hard to believe the new media critics and game enthusiasts live in the same reality. How could one group be so convinced that we're steadily getting dumber and the other be so convinced that video games are cognitively, socially, and educationally positive? Well, to be fair, they're arguing about slightly different things. For one thing, although Bauerlein and Jacoby specifically mention video games (as we'll see below), they're setting their sights on a much bigger phenomenon: the entire digital media environment. Scholars such as Gee and McGonigal, however, are talking specifically about games. For another, the media critics are primarily focused on the way things actually *are* (with some vague forecasting of how things will be getting worse), while many game boosters focus much more on the *potential* of the video-game medium (with some attention paid to current research). The two sides do, however, lock horns directly on a number of occasions.

Steven Johnson admits that the changes in media practices may cause an atrophy of certain kinds of mental skills. He believes that the decrease in book reading, for example, is likely to lead to a decrease in the ability to concentrate on long, complicated arguments. But he believes that such a decline is accompanied by other benefits. His key piece of evidence is the Flynn Effect, which notes that the American population has seen steadily rising IQ scores since about the middle of the twentieth century. The IQ test measures abstract, puzzle-solving mental skill, and the increase shows that our media environment is sharpening our logical skills.[20] Bauerlein and Jacoby grant that video games (and other aspects of the new media environment) may have cognitive benefits—but contend they are the wrong kind. "The more sophisticated video games," argues Jacoby, "require intense concentration, but in the end, the cognitive reward for the master of the game amounts to little more than an improved ability to navigate other, more complex video games."[21] Bauerlein believes that this abstract thinking is devoid of the contextual richness needed to produce good citizens—video games might help process information and engage in context-free problem solving, but they don't demand or reward rich historical and sociological knowledge.[22]

Give and Take: How Media Help *and* Hinder

On the whole, though, these groups don't really directly address each other's points. So how do we put this discussion in proper perspective? I don't think the Bible or the Christian tradition provides very specific answers; there's very little discussion of media in the Scriptures. This makes sense, because other than the invention of writing (which biblical authors don't seem to have dwelled on much), there wasn't much innovation in communication tools during the time period of the Bible's composition. In fact, there is little commentary in the Bible on technology at all.[23] However, the values of the gospel message can still inform a Christian evaluation of culture. Does our media environment help us to do justice, love mercy, and walk humbly with God (Mic. 6:8)? Do video games help us to live out the full human potential that God placed in us? The Christian tradition and the example of Jesus call us to develop virtue and—to the extent we are given grace—combat our weaknesses and failings. The tools that we use to express ourselves and to build society are a key part of fulfilling that call.

Media Ecology and the Morality of Technology

All of the arguments that we have seen so far assume that the technology we use impacts our culture. This idea agrees very much with the scholarly theory called media ecology, which is based to some degree on the ideas of Marshall McLuhan, famous for arguing that "the medium is the message." The main theme of this scholarship is that our tools of communication shape how we interact and thus indirectly mold the way we think and what we value and pay attention to as a culture.[24]

A simple example: we know intuitively that if a person initiates a breakup via texting, he or she will send a substantially different message than breaking up in person, even if he or she uses exactly the same words. Texting isn't typically a very personal medium. While this might seem like a small quirk, according to media ecology theory, little things add up. That's because every medium makes certain kinds of communication possible or easy and others impossible or difficult. For example, writing makes it easy to keep precise records of events, ideas, and facts—and in turn removes the need to memorize human knowledge. The overall media environment or ecology of a society—its complete set of tools and practices of communication—shape the way we live just as our physical environments do. The residents of Alaska and Bermuda and the residents of print culture and digital media culture think and live in different ways because of their settings.

This is not to say our media environments absolutely *control* us—such a notion would be called technological determinism, something that many scholars hate because it implies that we are helpless before the power of our tools. Just as we can reshape or ignore our physical environment—we can, for instance, tunnel through hills or dig them up if we want to travel past them—so we can interact with our media ecology in unexpected ways. It *is* possible to send a really touching, personal message via texting. But our environments—physical or media—tend to encourage certain things and discourage others. It's easier to go down a hill than up, and it's easier to use texting for impersonal messages than personal ones. While a cell phone, a human creation, would seem more malleable than a natural hill, the physical reality of a technology sets limits we can't wish away: sadly, a cell phone cannot, by itself and without significant modifications, make a good mochachino. So, as McLuhan put it succinctly: we make our tools and our tools make us.

One of the key themes running through much of the theory of media ecology is that we have a moral imperative to judge the strengths and weaknesses of our media environment. It is not enough, some media ecologists argue, to simply note the changes that result from a shift in media.[25]

Adopting any medium involves a trade-off—every gain is accompanied by a loss.[26] So the correct question to ask is not whether video games are educationally, mentally, and socially good for us. The question is what a video game–influenced culture gains and loses by adopting the medium.

It seems to me that this is partly why the arguments of the game critics and enthusiasts don't quite connect with each other. To a large extent, each party is talking *past* the other because each side relies on its own standards. If we use the standards of the print people, as Bauerlein and Jacoby do, their critiques of our media environment make sense. If we use the standards of the digiterati, however, as Johnson and McGonigal do, video games look great and promise great things in the future. What we need is a balanced evaluation, one that looks at the pluses and minuses together.

Evaluating What We Lose in a Video-Game World

To start with, I do think the critics of video games and the digital media environment have some valid points. For example, it's fair to argue that video games—and especially the overall digital media environment they are part of—disrupt the long attention span and capacity for complex logical argument that print develops. Reading is a remarkably challenging form of communication to master. It requires significant mental focus. It also has a bias toward sequential communication: one sentence leads to the next, one page follows another (although stories frequently mess around with time lines via flashbacks and flash-forwards). Because it is prepared in advance and allows for significant editing, print allows for the creation of complicated statements and ideas that are much harder to compose orally—there's a reason it takes a long time to write a book![27]

The profusion of screens and audio pollution in today's environment kills the ability to concentrate and focus. Video games themselves can actually encourage intense focus, as we've already discussed. But the overall media environment they reside in is one of a million options and thus potential distractions. It's very easy for us to drop a book for a game, a game for a status update, a status update for a video, and so on—or more likely, we carry on a few of these things at the same time. This sort of stream-of-consciousness surfing and multitasking is not good for complex, sustained thinking. Research shows that we are much worse at multitasking than we think we are. When we try to balance multiple cognitive tasks at the same time, such as texting and driving, we do all of them worse than when we focus on one at a time.[28] I don't think video games are at fault for this, but they are certainly one very big blinking light in a world that is full of blinking lights.

In addition, the proponents of teaching or social engineering with video games (the popular ones like McGonigal or Johnson more than the pure academics) tend to make problematic arguments. For instance, some pro-game analyses seem to assume that all video gamers are similar, when in reality, all that ties them together is game playing. Not all gamers, for instance, like competition. Some get other kinds of pleasures from games. Yet many design discussions about educational or alternate-reality games such as *Chore Wars* seem to assume shared interests for all gamers. McGonigal also repeatedly makes utopian claims about gamers banding together and building a better, more fun, more motivated world; but anyone who's suffered through a bad session of *League of Legends* knows that foul-mouthed, squabbling gamers can quickly poison any naive notions about the goodness of humankind.

The biggest problem with video games as a teaching tool is that the knowledge and skills gained while playing a game are naturally geared to that specific world.[29] There may be logical connections between games and nongame activities: organizing complicated business in *Railroad Tycoon*, for example, might well have important similarities to managing companies in real life; when my daughter learns how to get three stars on a level of puzzle game *Cut the Rope*, she is developing logical thought patterns that would solve real-world puzzles. But it is unlikely that a player is going to automatically make those connections. The biggest challenge for educators using video games is to help students construct a bridge between the worlds inside and outside of the video game. It is possible to do this, to be sure, but it is a lot of work. That is why, from my perspective as an educator, video games are not cure-alls for the educational ills that beset us. They are tremendously time intensive. Even games made specifically for education, such as the hallowed and venerable *Oregon Trail*, will struggle with this limitation. I may learn how the game wants me to shoot digital deer for food, but I may not connect that to the experience of settlers without some help.

At the same time, the arguments against today's media environment have some flaws as well. If we connect book culture and its long-form, complicated, linear thought with the development of democracy, the modern university, modern science, and other good things, then we must in all fairness connect it with the bad stuff: horrible wars, global imperialism, awful abuse of labor, and so on. Obviously, the printing press is not responsible for all of this. The bigger point is that rationality and the other benefits of print are not everything they're cracked up to be. McLuhan, for one, was not a big fan of print culture. He thought it overemphasized certain aspects of humanity, denigrating the values of sound and the tribal wholeness associated with orality.[30] The point is not that print (or the broadcast media that followed it) is wholly evil; it's just that it does not represent the pinnacle of perfection that some bibliophiles attribute to it.

In addition, I believe that the death of reading is a bit overblown and that the fears attached to the cultural changes in reading are exaggerated. Bauerlein, Jacoby, and others see a tremendous decline in our culture, but history tells us there has always been an elite worried about society rotting away.[31] As I mentioned in chapter 1, that doesn't mean there's *no* substance to the specific complaints, but it does suggest that the new media environment isn't inevitably leading to the apocalypse. The profusion of online text indicates that people read quite a bit today—probably less book-length stuff than a generation or two ago, and that is significant, but not the same as saying that there's no engagement of the written word.

The terrible test results that worrywarts often cite are geared toward methods of learning and subject material that is important in a print culture—is it any wonder that we don't see things improving through that data? I think it's valuable for people to know where Iraq is, but if they don't, they can find out with five seconds and a cell phone. It's less important for today's education to teach data and data recall, and much more crucial to teach how to find and critically evaluate data.

Evaluating What We Gain in a Video-Game World

Still, this doesn't get to the heart of the *positives* of video games. Despite their inevitable limitations, video games should be a valuable tool for teachers—and not just because kids like them (although that *is* a plus). The deeply social aspect of games gives a reason and a venue to get people together to act collaboratively. Even single-player games encourage cooperation in the form of strategy discussions and tips for better play. And because video games are computer programs, we can distribute the same game to millions of people, meaning game sociability can be played out on both a small and huge scale.

Video games also excel at creating imaginary places and spaces with reams of information and detail.[32] Interacting with tangible fantasies is an aesthetically powerful experience. But it's also educationally valuable: rather than divide and categorize a problem as a textbook would, a video-game player has to encounter, say, the effects of an economic recession or an invasion or being in a rock band in a relatively holistic way. Real life doesn't split problems into categories; video-game worlds can simulate the inter-related play of factors very well. For example, *Third World Farmer* shows players how politics, global markets, climate conditions, sociocultural expectations, and technology all affect the survival of families involved in subsistence farming, and it does so in a seamless fashion.

But to my way of thinking, many of the greatest cognitive and educational benefits that proponents of the medium have noted come from its great distinguishing characteristic: video games are interactive symbolic machines. A little review is in order to make the point. A video game is like a machine built of symbols, a machine that we can manipulate, but that has a somewhat unpredictable interaction of parts. Pressing the right trigger in *Red Dead Redemption* may always result in my character firing a gun, but exactly what the bullet hits is dependent on where I'm aiming and what's on the screen. Contrast this with other forms of communication. Print is effectively noninteractive—we *can* rewrite a book with a pen, but it's not terribly easy. Live oral storytelling or conversation or performance is interactive, but it is not recorded and able to be mass produced, and it is not bounded by game rules and computer programs.[33] Broadcast media such as radio and television have the live feeling of oral communication, but are as noninteractive as print. Some other digital media are interactive systems, such as hyperlinks on web pages, but the interactivity is very limited. Video games are mass producible *and* deeply interactive.

Certainly there are downsides to the systematic nature of video games. For one, although we wouldn't know it from the praises of some game enthusiasts, video games cannot be completely free-form. All games have rules and must run according to programs, so even though we might be able to imagine something, the game may not let us do it. I might want to play John Marston of *Red Dead Redemption* nonviolently, but the game won't let me—at least not if I want to advance the narrative. I might want to introduce a third party into *The Redistricting Game*—a wonderful political-education game—but it's not part of the program. This may be partly why romantic souls rebel against the cage of the machine. Movie after movie proclaims that technologies such as computers (think *Termi-nator*) or bureaucracy (think *Office Space*) are essentially inhuman and will take us over and destroy us in the end if we let them. We often see the worst of this when players try to optimize their success in video games. They tend to find an optimal strategy and start repeating it ad nauseam, becoming machinelike (in a bad sense) in their play. MMOs are particularly famous for requiring players to level up by "grinding," repetitively killing monsters or crafting items in the same sequence of actions over and over again for hours at a time.

Yet, in an odd way, systems can breed tremendous creativity. Some of the most interesting works of art result from creation within strict self-imposed rules. An easy example is haiku poetry:

> *Set syllable counts*
> *Force clever poets to write*
> *With economy*

The strict rules still leave room for nearly infinite varieties of poems. Likewise, gamers can demonstrate tremendous capacity for creation when they enter a game world. A common example is when they find strategies that the game makers didn't anticipate: complicated games such as *Civilization* and *League of Legends* get periodic patches that alter units and rules because gamers have found strategies that make the game unexpectedly easy. But even more clearly, players find ways to express artistic creativity in games. *Minecraft* is an excellent example. This retro-style indie game is essentially a giant digital box of Lego blocks that allows players to construct whatever they want—but they're limited to cubes, and working block by block. This low-tech game has spawned a vibrant community of enthusiasts, some of whom use *Minecraft* to make bizarre, fun, and unanticipated tributes to all kinds of pop culture items (see the illustrations on p. 124).

Humans use systems to organize the world, and systems are obviously crucial to all kinds of work—science and finance and politics, even the business of art. As video-game-education proponents have noted, games encourage us to be puzzlers and tinkerers, to play with problematic systems and make them work. And because video games are dynamic symbol machines, they adapt to players extremely well, cognitively challenging them at just the right level. To not integrate such valuable tools into our education systems or to ignore their benefits on society in general is to miss out on a great opportunity.

Here's a very small sampling of the thousands of objects that *Minecraft* enthusiasts put together. Go online and search for "Minecraft art" to find many more.

The Moral Imperative of Technology Studies

There is a deeper issue here, though, than just the question of whether we should use video games as teaching and social-shaping tools. We certainly need this *specific* discussion, but the larger issue is how we manage and use technology. One of the key points of another set of scholars that I rely upon—the social-construction-of-technology perspective—is that we are under no obligation to accept technology and its impact. In fact, scholars in this tradition argue that technology is to a large degree what we make it to be. No amount of wishing or hopeful thinking will make my dead hard drive spring to life, so as we've already noted, the technology itself has some power. But we invented the hard drive, we purchase and deploy it, and we decide what it is used for.[34] Likewise, video games do not operate by themselves. We make them, and we decide how to think about them and what to do with them. We are not powerless, and so we have an obligation to carefully think about the cultural and cognitive impact video games have and then act to encourage the positive and discourage the negative.

We can do that in and through education. Sometimes it means adopting new technologies and employing them wisely. A website where kids or adults can collaboratively imagine a world without oil (*World without Oil*) or try to draw the boundaries of electoral districts (*The Redistricting Game*) are instances in which the use of game technologies and techniques can be really positive. But I also believe that education is a possible area for resistance to problematic social trends. Schools should be a space where students are free of the consumer commercialism that floods the rest of our lives. And I have no problem with teachers employing the supposedly out-of-date techniques of lecture and note-taking, if they are done in a way that fosters concentration, memory, and complicated linear thinking. These things are truly imperiled in our current media environment.

If properly deployed, video games can be a part of our new culture without destroying what is valuable in existing culture. Video games aren't stupid: the question is whether or not we'll be stupid in how we use them.

◄ ⑧ ►

Making a Different World

Christians Building Video Games

Horror Stories—Tales of the Dark Side of Making Video Games

- In 1982, Atari rushed the production of a game based on the movie *E.T.* just as the public was starting to get tired of poor-quality video games. It was so bad and sold so dismally that Atari dumped millions of unsold cartridges in a New Mexico landfill.[1]
- High-flying John Romero—the famous cocreator of early 1990s hit *Doom*—founded multimillion-dollar-studio Ion Storm to produce his dream game, *Daikatana*. Although promoted aggressively by an arrogant advertising campaign, the project was a disaster. It arrived five years late, millions over budget, had terrible reviews, and miniscule sales. The studio closed down shortly after the game's release.[2]
- In 2004, anonymous author ea_spouse touched off a firestorm in the game industry by posting the online essay "EA: The Human Story." The piece detailed systematic abuse of developers at giant **publisher** EA, such as eighty-five-hour workweeks for many months in a row, which caused health problems and put a tremendous burden on developers' families. Within a year, the public embarrassment had resulted in class-action settlements for workers and changed labor practices.[3]

People like to complain, and entertainment is often a target, even as we continue to consume it. But criticism of the video-game industry seems particularly virulent at times. Game enthusiasts complain that many games are totally derivative, lacking creativity. Fans moan about rushed releases of buggy, behind-schedule software. Industry insiders complain about horrendous workloads, cutthroat management practices, and stupid business decisions.

How fair is all of this? And how are Christians called to be a light to this video-game industry? This chapter will give a voice to some of the Christians working on video games for a living. Over the next few pages, we'll hear about the challenges they face and their visions for the industry.

Understanding Video-Game Development

To better understand the Christian game developers I interviewed, we'll take a quick look at how the video-game industry works. The industry as a whole includes several distinct lines of work. Developers are the companies that actually produce games—they do the design, the art, the programming, and so on. Publishers are the corporations that fund development and handle printing, distribution, and marketing. Game hardware (i.e., consoles) design and manufacturing is another distinct aspect of the industry. And finally, retailers—not only brick-and-mortar stores but, increasingly, digital sites such as Steam, Xbox LIVE, or Apple's App Store—sell the games.

Economics of Production

So how do these various parties make money? For many years, either very well or very poorly. In the first few Wild-West decades of the industry, many of the earliest success stories were built more on entrepreneurship and salesmanship than the steady and calculated management that typically leads to a stable business. Companies such as Atari went from tiny start-ups to billion-dollar giants in a matter of years, and then crashed just as spectacularly a few years later.[4] The classic retail system, however, offered a greater degree of stability between about 1990 and 2005. It centered on the game console, which was much cheaper than a home computer and easier to use. Console makers sold their machines cheaply and made their profit charging publishers for each game copy sold. Nintendo, for example, typically made $5 after costs on each cartridge for the NES.[5]

Game products were physical hardware requiring expensive shelf space, so major chain retailers such as Walmart and GameStop wanted mass sales to turn a profit. Simultaneously, improving graphics and sound resulted in a ballooning cost of production. Most developers needed production funding from large publishing companies such as Microsoft or EA (if they weren't outright purchased by them), who in exchange for their investment and ability to promote and distribute product to major retailers took in the lion's share of sales revenue, returning a small royalty of 10 or 15 percent to the developers. Thus the system favored big business and formulaic titles that sold predictably.

The industry, however, has undergone significant changes in the early twenty-first century. Since 2000, game makers have created a number of very different business models, largely due to new forms of technology. MMOs developed subscription-based revenue streams, where gamers pay monthly fees to play. The biggest subscription-based game, *World of Warcraft*, with more than ten million subscribers at thirteen dollars a month, makes billions of dollars each year.[6] Cheap-to-produce casual games often make money from advertising (e.g., Yahoo! Games) or using free games to sell upgraded versions (e.g., PopCap), and still others sell merchandise (e.g., Orisinal).[7] Today, many big-budget games—everything from MMOs such as *The Lord of the Rings Online* to combat game *League of Legends* to *FarmVille*—also use "freemium" models, where players can play the game for free, but the game invites them to spend money on extra options, power-ups, or special decorations. The other tremendously popular revenue model is that of micro-purchases: ninety-nine-cent games sold at the Apple App Store or Google Play, the current champion being *Angry Birds*.[8]

All this is important because, quite simply, it's opened up the system. Developers in the casual and app markets can make a good living (or at least *a* living) on games that don't require massive budgets to develop. They can find niche audiences for quirky or nonformulaic games. The old big-budget system still exists—although physical retailers are steadily fading in importance—but it's no longer the only industry. That doesn't mean that it's *easy* to turn a profit. Just about everyone I've ever met who makes games for a living is, on some level, focused on money because it's hard to make ends meet. Major publishers are under pressure to return substantial profits for investors, developers of top-quality titles are constantly chasing funding, and small-scale indie developers are worrying about how to pay rent. The technology of the internet and portable devices has opened up a new world of opportunities, but it's also tremendously unpredictable, financially speaking, and more competitive than ever before.

Culture of Production

Another issue we need to discuss before we turn to the interviews is the culture of production in the game industry. What is the work actually like? What I hear in conversation with developers and see in article after article is that making video games is a demanding line of work.[9]

Developers of any type—whether in major companies or small start-ups—work *extremely* long hours. They work weekends and work late—during a *regular* week. The last few months before a release is "crunch time" when everyone on the project works around the clock, sometimes sleeps at the office, and subsists on a diet of Coke and pizza. If self-employed game makers allow themselves slightly healthier schedules than their corporate counterparts, they risk running out of money before their projects are complete. The industry lore also paints the game industry as a harsh and often dysfunctional world. The locker-room-culture elements of game culture mean mistakes often bring harsh criticism and mockery rather than grace. The pecking orders in some companies can also lead to poor treatment of those on the bottom of the heap.[10] To top all of this off, job security is virtually nonexistent. Developers often pour themselves into a project only to be laid off when the game ships because the company has no more work for them.

So why on earth do people put up with this? It's the old law of supply and demand: more people want to work on games than positions exist for them. Just like Hollywood, the game industry beckons to thousands of young people (young men, mostly) with stars in their eyes, dreaming about the opportunity to work on the games they love to play. Desperate to get in on the action, once they arrive, they're willing to put up with an awful lot to stay there. So the game industry is full of passionate young people who—just as in Hollywood—get chewed up and spit out when they're used up. Most people can't hack the required work schedule of a beginner programmer or artist or quality assurance tester for more than a few years. Eventually, the lack of normal social interaction and the demands on the body catch up, and most people either get out, move up the ladder (if they can), or try to work for themselves as an indie (assuming they can afford to). I've met a few ex-game-industry workers, and they're not likely to ever get back in again.

I don't mean to portray work in the game industry as a horror show. It's very important to note that the best developers create much more healthy environments—most people can't say enough positive stuff about companies like BioWare and 5TH Cell, for example—although even these companies are still likely to require heavy workloads. And clearly, thousands of people love it enough to stick with it, at least for a while. Plus, we all know that complaints about work are universal. But I've heard from enough different sources to know that working in the industry is not an easy path.[11]

The Great Divide: Indie vs. Corporate Giants

I should highlight one final thing before we listen to the game developers themselves: the difference between corporate game production and indie game production. Giant game publishers like EA, Activision, and Nintendo, who are all worth billions of dollars today, totally dominated the industry from about 1990 through 2005 and are still tremendously powerful. Corporate control of the industry, however, was never airtight: there were always small companies making stuff outside of the mainstream, such as the small world of turn-based strategy war games. And the new technological and economic environment has made survival as an indie more feasible than ever before. Many newbies trying to break into the industry will start working for indie companies or start their own, and an increasing number of industry veterans are leaving major corporations to start new development companies.

The big game companies certainly have advantages. First and foremost, they are able to throw millions of dollars and hundreds of top-quality professionals into a project: the stellar visuals, writing, and voice acting of *Red Dead Redemption* couldn't happen on a shoestring budget. Major publishers are also able to properly promote games, meaning that they won't unfairly languish in obscurity, a terrible fate that can befall even high quality games.[12] They are also far more likely to have steady (or steadi*er*) revenue streams, so they can provide a kind of income stability that indies lack. In some cases, major corporations are able to implement some healthy limits on overworking that smaller companies simply can't afford to do.[13]

However, game makers who have chosen the indie path point to the huge advantage they have over their corporate counterparts: creative freedom.

They often don't know how they're going to pay the rent, they have to live on macaroni and cheese, and they may need to pick up extra jobs and work themselves to near-death, but they can follow their commercially unproven passion to build a game about squid ecologically restoring deforested regions through the power of pop music and dance. And in fact, today, many of the small companies making iPhone games are finding that they can live near-normal lives as long as they're not worried about getting terribly rich.[14]

Being Salt and Light: Discussions with Developers

Now that we have a little context, let's hear from some video-game makers themselves. Over a period of several months, I had the privilege of interviewing more than a dozen thoughtful Christian professionals working on video games in some capacity who were generous enough to share their time with me. The group are remarkably diverse, including Christians from a variety of theological perspectives, ages, and ethnicities, although they were mostly men; I interviewed only one woman (it's hard to find more in the game industry). Some people work on game programming, others on design and art, and still others on business and management. A few of the interviewees are long-time industry veterans, and others have worked on video games for only a few years. Some have worked in large corporations, others in small start-ups, and their games ranged from big-budget AAA titles to short casual games meant to be played on iPhones. I thank each of them for their time and for permission to include their work experience and their responses to my questions.

I asked all of them the same questions. After talking a little about their backgrounds and faith commitments, we spent most of the time addressing their experiences as Christians making video games. Specifically, I asked:

- How does faith impact making video games?
- What's a Christian video game, if such a thing is even possible?
- What's the general perception of Christians within the game industry?
- What would you like to tell Christians outside the industry about making video games?

I received a wealth of answers to these questions, but throughout the conversations, a number of themes emerged, so we'll look at each one in turn.

Christians Working in the Gaming Industry

Name	Company and Experience	Kind of Work	Games Worked On
John Bergquist	Soma Games and Code Monkeys	Writing and art	*G: Into the Rain, Wind-Up Robots*
Sherol Chen	The Expressive Intelligence Studio at the Center for Games and Playable Media	Artificial intelligence programming research	*EMPath* (experimental game), "drama manager" tools
Jon Collins	Kaio Interactive	Programming and game design	*Bounder, Codebearers: Viginti*
Seth Crofton	Wargaming.net	Business consultant, marketing	*World of Tanks, Principality*
Andy Geers	Old Testament Adventures	Programming and game design	*Ebenezer* (in development)
Brock Henderson	Paper Tower, Crawl Space Games	Business, programming and game design	*Float, Globs, Knife Toss*
Dan Hughes	Camp Skookum	Art, business, game design	*Camp Skookum* (in development)
Rustin Lee	Alpha Digital Network, previously: 2K Sports	Business, programming and game design	*Lands and Legends, NBA 2K, NFL 2K, MLB 2K, NHL 2K*
Rand Miller	Cyan Worlds	Game design and production management	*Myst, Uru, Bug Chucker*
Brian Poel	Homebrained Schemes, previously: Xbox Kinect, Wizards of the Coast, Oberon Media	Financial analysis, business development, user experience design	*D&D Insider, Noah's Ark, Kinect Fun Labs*
Lance Priebe	RocketSnail, previously: Disney	Production management, game design	*Club Penguin, Mech Mice* (in development)
Nate Sawatzky	Tiny Speck, previously: Disney	(Online) community manager	*Glitch, Club Penguin*
Chris Skaggs	Soma Games	Programming and game design	*G: Into the Rain, Wind-Up Robots*
Mark Soderwall	Authority 5, previously: LucasArts, Atari, Inc.	Art, art direction	*Star Wars: The Force Unleashed, Fracture, Terminator 3: Rise of Machines*

Name	Company and Experience	Kind of Work	Games Worked On
Joseph Tringali	5TH Cell	Business, production, studio general manager	*Drawn to Life, Scribblenauts, Hybrid* (in production)
Bobby Wells	Third Day Games	Business and game design	*Big Bible Town*
Kelly Zmak	Infinite Game Publishing, previously: Radical Entertainment, Sierra Entertainment (Vivendi)	Business, production management	*Prototype, Scarface: The World Is Yours*

Christians and Coworkers

"The way we treat people is the best reflection of our faith," says Kelly Zmak. While this might sound like common sense for Christians, it's a valuable attitude in an industry full of rotten and abusive behavior. The "only concern [for many companies] is that you spend all your time there, and they don't really care what the aftermath is," as Rustin Lee puts it. Christian game makers, however, have an obligation to treat people as Jesus would have. "The idea that 'business is business' is messing with the number one way that faith is supposed to impact our work," says Rand Miller. "'Business is people' should be the conviction of anyone who professes to follow what Jesus was saying." Whether dealing with peers or superiors, Zmak argues that it's important for Christians in the game industry to "treat people with honesty, candor, respect, and encouragement, discipline when appropriate."

Others note the importance of being solid employers. For one thing, as Lance Priebe notes, "one of the greatest gifts you can give people is a job, a career." Priebe lauds *Club Penguin* cofounder Dave Krysko for not only making job creation a life calling but also taking good care of his employees once they are hired. Jon Collins notes that responsible employers do their best to provide good benefits and structure their demands in such a way that "family time takes precedence over work. . . . That's my understanding of what God wants from me." Christian game makers can model a healthy attitude at the worst of times too, such as firing workers for not doing their jobs. "Even when we do difficult things," says Joseph Tringali, "we strive to do them in a way that looks out for the employee in terms of severances, in terms of generosity. We've done everything we can to be as good to people as we can." And Brian Poel stresses the importance of fair agreements: bad employers will try to use the small print of contracts to take advantage of inexperienced game makers.

Several developers also mentioned the importance of involving God in the workplace via prayer. Chris Skaggs notes that at Soma Games, if people on the team are facing challenges, "we'll just break from what we're doing. . . . Everyone gets together and we just pray." He even says that non-Christians will ask for prayer when facing significant problems. This wouldn't fly in a secular company, but private prayer is a feature of everyday work for other developers I interviewed.

Witnessing to the Industry

Some of the interviewees believe Christians are called to witness to the industry as a whole, not just people working in the same company. That's because the world of video games is often at odds with Christian sensibilities: "it's an amazing mission-field/minefield," according to Mark Soderwall. As Rustin Lee puts it: "It's kind of a boy's group, and they're all into just having a good time and partying. I hate to say it but they're into the sex, drugs, rock and roll."

Christianity, according to these game makers, has a varied reputation within the industry. Some developers and publishers are actively hostile to Christians. Nobody offered verifiable specifics, but interviewees claimed they knew horror stories of people being fired for their beliefs. More commonly, some members of the industry see Christians as hypocritical, repressive, and kooky—although several people note that such ideas are hardly unique to game makers. Chris Skaggs says that this negativity is often only "paper thin," and it goes away when non-Christians get to know real Christians. And in many cases, the culture of the game industry has nothing to do with Christianity—several developers reported that they never encounter or discuss anything to do with Christians or Christian faith at industry gatherings.

In such an environment, a person making it known that he or she is a Christian can be a strong witness, according to some interviewees. Skaggs says that when people find out he's a Christian, they often start up very interesting discussions. Seth Crofton has found that living a different lifestyle can really grab people's attention, and not necessarily in a hostile way. In his case, his commitment not to drink alcohol leads to late-night conversations at bars during industry conventions where he is able to explain what his faith means.

Looking Out for Gamers

Christian game makers, argue many of the people I interviewed, have a responsibility to treat gamers properly. For instance, protecting children is important. Collins argues that adult content shouldn't masquerade as kid-friendly stuff. It also means doing more than the bare minimum to protect children from predators and other risks: "I believe that if you're on my property, you're my responsibility," says Priebe, the cofounder of the online kid's playground *Club Penguin.*

Brian Poel points to the significant issue of addiction in the casual and social games that he works with. "The game itself has ways to manipulate your behavior to turn you into a tool for them, a tool to promote the game." Social games, he argues, try to create cycles of dependency to keep players and their friends hooked. When that happens, "it becomes a job and no longer entertainment." What's particularly bad about it, he believes, is that social games typically try to grab new gamers, which means "[game designers are] exposing people who have no white blood cells against these game-design tricks, because [these new players are] not gamers." Christian game makers need to find revenue models that are less reliant on antisocial behavior. "If you're designing gambling tricks into your game to extract the most money possible from the most vulnerable people, and the only reason they're spending that money is because you've hooked them into it, then the line between drug dealer and social-game designer is pretty thin."

Zmak suggests a third issue involving the paying public: "We talk about value all the time. I need somebody to spend a buck fifty on a microtransaction. They need to feel like they got three dollars in value. . . . I need to treat them well in my product. I need to treat them well in my actions . . . because I'm asking them to separate themselves from their cash." In light of Jesus's example of living for others, Christians need to think of more than the bottom line (as do non-Christians!); they are responsible for their customers in terms of safety, health, and giving customers fair value.

The Challenge of Christian Games

To this point, all the themes we've discussed apply to just about any kind of game. Whether a developer makes a first-person shooter or a cute puzzle game, a Christian approach can emphasize healthy relationships between employees, good witness to others in the industry, and a responsible attitude toward paying customers. But what about the games themselves? Does their *content* matter? What kinds of games can and should Christians make? The interviewees generally agreed that the nature of the game itself is important. As Skaggs puts it: "Every game, whether you like [it] or not, comes with a worldview." Christian game makers, many of the interviewees argued, need to take care with the kinds of ideas and worldviews their games adopt.

Yet the response to "Christian games" was truly universal: to this point in time, at least, they have been quite bad. Brock Henderson sums up the critiques: "Typically [Christian games] don't have the budgets, they don't have the production value, [and] they're very heavy-handedly preachy." Rand Miller associates them with "*conforming*, not *transforming*." John Bergquist puts it even more succinctly: "Honestly, [they're] something I don't play." Nate Sawatzky describes them as the kinds of games bought by Christian parents who are nervous about video games, and the kinds of games kids don't really play much. When I started to push past that initial negative assessment, however, the interviewees had some significant differences of opinion.

Defining Christian Content

The interviewees shared two common definitions of "Christian games." "Explicitly Christian" games feature Bible stories or passages, very clear presentation of the gospel message, and stories that very openly have a Christian worldview. Wells's *Big Bible Town*, designed in conjunction with Sunday school curriculum and focused on teaching Bible stories to children, is an explicitly Christian game. "Allegorical" Christian games have stories that are not necessarily openly Christian but have Christian themes or messages underneath them. Many cited C. S. Lewis's Narnia stories as examples of this approach.

Two other definitions popped up in a few interviews. "Christian-friendly games" are clean and safe, without significant violence, adult sexuality, swearing, anti-Christian worldviews, and other things that Christians might find offensive or disturbing. This would include puzzle games like *Bejeweled* or *Words with Friends* or the nonviolent MMO *Glitch*, which emphasizes crafting items (and is produced by the secular game company Sawatzky works for). And finally, "evangelical Christian video games" focus on sharing the gospel with people who aren't Christians. This is a visionary definition, since there aren't really any prominent examples that I know of or that any of my interviewees mentioned.

EVALUATING DIFFERENT VISIONS FOR CHRISTIAN GAMES

What are the pluses and minuses of each approach to Christian games? A few of my interviewees made a strong case for the value of explicitly Christian games. Sherol Chen believes that explicitly Christian content in games would be a natural outflow of a healthy relationship with God: "When you're in love with somebody, you think about them all the time, you paint pictures of them, and you sing songs to them and you do things for them. . . . If we were a people that were in love with God, we would see it everywhere." Andy Geers argues that the Bible is great subject material: "There's nothing boring or irrelevant about the Bible, and so if your game feels boring and irrelevant then it's not really teaching the Bible." And Lee says a Christian video game "needs to be pretty literal [in its Christian content] to really make the kind of impact that needs to happen out there."

Nevertheless, explicitly Christian video games face some significant challenges. "You can't get a [Christian] video game into retail," explains Bobby Wells. "So you've got to find an alternative marketing and distribution strategy." A physical retailer wants to stock on their precious shelf space something that's a predictable seller.[15] Explicitly Christian games are also far more likely to end up in the middle of theological conflicts than a more ambiguous allegorical game, Crofton notes.

Some developers level more fundamental criticisms at explicitly Christian games. For one thing, as Dan Hughes points out, "I don't think a book can be a Christian, I don't think a movie can be a Christian." Being a Christian, in other words, isn't about media content, it's about a relationship with a living God. A bigger issue is that explicitly Christian content can mask a lack of creativity and a poor understanding of games. In Christian games that Poel has seen, the developers "just took an existing game concept and they skinned it with some spiritual dressing. I've got *Bejeweled*, but instead of abstract gems, there are [Bibles]. That doesn't make it Christian." Crofton offers a similar critique: "[The church] tries so many times to replicate what the world is doing when we shouldn't be. We should be doing it ourselves first and then giving it to the world."

What about using explicitly Christian games for evangelism? Crofton argues that the medium is well suited for such purposes. "[Games] can reach people faster than getting Bibles to them, that's for sure. We're see-ing that in China right now and Indonesia, where people can download that content and then share it with friends . . . and at a cheaper cost [than Bibles] as well."[16] In addition, argues Wells, "People who love the Lord have used the technology of the day, whether it be the printing press, radio, television, the internet, or whatever as a medium for trying to communicate the gospel to people." Crofton agrees: "Christ told parables. And people learned from them. He used the media of the day and . . . the medium of the day right now is games."

Other developers question the goal of using video games for evange-lism. The most common complaint about such games (and explicitly Christian games in general) is that they tend to be preachy, which doesn't fly in our culture. Skaggs also points out a problem unique to video games: we don't participate in a conversion experience in a movie or novel, "but in a game, it's the nature of the medium to be interactive and so if I force someone to go through a conversion experience in the game . . . I think that I'm coming really close to violating their free will." Zmak raises the point that mass media may not be as effective for evangelism as many Christians assume. "I don't know how many people accepted Christ after watching Mel Gibson's *The Passion*. I look at those [kind of movies] and go, 'are those converting souls?'" With perhaps a few notable exceptions, he argues, most people become Christians because people they know are Christians. For good reason, says Miller. "The kingdom of God that Jesus talked about was not primarily about mass communication or a media agenda. It seems to me that what Jesus was demonstrating had more to do with '*doing* on a small scale' than with '*saying* on a large scale.'"

So what about allegorical Christian games? Such games have two big things going for them, according to my interviewees. First, as Crofton puts it: "It's far more likely [compared to explicitly Christian games] for the world to be able to say, 'Oh this is cool, let me try it out!' and find out what's behind it." Second, Collins argues that broader acceptance translates into financial feasibility, especially in comparison to explicitly Christian games. Some of the developers, however, caution that allegorical Christian games have their limits. Lee argues that such games are usually not going to get the point across: "I think Narnia did it well . . . but I think that was the exception to the rule, and I think most other people need . . . it [delivered] literally to get the point across."

What about the value of Christian-friendly content? First, making things inoffensive is often good business: Zmak points out that games that are *too* disturbing can actually backfire and result in terrible sales. Second, Poel argues that "[not] everything you make has to be laden with deep and life-changing stuff." Most entertainment he consumes "is just popcorn. But I like my popcorn." Henderson puts it this way: "I think it's okay to make games that are just purely fun without trying to be heavy-handed in trying to teach or anything like that. I think God created fun and he likes it when his kids have fun sometimes."

At the same time, very few advocated calling inoffensive games *Christian* games. It felt more like the interviewees were trying to say that Christian-friendly games were simply okay for Christians to work on. And therein lies the challenge with this discussion: for all the great ideas being thrown around, the participants still seemed to have a particular notion of Christian games, a notion that's tied to the idea of the Christian market segment.

MAKING CHRISTIANS A MARKET SEGMENT

"I think," says Priebe, "that just like the music industry, there should be a gospel [video game] category." Many of the people I spoke to think the same thing. All the major media corporations have divisions for producing entertainment aimed at Christian consumers: Casting Crowns for Christian music fans, *Soul Surfer* for Christians going to the movies, Max Lucado books for Christians who prefer something a bit safer, and Donald Miller for the more edgy Christian literati. These are all highly profitable. Yet there isn't currently an equivalent with video games. "From a secular business perspective," says Zmak, "there is a clear awareness of a market. What there isn't clarity on is how to be successful in that market." Priebe echoes this: "The problem with Christian gaming is it hasn't had its [breakthrough] piece. Christian videos have. *VeggieTales* broke through."

But we should be careful what we wish for. While a Christian market segment makes economic sense, several developers pointed to the dangers of developing such a market. To start with, it makes Christian culture insular. "Very rarely," notes Tringali, "does a non-Christian pick up a Christian video game and say, 'I want to play this because I'm interested in Jesus.'" Poel believes customers of explicitly Christian games are people who want "the exact same gameplay [as popular secular games] and they prefer to surround themselves with Christian symbology." He holds up as an example the board game *Settlers of Canaan*, which is a Christian clone of the popular *Settlers of Catan*. "If that gets *Settlers of Catan* into a Bible-belt Christian store and has somebody buy it? Great. But what's funny is that it's not about stealthing someone's Christian values into somebody's house. It's stealthing European game design values into somebody's house using Christianity as the Trojan horse."

Zmak raises another challenge: mixing faith with commerce. "What we're taught in business isn't what we're taught in our faith. . . . The conflict is inherent in receiving profit. Nowhere in the Bible is there a business plan that says 'Okay, so you can make a nice 12 percent return on the Christian community if you follow the standard.'" Obviously, as a Christian in business, he's not against making money, but he points to the risk of profiting from making explicitly religious material. "The Christian video games . . . category was created out of the desire to do something that impacted people's lives. It's now become . . . 'How do we positively impact people's lives and make money? Because this is what I want to do for a living. . . .' Well those aren't necessarily in line with each other."

In any case, argues Priebe, a market category can't be a defining characteristic of Christian games. "At the end of the day, there is no Christian music, there are no Christian movies, there are no Christian games. There is just great music, great films with stories, and great games. And that's how you should see all of it. Sadly, our industry has to put things in their pigeonholes. So for us to succeed as an industry, we have to have stuff to put in that hole."

Toward an Inclusive Vision: Should the Definition Be Broader?

So should we broaden the definition of Christian content to include all of the above? Certainly it makes economic sense to do so. Collins believes that explicitly Christian games, allegorical Christian games, and Christian-friendly games are all financially important because "if you're looking to try and make a viable company that's going to be self-sufficient, just on one of those three genres, you're going to be stuck." But it's more than just economics that suggests an inclusive approach to making Christian games. God made people to think and interact and play in many different ways. "There should be the full gamut [of video games]," says Henderson. "There should be games where Christians learn Bible verses and games that are just fun."

But is Christian content necessary at all? A few of the game makers I interviewed suggest that we can learn a lot about humanity and about God even in seriously problematic games. In his decades of work on big-budget games in the secular industry, Zmak helped produce games that he sees as troubling. "But like everything else in literature, everything else in movies, everything else in entertainment, there are moral stories in it." I think he means that it's not so much that such games aim to *teach* morality but that they have narratives that reveal some aspect of being human. For example, the überviolent *Prototype*, which Zmak worked on, focuses on the story of a man with godlike powers and a kind of god complex; while it is dark and disturbing, Zmak argues that it is an excellent study on the weaknesses of humans and the dangers of egoism, both of which Christian teaching warns about.

Skaggs suggests it's not an accident that so many stories are relevant to Christians: these narratives are evidence of God working in the world, even when unacknowledged. Skaggs notes the work of Joseph Campbell, whose famous book *The Hero with a Thousand Faces* describes how the myths of cultures all around the world have striking similarities. Skaggs argues that Christians realize these different narratives are "all drawing on the One True Story." This would suggest that there is value in Christians making many games that wouldn't fit in *any* category of Christian content as people normally define it.

Is Christian Content the Content Christians Make?

This brings us to a final suggestion—one that nobody said explicitly but that seems to be underneath some of the arguments. Perhaps the idea of producing Christian content is not the right goal. Perhaps Christians can make *any* type of game. Lee argues—for clarity's sake, I think—that not all games that Christians make are Christian. But many of the interviewees made points that suggest the work of a Christian in the game industry is justified by something other than neat biblical lessons in a game's narrative.

What many developers emphasized was the big picture, rather than specific doctrinal points. For Bergquist, producing work of high quality is a sacred calling: "I see that whatever I do is a reflection of how God made me. And if I'm producing crap, I'm kind of stepping on sacred ground." Miller says that when he's open to it, "sometimes a (so-called) secular song has a wonderful aroma that touches the deep recesses of my being." This suggests that for Christians, then, as Miller puts it, "The goal is not to try to make *Christian* things but to make things that have that wonderful positive effect—things that *smell* beautiful." Soderwall makes a similar point: "We've been given gifts, all of us. And how we choose to use those gifts (or better yet, *who* we choose to use those gifts for), either it's a selfish act or it's for something greater." Chen puts it this way: "When you make a game and you're making it for God as an act of worship . . . it's Christian. . . . Our life's work should go to God." And Priebe believes that whatever it is we do, "God calls us to be great."[17]

Of course, this is a lot less clear than a checklist of elements that a Christian should include (or not include) in a video game. But that's precisely the point for some of the people I interviewed. Tringali, for example, thinks there is a place for a lot of challenging things—like violence—in video games made by Christians. The real question is "what you're glorifying." And Sawatzky argues that there's no one right way to make games as a Christian. Chen believes the right path of the Christian game maker is a mystery (in the good sense): it means following the leading of God and the Holy Spirit. "We should do what helps us get to know God better. . . . As long as our hearts are right, I think what we do is fair game because Jesus says there is no condemnation."

The Message of Game Makers to Us: Support and Engage!

When I offered the game makers the opportunity to say something to Christians outside the industry about their chosen profession, they gave many answers, but the main theme was that they want those of us outside the industry to engage the medium. In a complaint echoed by many of the interviewees, Skaggs notes that "the truth of the matter is, we've had a wonderfully positive response from the secular world. . . . Where we actually get poked at quite a bit is from the church." Christians often believe "that video games are the devil's work," according to Wells. Unsurprisingly, the people I interviewed see this as a big mistake.

To start with, many expressed a firm conviction that God wants them working on video games. Hughes claims, "When I am doing my artwork and I'm into the groove, that's when I feel closest to God, because I feel like I'm doing what I was called to do. . . . That [is] my form of worship." That clear calling motivates many of the game makers to persist in the face of challenges. Wells, for example, says, "We believe we're doing something that's God's will for our lives and you don't get into the Christian video-game business to make a lot of money, to get rich." Henderson likewise notes the financial challenges of being an indie: "You know, there have been times where it's been super stressful and freaked out, but I've really come to learn that God's going to take care of you just like he says in his Word."

The greater Christian community also needs to wake up to the scope and influence of video games on today's culture. "The game business," notes Collins, "is very much a growth industry. It has been for a number of years, and people may have let it go past without noticing it, but it's now bigger than Hollywood." In addition to being popular, the games are inherently powerful, as we've noted throughout this book. Multiple interviewees note that video games deliver stories in a particularly involving and powerful fashion. Bergquist loves the multimedia characteristics of the medium, the fact that "video games bring in so many pieces of art. The writing, the technical art, and then the selling of the games and communication and community building and all those things." Priebe highlights the social joy of video games: "four of us are on the couch and we're playing *Super Mario Kart* and we're laughing as a family and we're having fun and we're making memories and we're bugging the nine-year-old to keep up. . . . This is a powerful place for games." And Wells speaks highly of the educational merit of video games: "If the content is good, you'd really rather have your child spending ten hours a week playing that video game instead of doing what I did when I was a child: spend ten hours a week watching television. They're going to learn something through the process of playing that game."

Video games, says Bergquist, are just as open to good use and abuse as anything else, "just as much as music, like the radio, the television, the movie theater. . . . They're as much of the devil as anything, as a spoon is. It's what you do with it [that matters]." There is, in other words, no need to single out this medium as inherently evil. Chen puts it a slightly different way: "Stop thinking that God is so small that man's creation would somehow trump his validity. Twitter and Facebook and video games . . . [stop thinking we] need to squash those things because God's going to become illegitimate because man created this other technology."

And above all, the game makers plead with Christians not to abandon the medium and the industry. It is remarkable how many of the interviewees use the same historical parallel to point out what they see as today's Christians' fear of video games: "The industry is very much like Hollywood was in the early days," says Collins. "We've got an opportunity to abandon it or embrace it. If we abandon it, we will be in the same situation we are with Hollywood." Christians had a tentative and often negative experience with the early movie industry, meaning they largely avoided working there and lost the ability to influence its morality and its narratives. This has been a common pattern in the last century. "Christians have withdrawn from the battle," as Tringali puts it, "to shout from the sidelines." To do the same with the video-game industry is to shortsightedly repeat a bad mistake. "Christ went to places that were unpopular [with godly people]," argues Soderwall. "He went and visited these tax collectors and these individuals that were less than wholesome. . . . He went to the lost. . . . Even though there are certain video games I don't condone, if there aren't [Christians] getting in there, who's going to witness to [the lost]? Who's going to be the light in the darkness?"

That *doesn't* mean every Christian should try to make games. "Christians don't get a pass because they're Christians," says Tringali. "Don't get into video games because you see this opportunity. Get into video games because that's your passion and your heart. . . . All you're going to do by making crappy . . . video games is . . . make Christians look incompetent." Likewise, the game makers are not advocating a kind of blind acceptance of video games. Poel, for instance, warns about the dangers of addiction, and Lee advises parents to carefully monitor what their children play.

While they certainly encourage talented Christians to get into game making, what these game makers want most is active and critical Christians. Wells believes Christians "should look for Christian alternatives in the marketplace, and when they don't find them, they should demand them. If people wrote letters to Walmart and said, 'Why don't you have any Christian video games in this store?' that would change things." And Zmak emphasizes becoming an informed and constructive critic: "If you want to judge a product, judge it on its value, judge it on its lack of value, but you can't judge it unless you play it. You want to become a critic of an industry or a product? You must play its product in order to become a critic. Do you want to become a critic of people? You're in the wrong faith."

A Call for More Salt and More Light

When I started researching the Christian presence in the video-game industry five years ago, I was dismayed at what I found. I could locate very few Christians, the games that were called Christian were few in number, limited in genre types, low in quality, and represented only a few of the many perspectives in the church universal. After working on this book, however, I am far more optimistic. Part of this is because I did a better job of digging and using connections to find out that more Christians are making games than I previously thought. Partly, I am encouraged because I'm hearing more and more principled discussions of game design and development throughout the game industry. Plenty of non-Christians are concerned with making better games via more ethical processes, and they can be a real inspiration to Christians. But a lot of these shifts are due to today's changed technological landscape, where small-scale productions are no longer necessarily of poor quality or destined for obscurity.

The opportunities have never been greater. Facebook, the App Store, and other internet-based forms of distribution give game makers access to potentially huge markets. The tools of development are steadily getting cheaper, and the mass market has gaming tastes that don't require an investment of millions to satisfy. All of this allows for greater experimentation and a greater diversity of games, which leaves an opening for Christians to make their mark. That doesn't mean any of this will be easy, only that it is more possible than it was even a few years ago.

That said, I still think we need a lot more salt and light in the video-game industry. We need talented programmers, artists, writers, designers, project managers, public relations practitioners, and salespeople who follow Jesus. We need a greater diversity of Christian perspectives. The family of God is a big one, and the huge variety of theological and denominational perspectives all have something to contribute to the kingdom and to making video games in different ways. We need Christians in as many different kinds of companies as possible. While I am ideologically geeked by the creative freedom of being indie, the real money and some of the greatest influence in the industry is still in those predictable giant corporate structures that turn out video games with the highest quality production values.

Likewise, we need Christians making lots of different kinds of games. The gaming world is huge, and if we want to be a widespread positive force, we need followers of Christ working on puzzle games, RPGs, strategy games, first-person shooters, and more. I don't think we should be limited to explicitly Christian games, either. God made us playful meaning-makers and storytellers. Our pieces of art should develop those gifts. That may sometimes mean a Sunday school game, but it may also mean a game that makes no mention of Christ.

If the calling of Jesus is to bring the healing, the wholeness, the shalom of the kingdom of God to the whole world, then we need God's followers at work, whether it be on games that are explicitly Christian, allegorical, or simply good games. Our culture is blessed by the creation of new worlds, and who better to create them than those who deeply love and respect the original Creator?

Plays Well with Others

The Social Side of Gaming

Who *Are* These People?

At the end of August, I made a pilgrimage three hours down the road to Seattle to see grown men dressed as mushrooms. No, this didn't involve illicit substances—at least, not on my part, and I'm pretty sure not on theirs. I was attending the mother of all game-fan conventions: the Penny Arcade Expo, usually known as PAX. Twice a year—Seattle in August and Boston in March—well over sixty thousand gamers from all over the world get together to celebrate all things games.

It's a wild atmosphere. I don't mean that in a frat-party sense. Huge booths and displays sport life-sized posters and statues of video-game characters as developers and publishers seek to outdo one another in the race to impress gamers. Noise and music blare everywhere. Many of the attendees are dressed in outlandish costumes representing their favorite characters (the mushrooms were human-sized versions of the weapons dropped by *League of Legends* character Teemo, who was also portrayed by a young woman in costume). And in room after room, legions of enthusiasts play all types of games, old and new, video and board, cooperative and solo.

But what's most notable about these events are the game-crazed people there. Just about everyone is friendly, and unlike some game conventions, whole families attended, complete with little kids. It's remarkable how easy it is to start a conversation with complete strangers, and, of course, attendees can play games with just about anyone, even if they look like carnivorous plants or zombies. It's rare to find such a concentration of camaraderie, creativity, and frivolity.

Who *are* these people? They're gamers, of course, and they're busy demonstrating how incredibly social games are. People who still think video games make people withdraw from society need to read this chapter. Video games absolutely do not need to be solitary activities. Rather, they are social spaces. They are clearly not the same shape as other social spaces, such as restaurants or offices, but they are social spaces nonetheless. Gamers have occupied the universe of video games en masse, and today's game community is huge and vibrant. This chapter examines that community, considers its challenges and its wonders, and puts special emphasis on the role of Christians in these video-game spaces.

The Lonely Gamer Stereotype and Why It's Wrong

But aren't video games for lonely people? For many years, if we were to see a cartoon caricature of a gamer it would almost certainly be a white teenaged guy hunched over a console in front of a big screen all by himself in a dark basement. And to be fair, that wasn't entirely without reason. That was kind of me—although I played *computer* games growing up, not *video* games.[1] All my favorites, such as *Railroad Tycoon*, *Quest for Glory*, *Civilization*, or *The Bard's Tale* needed input only from me; they replaced human opponents with computerized ones. Some of the highest-profile video games did and still do emphasize this single-player mode.

Even in the good ol' days, however, video games were never solitary, and they've gotten only more social over time. Many of the earliest and most popular video games, such as *Spacewar!* or *Combat*, were in fact meant to be played by at least two people on the same computer. And even single-player games could be intensely social back in the day. The stinky, loud arcades of my youth were such popular hangouts that worried moralists sometimes tried to close them down, fearing juvenile delinquency. And cooperative play went on in countless living rooms and basements: I distinctly remember huddling around our Commodore 64 with my siblings while playing games, and my college dormmates and I collectively solved the first *Monkey Island* adventure game.

None of this in-person socializing has gone away over the years, but there are more and more options for playing together. Game systems have added more controllers, making it possible to have many people in the same room playing cooperatively, such as in *Gears of War 3*, or playing group games such as the *Mario Party* series or the *Rock Band* games. Online play, while around in some form or another since at least the late 1970s, has also boomed since the rise of high-speed internet in the late 1990s. Online servers, local-area networks, and console networks such as Xbox LIVE can host multiplayer games, such as the terrorist-vs.-counter-terrorist shooter *Counter-Strike* or the überpopular *Halo* series. MMO games, such as *The Lord of the Rings Online*, take things a step further by establishing online countries with well-populated towns and fully functioning economies (see the image below).[2] In these games, any player with internet access can create an avatar and run that character through a huge imaginary world while thousands of other players are simultaneously playing in the same world.[3] And finally, Facebook games, such as *Words with Friends* or *CityVille*, are also broadening the social reach of games to casual gamers.

My adventurer, Aethyn of Dale, overlooks the famous town of Bree in Middle-earth in *The Lord of the Rings Online*. Down in the town at any given moment, there are plenty of other adventurers.

On top of all this, players can socialize on websites, via chat software, and at conventions or meet-ups. The bigger point is that video games are not solitary—at least, they don't have to be—and millions have chosen to make them just as social as board games.

Manifestations of Gamer Community

Game communities are so numerous and have so many interesting characteristics worth mentioning that I could spend a whole book on them. Rather than go into that level of detail, however, I'll note a few of the most popular and common features of video-game culture just to give an idea of what goes on in the gaming world.

Since the 1990s at least, gamers have banded together in groups that go by all kinds of different names: clans, guilds, kinships, you name it. They're kind of like sports clubs. Members chat together online, they may play competitively against other teams, and they may use their servers to host intra-squad games. With names such as Elite Artificial Soldiers, ODST Artillery, Tribe of Judah, and Soldiers of Christ, these clans can develop long-standing traditions and relationships and may share histories on their websites.

Gamers often set up their own discussion, news, and review sites. There is a handful of giant game news providers (e.g., IGN, GameSpy, and GameSpot), but these are no more personal than the online sites for CNN, MSNBC, or Fox News. Myriad smaller-scale sites, such as Everyday Gamers or Play This Thing!, may number their monthly visitors in the thousands rather than the millions, but they tend to house much tighter communities. They do their own podcasts, game reviews, and critical blog postings, as well as host web forums for gamers to get to know one another. Fans of these sites may or may not game together, but they often get to know one another very well.

Then, of course, there are meet-ups and conventions. PAX is an unusually large gaming convention—one of the biggest out there and the focus of a huge amount of industry attention. However, there are hundreds of much smaller gatherings all over the world, driven less by marketing and more by love of the games. These range from a few dozen people getting together for a LAN party (setting up a bunch of PCs in a room and gaming together) to regional MMO meet-ups where gamers can congregate in person. Even when they take up only a small meeting room in a hotel and don't have all the bells and whistles of the big industry-sponsored events, these are intense experiences—for the space of a few days, gamers spend all their time together, sharing laughter, competition, stories, and sleep deprivation.

Gamers also sometimes fall so in love with games—or are so inspired creatively—that they take to changing or "modding" (modifying) them. Game mods can consist of very small tweaks, such as allowing players to exit the Thieves' Guild more quickly in *The Elder Scrolls V: Skyrim*, or they can be total overhauls of the programs, turning history-themed *Civilization IV* into a Fantasy-genre game with the *Fall From Heaven II* mod, complete with new art, units, and story lines. The more ambitious the mod, the more time and energy it takes, and so modding is often a communal activity; people involved with the project essentially work as an informal or nonprofit game-development company.[4]

Finally, gamers can also be passionate advocates. Every gamer has their video game causes to champion, be it an underappreciated series, an indie company, or a cultural issue surrounding games, and they sometimes band together to address their concerns. One of the most dramatic demonstrations of this occurred in the spring of 2012 with the game *Mass Effect 3*, a tremendously long and narratively complex sequel to two highly celebrated space-themed role-playing games. While the release of the title was highly celebrated, many gamers were disappointed with the ending—*so* disappointed, in fact, that they started a massive protest movement that essentially forced Bioware, the game's developer, to create extra material to help wrap up the story better.[5]

Christian Game Communities

The rest of the chapter will focus on Christians in game communities. Contrary to what some might think, there are plenty of self-identified Christian gamers out there. To start with, quite a few Christian game sites share news and do reviews, podcasts, or other kinds of commentary. Some, such as Christ Centered Gamer, are quite explicit about their faith commitment, but others, such as Everyday Gamers (see the image on p. 154) or 3 Day Respawn, are a little more muted—the site's leaders have noted that they have many non-Christian visitors. Either way, the quality and maturity of these sites have progressed by leaps and bounds in the last several years. If I were writing even a few years earlier, I would have complained about simplistic reviews and poor web design. But today, many of these sites have very thoughtful commentary and slick, professional design.[6]

The website for *Everyday Gamers*, a well-designed site with all kinds of news, reviews, and commentaries.

Clans and guilds can form around pretty much any game, idea, philosophy, or characteristic, so it's not at all surprising that games such as *World of Warcraft* (*WoW*), *Lord of the Rings Online*, and *Minecraft* have Christian gaming communities. While they might be only a small drop in the bucket of the gaming world, these explicitly Christian clans are actually quite numerous. The Christian Gamers Alliance, for instance, lists twenty-two explicitly Christian guilds and another seven led by Christians just in the game *WoW*. There are dozens of other sites for Christian groups dedicated to just about every major video game that has a popular multiplayer mode. Some clans have been around for many years. It's also not unusual to find stories of gamers who have jumped from game to game and community to community for quite some time, often with the same core group of friends. For example, the guild master of the *WoW* guild The Forgiven created one group to play *Rainbow 6* and then *Counter-Strike* before creating his current community.[7] Thus, while communities appear and disappear over time, there may be greater continuity than it would seem from an outsider's perspective.

Some Christians even focus on evangelizing via video games. Probably the most prominent example of this is the Gamechurch group. Starting from a room full of computers for playing games, this ministry has expanded to include a content-packed website of news and reviews.[8] It also rents out prominent booths at major conventions such as PAX, where I stumbled across a friendly young man giving out little booklets. I was surprised to see the cover had a picture of a nineteenth-century beatific Jesus with a headset and a game controller and a big title *Jesus, For the Win!* along with the subtitle: "A little book about a guy named Jesus, his Guild, and his ultimate quest to save a land known as Earth." Inside was the entire Gospel of John and a brief explanation of the Christian faith. The booklet's cover art and hipster writing style typified the hardcore-gamer-friendly, grungy, visually jarring, counterintuitive approach of the ministry. Another example is the 2011 online Gamechurch video reporting on E3 (the enormous annual game industry expo), which featured inter-views with big-name developers, a hyper gamer hitting on booth babes (the scantily-clad models hired to promote games), and a guy pretending to be Jesus interviewing expo attendees. In a 2011 interview, Mikee Bridges, the founder of Gamechurch, was unapologetic about potentially offend-ing Christians: "I want Joe Blow atheist guy to come on my site, see some cool stuff; I want to speak his language. I want him to think, 'Those guys are Christians but they aren't trying to convert me or anything. They are actually being really cool.' And that is what we have been seeing a lot of all year—a lot of people who would never be introduced to Christianity by going to the average church."[9]

Christian Gamers Speak about Community

About the Survey and This Section

When I wrote about Christian gaming in the past,[10] I worked solely on the basis of what I could find on websites. But typically, gamers are busy *gaming* rather than constructing websites. So this time around, I decided to talk directly with gamers. I posted on as many Christian game forums as I could a request for gamers to take a survey, and in less than month I had completed responses from 125 Christian gamers and another five from non-Christians (whose answers aren't included here for the purposes of clar-ity) who were willing to talk about their gaming habits, what they thought about their gaming communities, and the connections they saw among faith, gaming, and community. The respondents were *not* representative of gamers as a whole: by posting my survey on sites for Christian gamers and explicitly framing it as a survey about faith and the game community, I automatically limited the scope of who would respond. Nevertheless, this is a pretty sizable sample of responses, and it helps us draw a picture of what kinds of people frequent Christian game-community sites.

The occupations of the respondents were tremendously diverse, ranging from "farm worker" to "artist" to "youth pastor" to "sleep technician." The most common responses were "student" (29 percent), some kind of technology-related occupation (15 percent), and "homemaker" (10 percent). Unsurprisingly, the vast majority (86 percent) of the respondents were male. They were also not particularly elderly: 84 percent were between the ages of 16 and 40, although the age groups were evenly spaced within that range, and a few gamers fell into the 56–60 bracket.[11]

They didn't report playing games as much as I anticipated. More than one in eight (14 percent) barely played at all, reporting only 0–5 hours per week. Very heavy play was even less common: only 12 percent of the respondents reported playing more than twenty-five hours per week (although 3 percent reported playing over forty hours per week). The most common answer (31 percent of respondents) was 6–10 hours; almost half (48 percent) played 6–15 hours per week. That means a majority of players played two hours or less per day. To put this in perspective, a recent Nielsen report claimed that the average American watches just shy of five hours of television per day or thirty-five hours per week.[12] The respondents to my survey spent most (65 percent) of this time playing with other people, most commonly in MMOs. Very few reported spending significant amounts of time on social-networking games, indicating that this is a fairly hardcore, not casual, gaming demographic.

Respondents reported playing most with close friends and families, followed by acquaintances, followed by strangers. Nevertheless, the gamers still stated that on average they spent 27 percent of their multiplayer time with strangers, which suggests that gaming communities are not formed solely on the basis of previous relationships—the games are what bring them together. This was further reinforced by the fact that the respondents reported that over half of their play time (58 percent) on average involved playing with people they primarily interacted with online. However, this didn't mean that their gaming relationships were insubstantial: when I asked if they were currently good friends with anyone they had met first online, 70 percent of the respondents said yes. Fifty-four percent also said they had met people offline whom they first met online.

What Is Community and Do Your Game Groups Count?

All this gives a rough sketch of the survey participants' attitudes toward games and other gamers, but the most valuable information is what the gamers said about their experiences. The first major topic was the concept of community and whether the respondents' gaming groups fit their own definition of the word. I was curious to hear what they had to say about this because *community* is a word with history. Throughout the twentieth century, it was often used as a contrast for the impersonal *society* of the modern world, the loose social ties of huge cities filled with people who don't know one another. *Community* was a word that connoted close and warm relationships and connections.[13] When the internet was new and full of utopian potential, digital enthusiasts therefore called their social groups "communities" to indicate the forging of a new kind of social grouping. Since that time, however, "community" has been marketed to death on the internet and lost much of its utopian meaning. So I wanted to know how gamers thought about the people they played and talked about games with.

The vast majority (95 percent) of the survey participants *did* consider their gaming groups to be communities. And they certainly associated the concept with positive ideas. Most agreed that community is built on common interests, common goals, and common experiences, such as shared faith, a shared love of games, or a shared goal of putting the best interests of others ahead of one's own.

The participants also associated community with rich relationships. GodsGameFreak[14] said that "a simple group of gamers is one thing, but a community is a group that truly cares about its members, and interactions exist outside of the video games." People in a community are people who can hang out together (Xyrak: "[It's] like going out for coffee [in real life] and playing games together"), people who like and get along with one another (although, as gamer Romans58NRSVD put it: "There can be respectful disagreements"), people who are loyal to and can trust one another, people who encourage and care about one another, and people who can share their struggles. Narius described game community as "a family of friends to play with."

Respondents talked about the importance of healthy interaction and communication. A true community, they felt, has a shared vocabulary (complete with inside jokes); is marked by honesty, courteousness, and patience;

is in contact regularly; and has ongoing conversations. Communication should be positive, with gamers cheering other gamers on, even though a game community is also marked by healthy competition. And a *Christian* game community is marked by clean and safe conversation that creates, according to NeoJabez, a "family-friendly atmosphere where gaming isn't ruined by bad language or behaviors."

A proper Christian game community is marked by a faith commitment, said survey participants. Many highlighted the value of Bible studies, outreach to nonbelievers, and prayer support. More than a few highlighted the fact that a Christian game community needs to put faith above play, a notion summarized by this commonly cited mantra: "Christians first, gamers second."

And finally, respondents argued that community sticks together through times of trial. R3NNiS, the president of the Soldiers of Christ (SoC) community, summarized this eloquently:

> I don't want to give the impression that community is only good times, unity, and everyone agrees. Community is not all happiness nor friendship, and we've tried to be honest about that in SoC. . . . But there is a goodness to it that helps us treat each other with uncommon honesty, courtesy, and patience working through problems. No community is impervious to being torn apart. . . . We've had big ups and downs from the leaders right on down to the newest members . . . and there is something of a miracle (we believe in God) that keeps our fragile community together and growing. Community is never an achievement, it's work. . . . It's good work though.

The Challenges of Building Community

Aware of some of the difficulties that R3NNiS mentions, I asked participants in the survey to talk about some of the challenges of building game communities. The problems seemed to fall into two broad categories: the character of the video game medium and the difficulties caused by other players. To start with, many of the challenges these gamers mentioned were clearly related to the nature of video games. For instance, several respondents described communication breakdowns as serious challenges to building community. Since video gamers typically communicate via typing or voice chat, Xyrak reported "missing facial expressions or nonverbal cues." Others noted that it is easy to misinterpret innocent remarks or things said in the heat of competition.

Some participants noted that video games are a hard context in which to build meaningful relationships. "With an offline friend," said Valyrius, "you are able to enjoy a variety of activities and experiences together. With an online friend, you are often heavily restricted to what can be done at your computer for interaction." Others argued that it is risky to share too much information online, making deep relationships and friendships with accountability difficult to forge. }SoC{1-Bar pointed out that "it's difficult to help others with difficulties in life without being with them physically." Finally, participants believed that, while the global nature of gameplay can be exhilarating, cultural and language differences can cause barriers to building community.

The video-game medium also causes time problems. For instance, several respondents noted that trying to find gaming times that worked for everyone—especially when operating across time zones—is a consistent challenge. More commonly, however, the gamers talked about time management and worried about how video games and video-game communities tend to take up a lot of time, detracting from family, friends, and schoolwork. In fact, respondents said trying to be a good teammate can lead to more playing than is probably healthy.

However, most complaints focused less on the medium and more on game players and the kinds of attitudes and behaviors that are common in the video-gaming world. To start with, even when gamers play with people they like, the gameplay can generate some bad feelings. Some respondents complained that their fellow gamers can be too intense and serious about the video games (it's only a game!) while others lamented that it's frustrating to play with people who don't care enough. Others noted that the attitudes and behaviors of younger and older gamers could cause friction. And a number of gamers noted that when people playing together have uneven skill levels, the better player can feel impatient, while the less-skilled player feels overwhelmed. |CoR| Deacon called all of this "drama @ internet speed—someone always gets their feelings hurt, someone will always be offended."

But if friends can cause problems, strangers can be even worse. Respondents listed a whole series of problems in the video-gaming world that can really harm the creation of healthy community. One of these was the habit of some gamers to be extremely harsh, criticizing the play of everyone who is not up to snuff. This is especially problematic when such critics target inexperienced players—pejoratively described as "noobs"—with a torrent of anger.

And it can indeed be angry speech. I can attest to this personally—many online games apparently cultivate a kind of harsh environment where gamers can and will say just about anything. Respondents noted that gamer speech is often full of offensive language, racial slurs, sexual advances, misogyny, references to drug and alcohol abuse, and blasphemy. Along with many other respondents, Durruck argued that anonymity is a major factor because it "generally tends to allow immature people to become trolls and ignore social norms of decency." "Troll" is a common term for individuals on the internet whose words and actions are designed to upset other people—they get joy from seeing other people upset. They're hardly limited to video games, but many of the respondents noted that they are quite common in multiplayer game settings.

A related problem is that of bad play. NeoJabez put it this way: "Most games cost $50–$60 now, and you install them, begin to play, and POW! There's a fourteen-year-old child with an $8-a-month cheat running the scoreboard through the ceiling." Using computer hacks to gain unfair advantages, respondents said, shows disrespect for the game and other players. Other participants in the survey noted that some gamers play in a selfish way even when they are part of a team, taking the best treasures for themselves and refusing to share. Some trolls can be particularly malevolent and kill teammates.

Even when other players *aren't* being purposeful miscreants, however, it's easy to have bad gameplay experiences that could damage communities. For instance, Halcyon Lioness stated that "coordinating with gamers is like herding cats. Just ask any *WoW* raid leader."[15] And even when everyone is on the same page, the game—especially if it's an MMO—can settle into a highly monotonous rhythm gamers call "grinding," which can feel a lot more like work than play.

Finally, many of the survey participants mentioned challenges specifically relating to their faith. For one thing, quite a few people discussed how the video-game communities they were part of could sometimes encourage bad behavior or spiritually unhealthy gameplay. Sakura admitted, "I sometimes might become too caught up in the game and become upset, ruining my witness." Others noted that communities and players that openly identify themselves as Christians are likely to get targeted with some hostility. Witts suggested that "agnosticism/atheism/anti-Christian feelings seem to be more readily displayed when there is anonymity!"

The Joys of Healthy Community

For all the difficulties of building a good game community, the survey respondents were clearly excited by all the benefits of belonging to one. What was the most obvious advantage? Fun. Video games are amusing and playing them with others reduces stress. But even more than that, "good experiences are better when you share them with others." Why? First, it's more challenging—and thus more enjoyable—to play real humans rather than artificial intelligence. Second, having someone to chat with can make annoying parts of the game (like grinding) less burdensome. And on top of that, Loneshadow noted playfully, "when you individually do well, you have witnesses to brag to."

A second major advantage mentioned in the responses was that game communities allow gamers to help one another. Community members are more predictable than strangers, and thus safer. One respondent noted that online gamers were less likely to judge people on the basis of appearance, and another noted that while anonymity has its problems, it can also make it safer to share personal feelings and thoughts. Kyrel suggested that sharing is a big part of her community: "Sometimes the teens need help with their issues and trust a good solid Christian to help them through the Word of God as a counselor. We pray for one another, laugh and cry with one another." This sense of support helps justify the gamers' choice of pastime. Ghinao noted that "many Christians want nothing to do with video games and look down upon those (especially adults) who play video games in their spare time," so it is a comfort to have other Christians to play with. Game community members also help one another by teaching. "My guild," said Obi Kaybe, "is a great resource for learning how to better play and enjoy the game. They've done a great job helping me understand the dynamics of the game we play." Respondents reported that they get extra feedback, news, tips, and great discussions about games from their communities.

A third idea that participants noted is that game communities are a prime place to build relationships. Nacho Cheese said that a game community "provides a normally introverted person like myself a chance to socialize with others who share my interests." A few of the older survey respondents noted that playing games helps them connect with today's youth, and one respondent even described how talking about video games helped create a relational bridge with a former gamer in the office. Video-game communities, according the respondents, provide opportunities to get to know diverse types of people and perspectives they might never encounter without the common bond of gaming. And more than one respondent talked about game communities being instrumental in building effective teamwork. "Multiplayer video games," claimed 'Cuda, "teach communication, planning, and leadership skills. The teams that plan and communicate can often defeat a group of players that may have better reflexes or more talent but doesn't play as a team." And, others pointed out, such effective teams teach people to be reliable, another key relational skill.

Finally, many of the respondents commented on how such groups nurture growth. The participants, for instance, believed that Christian game communities help gamers strengthen their faith and evangelism. Crosser claimed "the Christian Crew Gaming community contributes to my faith life. There is a weekly Bible study and daily prayer requests within the community and knowing that someone out there is praying for me is encouraging." More broadly, survey participants saw video-game communities building up the character of gamers. Playing with friends, if nothing else, keeps people out of real-life trouble. More positively, gaming with the right people helps gamers develop self-control, teaches how to deal well with losing, and encourages healthy communication skills. In short, while respondents were well aware that video-game communities have their warts, they felt that they gained many important benefits by participating in them.

Faith and Game Communities: How Does Faith Matter?

The survey also addressed the impact of faith on video-game playing and video-game communities. Given that all the participants analyzed were Christians, I was surprised at how many of them said their faith didn't substantially impact the way they thought about the video games— especially since many saw their faith connected to interactions with their communities. Many respondents said something along the lines of "games are just games," that most secular games have little to no religious content, and the content that exists is either non-Christian or is kind of boringly obvious. A few argued that looking for religious meaning would diminish the entertainment value of the games. And although most such comments focused on the games themselves, a couple of respondents noted that there were few Christians in their game guilds and that their faith was simply not an issue for their groups (either positively or negatively).

The *majority* of participants, however, argued that their faith significantly impacted their gaming. To start with, many people talked about faith drawing boundaries. For instance, many participants noted that their faith helped them decide which gaming groups to join: many said they would join only a Christian game group, and many others said they would avoid gaming communities that were anti-Christian or characterized by offensive behavior such as foul language. Many respondents noted that they tried to avoid sexually explicit material and conversations, bad language, discrimination, and the vicious arguments among community members (sometimes called "flame wars"). Other gamers noted that they tried not to play games that mocked religion (especially Christianity) or those that fell into the horror genre and featured demonic themes or witchcraft. One participant also put a priority on not playing mature games while children were around. At least one participant also avoided playing games that forced a player to do evil actions, such as the *Modern Warfare 2* plotline that had the player act as a ruthless terrorist.[16]

But rather than just be *against* problems, survey respondents connected their faith with upright behavior in games and game communities. "I act in gaming communities exactly how I act [and] respond in real life," said Kunkali. "I strive to portray godliness and Christlikeness as much as my spiritual growth allows." A Christian faith entails all kinds of good behavior, according to the respondents: looking out for others, striving to create unity, treating others with respect, and playing with honor, as well as being encouraging, positive, fair, self-controlled, peaceful, humble, and polite. It also means being a good gamer: learning to play well and being a good loser when necessary. Others stressed the importance of openness. "I afford the same religious respect to others as I would want afforded to me," claimed x pathf1nder x. Upright behavior also includes community building: setting up effective and useful rules to guide community life and investing in the lives of others. Some even said that building the community is more important than playing.

Several participants noted that Christians were witnesses or spokespeople for their faith. This might include choosing Christian-themed user and clan or guild names—some of which are in this chapter—to make it clear Whom they belong to. Another gamer described himself as representing his Catholic faith to others in his mostly Protestant game community and to players outside of the community.

For many survey participants, their Christian faith called them to a critical engagement with the games they played and the communities surrounding them. For some, that meant warning or reminding others about the risks or problematic effects of games or maybe even asking people to stop cursing. For many others, it meant looking more deeply for the meaning in video games. For example, }SoC{DrBob argued: "We play games because it takes us to a more perfect world. It's not because we don't like reality, but who hasn't liked a superhero? . . . Since the fall, we long for a more perfect place whether we like it or not." Respondents talked about analyzing the themes and worldviews of video games, trying to gauge what the game makers were trying to say in the game, and perhaps even finding biblical parallels in secular games such as *Dragon Age*. Video games and the players of video games, argued one participant, could also show how Christians look to people outside the faith. Some survey participants went a step further and suggested that some video games could positively impact the way they live offline as well as online by being an inspiration—just as any story from any medium can change our lives. The value of a critical approach, argued Durruck, is large: "Even if the game developers have no desire (or are even forbidden) to insert Christian themes into their work, [that] doesn't mean God won't use it to reach out to the lost."

Game Communities and the Church Outside

Finally, I asked the survey participants what others in their faith communities thought about video games. The most common response? "The topic hasn't come up," said MJCaboose. Others, like Shrmn4Life, noted: "Most of the older people don't get why people play them, but they don't fuss about it." A few participants noted that the technological bar keeps many nongamer Christians ignorant of what was going on. It is hard, said one respondent, to find people in "real life" to play games with.

Others reported more negative responses. For one thing, gamers reported that nongamers in their churches see video games as a waste of time. Parents, for instance, want their children to be more productive. Some participants saw this as hypocritical; toj_Abea pointed out with a (digital) wink: "Those that don't get into computers or games think it's a waste of time, but they watch more TV than I do." Survey participants also noted that church members worry about excessive play and how that could damage relationships or cause family conflicts. Some church members raise the specter of addiction and argue that it is hard for gamers to build relationships with true accountability when playing too many video games. (It's worth noting that some survey participants shared these same fears.)

And some Christians, said the respondents, simply see video games as inherently bad. Romans58SNRSVD admitted that some members of his faith community respect the video-game medium and some are merely confused by it, but "others see it as nothing but a source of violence and the work of the devil." The violence and overt sexuality of many video games make them highly suspect objects to some Christians, according to survey participants. The members of SB Leader's faith community are "usually pretty skeptical. I've found it to be seen with disdain by quite a few at my church. 'Gamers' [are] kind of . . . social outcast[s] to them. Some people can't reconcile violent video games with Christian outreach."

Nevertheless, not all gamers reported hostile Christian reactions to video games. At the very least, as Loneshadow claimed, "Most of the people I interact with view it as a relatively harmless, if nerdy, pastime." Puddleyc agreed that many Christians hold that kind of view: "At least I am not out drinking or doing drugs." More often, survey respondents reported that people in their churches suggest caution with video games but not necessarily banning them. "For most it's a matter of getting priorities straight," said one participant. "Games (and entertainment in general) need to be placed in proper priority in one's life. Game content is also very significant—there is certain material a Christian should not be exposed to or participate in." Kyrel reported a similar sentiment: "All things in moderation. If it is taking you away from your relationship with Jesus, then you should be cutting back." Church members often appear to say video games are okay as long as they don't become idols.

Some survey participants reported clearly positive feedback from their church communities. "Many of them are curious," said R3NNiS, "and fascinated with the idea of a gaming community, and even more, some [are] incredulous that there is such a thing as a Christian online 'community' and that we actually have Bible studies." Some respondents reported that nongamers are often excited about the evangelical outreach possibilities of video games. And lots of Christians think video games are fun, according to the responses. In fact, several mentioned that their church's youth programs use games as part of their ministry.

Conclusion

I wish I had space to share more from the survey. There were some wonderful insights, and many of the comments expanded beautifully on themes we've covered in this book. I want, however, to highlight the main point I see in the mass of material given me by the survey participants: video-game community, even though it is not physical, is very real. If community is a collection of people bound together by a common purpose, this is it. If community features strong friendships, this is it. If a community comes together to support and uplift its members, this is it. Some critics will want to discount the value of game communities because they are built on nonproductive activity. I argued in chapter 5 that fantasy can be very positive, but even if it were a waste of time, that wouldn't mean that game communities cease to be communities or that the relationships built there cease to have the benefits and drawbacks of real relationships. In any case, I think the participants in this survey have made a good case that despite the challenges, they've created some pretty cool social groups that can have truly positive effects on them and the world around them.

That said, I want to share a couple of warnings with Christian gamers. The first concern is something I found both curious and a little alarming when looking through Christian video-game community websites: they're here today and gone tomorrow. Some subsistence-level societies practice a kind of agricultural practice called "slash and burn," where they hack and burn down a bit of jungle, grow crops in the clearing until the relatively poor soil is exhausted, and then move on and do the same thing in a new area. This is a good metaphor for what I've seen online. Many web communities start up in the blink of an eye, take on dozens or even hundreds of members, and then after a year or two, as new games come out or new friendships form or life circumstances change, activity peters out, and we're left with a dead website—the community dies and nobody seems to notice. Of course, all communities have cycles of birth and renewal. Like so many internet-based groups, however, video-game communities seem to form and disband with astonishing rapidity.

I don't think this is necessarily a bad thing. Our lives move quickly in a digital age, and I don't believe that we need to chain ourselves to one form of entertainment—and I hope it's clear by now that I think there are other priorities in life than games. Not only that, but as Durruck pointed out to me in an online conversation, even though the websites for the communities die off or people stop visiting, they often move on to new games together or keep in contact in other ways, and the relationships survive.

However, if these slash-and-burn communities are our *only* form of community, we have a problem. God built human beings to live in *true* community, which means dealing with all the difficulties that follow from making a commitment to someone. Thus, we need to make sure we *invest* in some community somewhere. We need to pour ourselves into the lives of other people, and I don't believe that can happen if we're picking up and moving every few months. If our game communities don't provide the kind of serious, long-term relational investment we need to make in others' lives, that doesn't mean we should stop gaming, but it *does* mean we need more community than the groups that play games. I think typically that means being involved in communities in the physical world, where commitment is tougher and it's harder to find people who share all our opinions, but where the results are deeper and stronger. I will not discount the possibility of creating that difficult-but-necessary community online or in the video-game world—but I *do* think it's harder than trying to form local and church-based communities.[17]

A related issue is what I would call the "inward turn" of video games. By this, I obviously don't mean that games aren't social—this chapter is dedicated to proving the opposite. Rather, I mean to highlight two potential problems: that video games tend to be self-focused and that Christian game communities can easily become insular. Neither problem is unavoidable, but they're both worth mentioning.

The first issue is that video games, as something we primarily use for entertainment, easily become self-gratifying. This can seep into all aspects of gaming: we get petulant when our products aren't exactly the way we want them to be, we denigrate games and gamers we don't enjoy, we see others as worthwhile only inasmuch as they help our entertainment. And most important, games can distract us from truly serving the world around us. A good attitude isn't enough if we want to be true followers of Christ—we are living in a real, physical world full of real, physical injustice and real, physical needs. The tyranny of the material world shouldn't completely destroy entertainment or storytelling or cultural expression, but we can retreat so far into those things that we fail to donate to charities, fail to volunteer at soup kitchens, fail to teach Sunday school, fail to become politically educated and active. God calls us to be light and salt to the world, but some Christian gamers spread that light and salt only in the virtual world. Perhaps a few are called exclusively to that, but I don't think most of us are. To be absolutely clear, I'm not accusing my survey participants of this! I have no idea what their lives are like beyond their gaming, and given that a third of them play only an hour a day, I'd suggest that their lives are probably pretty full of other things. At least one survey participant reported being housebound because of a disability, and in that case, video games were a way to get "out and about." I have no idea what the life circumstances are of the other people who play games for as many hours per week as a full-time job. My point is that Christians playing games need to think through whether video games and game communities encourage self-service rather than other-service.

The other issue was briefly discussed in the previous chapter: forming Christian ghettos. It's very easy for Christians to form clubs that are so focused on safety that members never have to encounter the outside world. Many of the communities I've looked at while researching this topic have statements that clearly indicate that non-Christians are welcomed, and the fact that I had non-Christians respond to my survey is proof that these organizations are not 100 percent Christian. Nevertheless, with a few exceptions, the gamers would be fooling themselves if they thought their clubs are truly open. The written and unwritten rules, the cultural practices and inside jokes, and the games played and not played can all function as barriers to outsiders. That a few non-Christians aren't turned off by all this doesn't necessarily prove that a community is outsider friendly. Christian game communities can become echo chambers, where the choir preaches to the choir and opinions are reinforced rather than critically examined.

Again, I don't think this is *necessarily* wrong. People of the same opinion have the right to congregate, and I think that Christians do a great service by creating gaming spaces that are free of the abuse that even crude gamers find offensive.[18] Christians even have a spiritual right to retreat from the world, as Jesus and the biblical church did for spiritual sustenance. But we should be clear that the end goal of the Christian faith is a relationship with God, *not* purity of language and behavior, and such an approach to life goes too far when everything we do is purposely cut off from anything we might find disturbing or problematic in the world. Christian entrepreneurs and media corporations have managed to create an entire ecosystem of Christian market alternatives for just about everything (except, ironically, video games), and this allows many churchgoers to be totally insulated from the rest of the world and perhaps pretend that they have somehow eliminated sin from their lives because their entertainment doesn't have any swear words. Christian video-game communities don't *have* to be part of that approach to life (in fact, many of my respondents made it clear that they were part of secular game communities as well), but they can be. And when they function in isolation, there's a problem. Christians are called to be *in* the world, in all its glory and misery.

On the whole, I'm increasingly encouraged by what I see when I look at Christians in gaming. There is something special about game friendships. I don't believe they are the same as relationships built around knitting, dog shows, or hiking. The vast majority of games are inherently social. They provide a wonderful excuse and setting for people to interact and to sharpen each other's wits, communication skills, and teamwork. My survey respondents were proof of that to me.

It's high time for the church as a whole to realize that this is not a passing fad, something to be ignored until it fades. Gamers are getting older, and while they may scale back on play time as they get families and full-time careers and mortgages, their video games are going to be just as much a part of our cultural landscape as movies, books, and television. The church has seen fit to engage these other media (especially books), and there's no reason to ignore games. God's people build communion and community in all kinds of situations. The fantastic worlds of video games certainly have room for us.

This mix of admiration and dismay that I feel suggests we're getting at the problem that Christians often encounter with video games—and with any kind of culture, for that matter—how can we be *in* the world but not *of* the world? How can we play video games, hang out in game culture, make video games, and yet not lose what makes us faithfully distinct as God's children? We have run into this issue over and over again throughout this book. Is it okay to shoot virtual people? If so, when? How much playing is too much? How can we be faithful men and women in our video-game play? How should Christian gamers build game communities?

The borderlines are hard to define and to police, and every Christian seems to have a different answer. As I've argued, I think the judgments we make need to be contextual. It may well be that Gamechurch's approach is the right one in certain situations and not in others. But I have consistently criticized some approaches or attitudes, and I want to encourage others.

Revisiting Christian Criticism

Contra Fear and Fanboyism

While I was writing this book, one friend giving me feedback made a very good point. Old technologies such as print and furniture, he argued, are things we're culturally familiar with; we have a pretty good sense of what their positives and negatives are. But a relatively new medium like video games is still untested, so it makes sense for us to be cautious with it. While I might quibble that we don't always understand old technologies as well as we think we do, I believe he's essentially right—I wrote this book because I wanted to work through this relatively new medium.

But *caution* is not the same thing as *fear*. When we are careful about what video games our kids play, when we monitor our own attitudes as players, when we look through reviews and educate ourselves before buying a new game, we are being *cautious*. When we make blanket claims about games being evil, when we rigidly reject any video game without investigating it, when we think that any possible flaws of a game will inevitably corrupt a player, we are moving into the realm of fear. Yet God says, "Fear not, for I am with you."[2] Knee-jerk reactions against video games—as opposed to thoughtful critiques—betray a lack of faith in a generous, loving, and protective God.

The Christian ghetto is often a manifestation of fear. The concern is that rock music with bad messages, TV with immoral content, and video games with non-Christian ideology are going to undermine the faith of believers. So the best thing we can do, according to this line of thought, is retreat into a world where all the stories are affirming and happy, all the good characters are Christian, all the lyrics are in tune with orthodox theology, and all the settings come straight out of a Martha Stewart magazine. We can even comfort ourselves by thinking this media is evangelical.

Now I happen to love *VeggieTales* and the music of Christian singers like Steve Bell, Andy Gullahorn, Jill Phillips, and Andrew Peterson, so don't think I'm arguing against Christian content. But when that media becomes a shield to protect us from (so-called) dangerous thoughts and ideas and to do so out of fear, we become the defensive, moralistic xenophobes that so many outside our faith believe we are. We also miss out on a heck of a lot of good stories, music, and video games, all of which can be uplifting or thought provoking, even if they don't conform in any neat way to our traditional beliefs.

But if fear is the wrong response, so, equally, is unquestioning acceptance. Caution is good for a reason: everything is permissible, but not everything is beneficial. I love playing games too, but they're not always good. To be perfectly honest, many of the justifications I've heard for Christians playing this or that video game are a little weak—at least without further explanation. I especially find that's the case with justifications of media violence. Yes, Jesus said he came to bring a sword, not peace, but I don't think he meant that it was okay to hack people to death for fun; and yes, the Old Testament is full of God-sanctioned bloodshed, but it's pretty clear that Jesus calls us to nonviolence to fulfill God's original plan. I'm sure we can develop deeper, thoughtful justifications based on these kinds of passages, but I haven't really seen any and they should be more common.

If we *really like* playing games, it can kind of seem beside the point to bother with such thinking. "Critics just don't get it!" gamers like me might say. But if we never carefully examine our practice—*especially* if we avoid critical thought after someone has challenged us—then we run the risk of falling into traps or not noticing we're already in one. Many gamers get tremendously defensive when people attack gaming, and while I understand that reaction (I get the same way), those attacks are actually doing us a favor: they force us to investigate. Clearly, not all critiques are correct—such as those of antiviolence crusader and disbarred lawyer Jack Thompson, who uses every public tragedy as an excuse to blame video games for violent behavior—but it's never a bad thing to question something we take for granted.

Toward a Healthy Christian Criticism

So what *does* a healthy Christian critical approach look like? Well, I hope I've modeled it at least somewhat throughout this book, even though I know readers will see plenty of flaws. But whether or not I've done it right, I believe solid critical Christian thought displays certain hallmarks.

To start with, good criticism is not automatically positive or negative. If we want to judge something fairly, we can't prejudge it (although it's impossible to completely avoid this). We also can't judge something without examining it. This might seem to be common sense, but it's remarkable how many people have very strong opinions on *Grand Theft Auto* games without having played them, watched them, read about them, or played anything like them. I do mention games in this book that I haven't played myself—that I've only watched or read about—but I don't use such games to back up key points.

Next, good criticism stands on careful attention to context. Partly, that means understanding where a game fits in gaming culture, in the gaming industry, and in relation to other games. It also means developing a historical perspective: no video game is developed *ex nihilo*, and the backstory to a production and game community matters a great deal. For instance, the prominence of military-themed action games in today's North American gaming culture and industry is hard to understand without knowledge of video games in the 1970s, '80s, and '90s. I have not done as much of this as I would have liked in this book simply because of space limitations, but for those who want to dig further, I encourage reading some video-game history books; most of them are quite accessible.[3]

Third, good criticism draws on or at least considers as many different critical perspectives as possible, even if we ultimately reject some of those ideologies. An argument that never considers other points of view is always weaker than one that can account for opposition; when considering other points of view, we may find ways to improve our own. Carefully considering non-Christian perspectives is, in my opinion, a healthy thing to do. Healthy Christian criticism is not defensive and prickly. And in any case, the idea of common grace suggests that we can hear and see echoes of God's wisdom in many different critical perspectives—even those that don't acknowledge God. Thus, for example, while I reject the atheistic materialism of Marxism, the ideology's focus on justice can help me to critique video games.

Fourth, my faith, the teachings of the Christian tradition, and the words of Scripture are by far the greatest motivator in my criticism. I critically engage video games precisely because I think that's what God calls me to do. My worldview is based on my belief in Jesus, and so I always try to turn first to Christian teachings when criticizing anything in culture. Sometimes those traditions are silent or are only tangentially related to what we're considering—such as the issue of video games and education that we discussed in chapter 7—and in those cases, we shouldn't try to shoehorn in some kind of forced faith lesson. But Christian understandings of morality, ethics, humanity, and the purpose of life are easily applicable to many issues.

And finally, good criticism leaves the door open to the possibility of a change in perspective. I get the feeling from some Christian reviews and essays that there can be only one right way for a follower of Christ to think about an issue. I'm not at all convinced this is the case when we talk about something like, say, gender in video games. In any case, even if there *is* a right and wrong interpretation of a video game, I believe very strongly in the notion of grace—if we get something wrong now, it is covered. We've been forgiven. What's left to us now is to try to think and then act as best and as honestly as we can.

Play On

I hope this book has suggested some possible approaches to a Christian engagement with video games. I say "possible" because I know there's so much more to say. This is not a definitive statement but rather the beginning of a conversation—or a continuation of many conversations. Many of the issues raised here need to be fleshed out. Some important topics aren't even raised. And in any case, video games and game culture change fast enough that even the day this book comes out it will be partly out-of-date. So there's a *lot* more to talk about.

We need to talk and think, because the playing is going to continue. For better and worse, we've opened the door to the DC Wasteland, digital farms, boxes with cute monsters hungry for candy, Los Santos, countless sports stadiums, Azeroth, unnamed planetary systems, Thedas, racetracks around the world, Hyrule, and pirate-infested Caribbean islands, to name just a few. Video games have sparked imaginations, aroused competitive spirits, and brought forth playful joy for millions. As in all areas of life, when we play and when we critique video games, our Savior calls us to combat that which makes us less human, less whole, and less healthy, and to cultivate that which brings healing, creativity, and shalom. Video games can be just as much a part of God's kingdom as anything else, if only we have eyes to see.

Notes

Chapter 1 Finding Balance in an Unbalanced Discussion

1. Video-game enthusiasts often like to claim that the video-game industry is now bigger than the movie industry. The North American box office take was $9.6 billion in 2008 (http://www.natoonline.org/statisticsboxoffice.htm), and the overall value of video-game sales was $11.7 billion in the same year (http://www.theesa.com/facts/salesandgenre.asp). However, this doesn't include all the product licensing, DVD and Blu-ray sales, TV payments, and so on that make up well over half the income of the Hollywood machine. When we include all those things, the movie industry is still probably larger than the video-game business.

2. Katie Salen and Eric Zimmerman, *Rules of Play: Game Design Fundamentals* (Cambridge, MA: MIT Press, 2004); Chris Crawford, *The Art of Interactive Design: A Euphonious and Illuminating Guide to Building Successful Software* (San Francisco: No Starch Press, 2003); Espen J. Aarseth, *Cybertext: Perspectives on Ergodic Literature* (Baltimore: Johns Hopkins University Press, 1997).

3. Salen and Zimmerman, *Rules of Play*; Jenova Chen, "Flow in Games" (MFA thesis, University of Southern California, 2006), http://www.jenovachen.com/flowingames/thesis.htm.

4. Googling "gaming friendships" pulls up lots of interesting postings and discussions. Some examples include Devilicus, "Gaming Friendships: Real or Virtual," *Epic Slant* (blog), February 11, 2009, http://www.epicslant.com/2009/02/gaming-friendships-real-or-virtual/; twistedcaboose, "Are We Real Friends?," *2Old2Play* (blog), February 6, 2006, http://www.2old2play.com/modules.php?name=News&file=article&sid=200&mode=nested&order=0&thold=0; "Higher purpose of gaming," *BoardgameGeek* (web forum), accessed June 22, 2010, http://www.boardgamegeek.com/thread/379039.

5. See, for example, Steve Weese, "Christians Playing Dungeons and Dragons," *Fans for Christ*, accessed May 5, 2012, http://www.fansforchrist.org/new/articles/article03.htm.

6. Mark Joseph Young, "Confessions of a Dungeons & Dragons Addict," *M. J. Young Net*, accessed December 9, 2011, http://www.mjyoung.net/dungeon/confess.html; Matt Richtel, "Thou Shalt Not Kill, Except in a Popular Video Game at Church," *New York Times*, October 7, 2008, http://www.nytimes.com/2007/10/07/us/07halo.html?scp=1&sq=halo%203%20church&st=cse; "Second Life Gospel: The Potential for Evangelism and Church Planting," *Internet Evangelism Day*, accessed December 9, 2011, http://www.internetevangelismday.com/secondlife-evangelism.php.

7. Guy Cocker, review of *Flower*, *GameSpot*, February 11, 2009, http://www.gamespot.com/ps3/action/flower/review.html?om_act=convert&om_clk=gssummary&tag=summary;read-review; Laura Parker, "Artistic Differences: The Games as Art Debate from a Developer's Point of View," *GameSpot*, December 10, 2008, http://www.gamespot.com/features/6202159/index.html?tag=result;title;6; Dave Kosak, "Gaming's Long Journey from 'Entertainment' to 'Art,'" *Gamespy*, February 1, 2003, http://www.gamespy.com/articles/489/489490p1.html.

8. An accessible, short example is "Deadening of the Heart," *Christianity Today*, October 2005, 31. A more dense, academic example is Nicholas L. Carnagey, Craig A. Anderson, and Brad J. Bushman, "The Effect of Video Game Violence on Physiological Desensitization to Real-Life Violence," *Journal of Experimental Social Psychology* 43, no. 3 (2007): 489–96.

9. Adam Holz, review of *The Sims 2*, *Plugged In Online*, accessed December 9, 2011, http://www.pluggedin.ca/games/2004/q4/sims2.aspx; Al Menconi, "*The Sims*: A Digitized Trojan Horse," review of *The Sims*, *Plain Games*, December 4, 2005, http://www.plaingames.com/articles/article.asp?id=31.

10. Mark D. Griffiths, "The Role of Context in Online Gaming Excess and Addiction: Some Case Study Evidence," *International Journal of Mental Health and Addiction* 8, no. 1 (January 2010): 119–25; Sabine M. Grüsser, Ralf Thalemann, and Mark D. Griffiths, "Excessive Computer Game Playing: Evidence for Addiction and Aggression?" *CyberPsychology & Behavior* 10, no. 2 (April 2007): 290–92; Darren Chappell et al., "EverQuest—It's Just a Computer Game Right? An Interpretative Phenomenological Analysis of Online Gaming Addiction," *International Journal of Mental Health and Addiction* 4, no. 3 (July 2006): 205–16.

11. Paul Cardwell Jr., "The Attacks on Role-Playing Games," *Skeptical Inquirer* 18, no. 2 (1994): 157–65; Kurt Lancaster, "Do Role-Playing Games Promote Crime, Satanism and Suicide among Players as Critics Claim?," *Journal of Popular Culture* 28, no. 2 (Fall 1994) 67–79.

12. Nancy Justice, "The Pokemon Invasion," *Charisma*, February 2000, 58–65.

13. For physically unhealthy, see Kaiser Family Foundation, *The Role of Media in Childhood Obesity* (Menlo Park, CA, February 24, 2004), accessed December 9, 2011, http://www.kff.org/entmedia/7030.cfm. For disrespect of parents, see Justice, "The Pokemon Invasion," 58–65. For control fascination, see Elizabeth Wirth, "For Mine Is the Kingdom . . . Playing God with Computer Games," *Re:Generation Quarterly*, Fall 2001, 21–23. For seeing people as a means, see Adam Holz, "*Grand Theft Auto* Is Back in the News," *Focus on the Family: Plugged In*, September 2005, 12. For poor appreciation of consequences, see Brian Belknap, "Reaching the Gamer Gens," *Group*, May/June 2005, 66.

14. W. W. Chartes, *Motion Pictures and Youth: A Summary* (New York: MacMillian, 1933), v.

15. Daniel J. Czitrom, *Media and the American Mind: From Morse to McLuhan* (Chapel Hill: University of North Carolina Press, 1982); Daniel J. Boorstin, *The Americans: The Democratic Experience* (New York: Vintage Books, 1974); Paul Dimaggio, "Cultural Entrepreneurship in Nineteenth-Century Boston: The Creation of an Organizational Base for High Culture in America," *Media, Culture & Society* 4, no. 1 (January 1982): 33–50; Herbert J. Gans, *Popular Culture and High Culture: An Analysis and Evaluation of Taste* (New York: Basic Books, 1975).

16. Czitrom, *Media and the American Mind*, 122–27; Lowery and DeFleur, *Milestones in Mass Communication Research*, 415; Walter Lippmann, *Public Opinion* (New York: Free Press, 1922); Brett Gary, *The Nervous Liberals: Propaganda Anxieties from World War I to the Cold War* (New York: Columbia University Press, 1999), 323; C. Wright Mills, *The Power Elite* (New York: Oxford University Press, 1956); Harold Dwight Lasswell, *Propaganda Technique in the World War* (New York: Garland, 1972); Glenn Grayson Sparks, *Media Effects Research: A Basic Overview* (Belmont, CA: Wadsworth/Thomson Learning, 2002).

17. Plato, *Symposium and Phaedrus*, trans. Benjamin Jowett (New York: Dover, 1993).

18. Neil Postman, *Technopoly: The Surrender of Culture to Technology* (New York: Vintage Books, 1993). Also see many of the writings of Jacques Ellul. To be fair, the utopian language of technological optimism is much louder in our consumer culture media than techno-pessimists' voices. But that doesn't mean the pessimists are nonexistent.

19. James W. Carey and John J. Quirk, "The Mythos of the Electronic Revolution," in *Communication as Culture: Essays on Media and Society*, ed. James W. Carey (New York: Routledge, 1988), 113–41.

20. Ted Friedman, *Electric Dreams: Computers in American Culture* (New York: New York University Press, 2005).

21. Boorstin, *The Americans*.

22. Friedman, *Electric Dreams*.

23. Ruth Schwartz Cowan, *More Work for Mother: The Ironies of Household Technology from the Open Hearth to the Microwave* (New York: Basic Books, 1983).

24. Lynn Spigel, *Make Room for TV: Television and the Family Ideal in Postwar America* (Chicago: University of Chicago Press, 1992).

25. David Nye, *American Technological Sublime* (Cambridge, MA: MIT Press, 1994).

26. Friedman, *Electric Dreams*.

27. My faith has been shaped by a series of writers, some of whom I will note specifically, but some of whom hide more in the background. I have probably read more from C. S. Lewis and J. R. R. Tolkien than from any other Christian authors. More recent writers who have influenced me significantly include N. T. Wright, Brian McLaren, and Donald Miller. In terms of Christian writing about the media and popular culture, my former professors Quentin Schultze and William Romanowski loom large, but I have also appreciated the ideas of Craig Detweiler, Barry Taylor, and Shane Hipps. There are also echoes of H. Richard Niebuhr's classic *Christ and Culture* (New York: HarperCollins World, 2003). Underneath all of this is my Calvinist upbringing and education (and current faith commitment) and the Bible itself, which I know better than any other book.

28. See, for example, Matt. 15:17–20; 25:25–28.

29. Craig Detweiler and Barry Taylor, *A Matrix of Meanings: Finding God in Pop Culture* (Grand Rapids: Baker Academic, 2003); William D. Romanowski, *Eyes Wide Open: Looking for God in Popular Culture*, 2nd ed. (Grand Rapids: Brazos, 2007).

30. Detweiler and Taylor, *A Matrix of Meanings*; Romanowski, *Eyes Wide Open*; Shane A. Hipps, *The Hidden Power of Electronic Culture: How Media Shapes Faith, the Gospel, and Church* (Grand Rapids: Zondervan, 2005).

31. Romanowski, *Eyes Wide Open*; Quentin J. Schultze, *Habits of the High-Tech Heart: Living Virtuously in the Information Age* (Grand Rapids: Baker Books, 2002).

Chapter 2 How to Understand a Video Game

1. See the glossary of gaming terms in this book.

2. For example, check out http://www.audiogames.net/.

3. Ludwig Wittgenstein, *Philosophical Investigations*, trans. G. E. M. Anscombe, 2nd ed. (Oxford: Basil Blackwell, 1958), 31–32.

4. Find a great summary of the definitions of games in Katie Salen and Eric Zimmerman, *Rules of Play: Game Design Fundamentals* (Cambridge, MA: MIT Press, 2004), 71–83, quote at 80.

5. McLuhan fans will be pleased to know we're going to consider his reversal of that idea in chapter 7.

6. It's worth noting that there are lots of different opinions here. In *Extra Lives: Why Video Games Matter* (New York: Pantheon Books, 2010), for instance, Tom Bissell argues that video games don't have to have the formulaic narratives and shallow characters that they do.

7. Janet H. Murray, *Hamlet on the Holodeck: The Future of Narrative in Cyberspace* (Cambridge, MA: MIT Press, 1997); Chris Crawford, *The Art of Interactive Design: A Euphonious and Illuminating Guide to Building Successful Software* (San Francisco: No Starch Press, 2003); Salen and Zimmerman, *Rules of Play*. I prefer Janet Murray's term "participatory" to "interactive" because it implies the player is working hand in hand with the game maker.

8. This section on interactivity relies heavily on Espen Aarseth, *Cybertext: Perspectives on Ergodic Literature* (Baltimore: Johns Hopkins University Press, 1997).

9. This same structure can work in other media—very easily on the computer via hypertext links and also with digital movies on CDs or DVDs.

10. In *Persuasive Games: The Expressive Power of Videogames* (Cambridge, MA: MIT Press, 2007), Ian Bogost describes communicative machines or systems as "procedures."

11. Murray, *Hamlet on the Holodeck*. Lev Manovich talks about something similar when he identifies databases as a key part of digital media in *The Language of New Media* (Cambridge, MA: MIT Press, 2001).

12. The best example I've seen of this perspective comes from Douglas Wilson, a talented game designer who works in academic circles. In a public LISTSERV discussion on games and communication, he wrote (Games Research Network LISTSERV, https://listserv.uta.fi/archives/gamesnetwork.html, January 18, 2010): "The perspective that games 'communicate' and/or 'represent' is not 'wrong'—it's just *boring*. . . . My worry here is that focusing on semiotics—and on concepts like 'expression' and 'rhetoric'—has led us (both theorists and designers) to neglect certain kinds of games. . . . I just think we need some fresh terminology, to shake things up."

13. A few of my favorite writings on communication are James W. Carey, "A Cultural Approach to Communication," in *Communication as Culture: Essays on Media and Society*, ed. James W. Carey (New York: Routledge, 1988), 13–36; Quentin J. Schultze, *Communicating for Life: Christian Stewardship in Community and Media* (Grand Rapids: Baker, 2000); Em Griffin, *A First Look at Communication Theory*, 7th ed. (New York: McGraw-Hill Higher Education, 2009); John D. Peters, *Speaking into the Air: A History of the Idea of Communication* (Chicago: University of Chicago Press, 1999).

14. This gets into the very complex body of theory called "semiotics." Daniel Chandler's introductory text *Semiotics: The Basics* (London: Routledge, 2002) is a solid introduction to the field.

15. Henry Jenkins, "Game Design as Narrative Architecture," in *First Person: New Media as Story, Performance, and Game*, ed. Noah Wardrip-Fruin and Pat Harrigan (Cambridge, MA: MIT Press, 2004), 118–30.

16. This is a very contentious issue. In a sense, we could talk about any game having a story, since it has antagonists struggling through a series of events that lead from a beginning to an end. My feeling is that "a once-empty space filled with blocks" is so spare a plot that it's not worth calling it a story. But reasonable people disagree. They're wrong, of course, but still reasonable.

17. For a fun alternate read on this, see Bernard Suits, *The Grasshopper: Games, Life and Utopia* (Toronto: University of Toronto Press, 1978), one of my favorite academic works. Written in a delightfully narrative style, this is a *very* easy to follow philosophical treatise on the definition of games. Aesop's grasshopper, as a creature of frivolity, becomes the wise hero of the story, since he is naturally predisposed to understanding game playing.

18. Ian Bogost has the most thorough and educated consideration (that I've seen) of how game worlds communicate in his book *Persuasive Games* (although he talks about "procedures," not "worlds").

19. See, for example, Stuart Hall, "Encoding/decoding," in *Media Studies: A Reader*, ed. P. Marris and S. Thornham (New York: New York University Press, 1999), 51–61; David Morley, *The Nationwide Audience* (London: British Film Institute, 1980); John Fiske, *Television Culture*

(New York: Routledge, 1987); Henry Jenkins, *Textual Poachers: Television Fans and Participatory Culture* (New York: Routledge, 1992).

20. This is *not* to say that it's a waste of time to play the game and give an opinion on it! I do that throughout this book. What I mean is that even if I'm really clever and thoughtful in my analysis of the game, I can't say with certainty what other players are going to make of the game.

21. To see gamers getting creative and misusing and abusing games, go to YouTube and search for "game exploit" or "game cheat." Gamers are endlessly creative and doing weird things with video games.

Chapter 3 Making the Immaterial Playable

1. Rona Jaffe and Tom Lazarus, *Mazes and Monsters*, directed by Steven Hilliard Stern, aired December 28, 1982, TV movie. The film was actually very loosely based on a real-life story of a teenager whose disappearance and eventual suicide were erroneously attributed to RPGs. See Kurt Lancaster, "Do Role-Playing Games Promote Crime, Satanism and Suicide among Players as Critics Claim?," *Journal of Popular Culture* 28, no. 2 (Fall 1994): 67–79; Paul Cardwell Jr., "The Attacks on Role-Playing Games," *Skeptical Inquirer* 18, no. 2 (1994): 157–65.

2. David Waldron, "Role-Playing Games and the Christian Right: Community Formation in Response to a Moral Panic," *Journal of Religion and Popular Culture* 9 (Spring 2005): http://www .usask.ca/relst/jrpc/art9-roleplaying.html; Lancaster, "Do Role-Playing Games Promote," 67–79.

3. On using RPGs to recruit for the occult, see Berit Kjos, "Role-Playing Games & Popular Occultism: Open Doors to Forbidden Realms and Spiritual Seductions," *Kjos Ministries*, February 3, 2003, http://www.crossroad.to/articles2/2003/occult-rpg.htm; Jack T. Chick, *Dark Dungeons* (Ontario, CA: Chick, 1984), http://www.chick.com/reading/tracts/0046/0046_01 .ASP. On the connection between game symbols and narratives and the occult as well as the Satanic spiritual forces in RPGs, see Kjos, "Role-Playing Games"; Berit Kjos, "Harry Potter and D&D: Like Two Peas in a Pod?," *Kjos Ministries*, 2000, http://www.crossroad.to/text/ articles/D&D&Harry.htm; William Schnoebelen, "Straight Talk on Dungeons and Dragons," (Ontario, CA: Chick, 1989), http://www.chick.com/articles/dnd.asp; J. D. Carlson, "Should Christian People Play Cards?," *European-American Evangelistic Crusades*, accessed December 9, 2011, http://www.eaec.org/bibleanswers/playing_cards.htm. On confusing fantasy and reality, see William Schnoebelen, "New Updated Research: Should a Christian Play Dungeons & Dragons?," (Ontario, CA: Chick, 2001), http://www.chick.com/articles/frpg.asp. On Harry Potter and Pokemon, see Kjos, "Harry Potter and D&D"; Nancy Justice, "The Pokemon Invasion," *Charisma*, February 2000, 58–65.

4. Jeremy Parish, "Hallowed Be Thy Game," *1UP.Com*, March 4, 2005, http://www.1up .com/features/hallowed-thy-game.

5. Drew Dixon, "Video Games & the Nature of God," *Culture* (blog), *Relevant*, September 26, 2011, http://www.relevantmagazine.com/culture/tech/blog/26868-video-games-a-the-nature -of-god.

6. I have written about these issues (and the subsequent arguments in this section) before in conference papers and in a scholarly journal article. See Kevin Schut, "Continuity and Discontinuity: An Experiment in Comparing Narratives Across Media," *Loading . . .* 1, no. 1 (2007): http://journals.sfu.ca/loading/index.php/loading/article/view/19.

7. Available at http://www.thatfleminggent.com/ultima/u4download.html. This is apparently legal; there is a long explanation at http://www.ultimaaiera.com/blog/concerning-ultima -4-or-in-which-i-have-to-be-the-wet-blanket/; also check out EA's history site: http://www .ultimaforever.com/.

8. Mark Hayse, "*Ultima IV*: Simulating the Religious Quest," in *Halos and Avatars: Playing Games with God*, ed. Craig Detweiler (Louisville: Westminster John Knox, 2010), 34–46.

9. Alex Wainer, "The Discarding Image: The Diminishing of the Mythic in the Cinematic Adaptation of the Fellowship of the Ring" (paper presented at the National Communication Association convention, New Orleans, LA, November 2002). And again, Schut, "Continuity and Discontinuity."

10. Thanks to Mike Terbeek for this point.

11. There are lots of other problematic cultural issues with this game. It's weird that Christians wear sweater vests and all rock musicians are bad, it's offensive that every character in the world is white and seriously problematic that women can't be evangelists. While many of these issues could be chalked up to requirements of the medium (in real-time strategy games, for example, all units of the same type should look the same so they're easy to identify), this further indicates the difficulty of using the medium in an overtly religious manner.

12. Not to mention the Salem witch hunts or the McCarthy anticommunist hearings. For more on this, see, for example, Scott McCloud, *Reinventing Comics: How Imagination and Technology Are Revolutionizing an Art Form* (New York: HarperPerennial, 2001), 86–88.

13. Found on the *Dragon Age: Origins Tome of Knowledge* wiki at http://social.bioware.com/wiki/dragonage/index.php/Cone_of_Cold.

14. Bill Walton mercilessly lampoons Christian worries about the occult connections with roleplaying; "Spellcasting 101," *The Escapist*, January 11, 2002, http://www.theescapist.com/index.htm.

15. For a thorough defense of RPGs from a Christian perspective, see Steve Weese, "Christians Playing Dungeons and Dragons," *Fans for Christ*, 2003, http://www.fansforchrist.org/new/articles/article03.htm; Mark Joseph Young, "Confessions of a Dungeons & Dragons Addict," *M. J. Young Net*, accessed December 9, 2011, http://www.mjyoung.net/dungeon/confess.html.

16. One of the most amusing examples of this is a well-known 1990s radio sketch by comedy troupe the Dead Alewives (it's easy to find by searching for "Dead Alewives Dungeons and Dragons"). It starts with a bombastic, threatening monologue about the evils of *Dungeons and Dragons*, but as soon as the actual game starts, we hear some dorky but totally harmless teenagers arguing about rules interpretations and finding snacks. This matches my own experience of RPGs. The ratio of something actually happening in the game to distractions from the game (looking up rules, getting snacks, watching the hockey game) is actually quite low. It's an event that's far more likely to make outsiders roll their eyes or cringe in embarrassment than shudder in fear (just ask my wife, who had the misfortune of sitting in on at least one session while visiting me in college).

17. Andy Chalk, "Dante's Inferno (Not Really) Protested at E3," *The Escapist Magazine*, June 4, 2009, http://www.escapistmagazine.com/news/view/92210-Dantes-Inferno-Not-Really-Protested-at-E3; Ben Fritz, "E3: Dante's Inferno Protest [UPDATED]," *Technology* (blog), *LA Times*, June 4, 2009, http://latimesblogs.latimes.com/technology/2009/06/e3-update-on-dantes-inferno-protest.html.

18. Stuart M. Leeds, "Personality, Belief in the Paranormal, and Involvement with Satanic Practices Among Young Adult Males: Dabblers Versus Gamers," *Cultic Studies Journal* 12, no. 2 (1995): 148–65, http://icsahome.com/infoserv_respond/by_article.asp?ID=36090; Lancaster, "Do Role-Playing Games Promote"; Waldron, "Role-Playing Games and the Christian Right."

19. See, for instance, Rom. 8:38–39.

20. See Gal. 1:6–7; 4:17–18; or 1 Tim. 1:3–7. Simon the Sorcerer's tale is in Acts 8:9–24.

21. Ten years ago, I would have said *Titanic*, before that, *Raiders of the Lost Ark*, and before that . . . well, we could go on.

22. William D. Romanowski, *Eyes Wide Open: Looking for God in Popular Culture*, 2nd ed. (Grand Rapids: Brazos, 2007), 163–84.

23. For those unfamiliar with these names, pretty much every one is from a different game. By correctly identifying these titles, you've earned "Trophy: Incurable Game Nostalgic."

24. It *is* possible to have "perfect information games" with no element of randomness. Chess is the classic example. But such games are relatively uncommon. See Katie Salen and Eric Zimmerman, *Rules of Play: Game Design Fundamentals* (Cambridge, MA: MIT Press, 2004).

25. Kevin Newgren, "*Bioshock* to the System: Smart Choices in Video Games," in *Halos and Avatars: Playing Games with God*, ed. Craig Detweiler (Louisville: Westminster John Knox, 2010), 135–45. Other chapters extolling video-game stories in the same book include Daniel White Hodge, "Role Playing: Toward a Theology for Gamers," 163–75; Chris Hansen, "From *Tekken* to *Kill Bill*: The Future of Narrative Storytelling?," 19–33.

26. Dreamers have been pursuing truly interactive human/machine narrative for quite some time now, and though there are some fascinating experiments, to this point they're not yet terribly successful. See Chris Crawford, *The Art of Interactive Design: A Euphonious and Illuminating Guide to Building Successful Software* (San Francisco: No Starch Press, 2003).

Chapter 4 Games and the Culture of Destruction

1. Lev Manovich, *The Language of New Media* (Cambridge, MA: MIT Press, 2001).

2. Tristan Donovan, *Replay: The History of Video Games* (Lewes, UK: Yellow Ant, 2010), 42–43; Steven L. Kent, *The Ultimate History of Video Games: From Pong to Pokemon and Beyond—The Story Behind the Craze That Touched Our Lives and Changed the World* (Roseville, CA: Prima, 2001), 90–92; Lauren Gonzales, "When Two Tribes Go to War: A History of Video Game Controversy," *GameSpot*, accessed August 9, 2011, 2, http://www.gamespot .com/features/6090892/when-two-tribes-go-to-war-a-history-of-video-game-controversy/ index.html.

3. Kent, *The Ultimate History*, 461–80.

4. Ibid., 544–55.

5. "Your Mom Hates *Dead Space 2*," YouTube video, posted by deadspace, January 15, 2011, http://www.youtube.com/watch?v=nKkPFDEiC6Q. A good summary of game controversies up to 2004 is Gonzales, "When Two Tribes."

6. Kyle Orland, "Breivik says he trained for Norwegian massacre using *Modern Warfare*," *Ars Technica*, April 19, 2012, http://arstechnica.com/gaming/news/2012/04/norwegian-shooter -breivik-says-he-trained-using-modern-warfare.ars. It is worth noting that news media coverage was inclined to disbelieve most of Breivik's ravings, but that this story seemed to gain some traction. For analysis on Breivik's claims, see Ben Crecente, "The truth about 'hyperrealistic' video games as war simulators," *The Verge*, April 23, 2012, http://www.theverge.com/ gaming/2012/4/23/2968888/the-truth-about-hyper-realistic-video-games-as-war-simulators.

7. Virginia Tech Review Panel, "Chapter IV: Mental Health History of Seung Hui Cho," in *Mass Shootings at Virginia Tech: April 16, 2007* (Virginia, August 2007), 31–62, http://www .governor.virginia.gov/TempContent/techPanelReport.cfm. For a more general take on all this, also see: Lawrence Kutner and Cheryl K. Olson, *Grand Theft Childhood: The Surprising Truth about Violent Video Games and What Parents Can Do* (New York: Simon and Schuster, 2008).

8. Ibid., 73. Also see Albert Bandura, *Social Learning Theory* (Englewood Cliffs, NJ: Prentice-Hall, 1977).

9. L. Rowell Huesmann and Laramie D. Taylor, "The Case Against the Case Against Media Violence," in *Media Violence and Children*, ed. Douglas A. Gentile (Westport, CT: Praeger, 2003), 107–30.

10. Information on Gerbner is widely available. For a readable overview of some of the key findings of cultivation theory, see Em Griffin, *A First Look at Communication Theory*, 7th ed. (New York: McGraw-Hill Higher Education, 2009), 349–58.

11. Christopher J. Ferguson, "Blazing Angels or Resident Evil? Can Violent Video Games Be a Force for Good?," *Review of General Psychology* 14, no. 2 (June 2010): 68–81.

12. Gerard Jones, *Killing Monsters: Why Children Need Fantasy, Super Heroes, and Make-Believe Violence* (New York: Basic Books, 2002), 99.

13. Ferguson, "Blazing Angels."

14. Huesmann and Taylor, "The Case Against the Case Against." The following articles go back and forth in a wonderful little conversation: Craig A. Anderson et al., "Violent Video Game Effects on Aggression, Empathy, and Prosocial Behavior in Eastern and Western Countries: A Meta-Analytic Review," *Psychological Bulletin* 136, no. 2 (March 2010): 151–73; Christopher J. Ferguson and John Kilburn, "Much Ado about Nothing: The Misestimation and Overinterpretation of Violent Video Game Effects in Eastern and Western Nations: Comment on Anderson et al. (2010)," *Psychological Bulletin* 136, no. 2 (March 2010): 174–78; Brad J. Bushman, Hannah R. Rothstein, and Craig A. Anderson, "Much Ado about Something: Violent Video Game Effects and a School of Red Herring: Reply to Ferguson and Kilburn (2010)," *Psychological Bulletin* 136, no. 2 (March 2010): 182–87.

15. Ferguson, "Blazing Angels"; Valerie Pottie Bunge, Holly Johnson, and Thierno A. Baldé, *Exploring Crime Patterns in Canada*, report for Statistics Canada (Ottawa, Canada, 2005), http://dsp-psd.pwgsc.gc.ca/Collection/Statcan/85-561-MIE/85-561-MIE2005005.pdf, 7.

16. Matt Richtel, "Thou Shalt Not Kill, Except in a Popular Video Game at Church," *New York Times*, October 7, 2008, http://www.nytimes.com/2007/10/07/us/07halo.html?scp=1&sq=halo%203%20church&st=cse.

17. Robert W. Brimlow, *What about Hitler? Wrestling with Jesus's Call to Nonviolence in an Evil World* (Grand Rapids: Brazos, 2006).

18. William D. Romanowski, *Eyes Wide Open: Looking for God in Popular Culture*, 2nd ed. (Grand Rapids: Brazos, 2007), 207–21.

19. Christians who support this kind of militarism might argue that violence isn't *desirable* but is often necessary. Given the cultural glorification of guns and martial prowess in some parts of the church, however, that defense sometimes rings hollow. As a Canadian Christian hockey fan, I am ashamed to admit I know all too well the joy of screaming for the opposing team's blood—and many Christians don't feel such shame.

20. Jacques Ellul, *Violence: Reflections from a Christian Perspective*, trans. Cecilia Gaul Kings (London: SCM, 1970), 93–108.

21. Ibid., 127–38.

22. Ellul himself joined the resistance. He talks about this somewhat in *Violence*. His firsthand experience of the conflict means he knew more about it than I do. But I've spoken with many people who *also* had firsthand experience, and they had quite different opinions.

23. Gonzalo Frasca, "Simulation Versus Narrative: Introduction to Ludology," in *The Video Game Theory Reader*, ed. Mark J. P. Wolf and Bernard Perron (New York: Routledge, 2003), 234–35.

24. I'm actually twisting Frasca's point just a little. He doesn't object to the simulation of torture and murder in the game, but that it is done for entertainment and without real regard for the consequences of such things (I'm not sure I entirely agree with his analysis of the game on this latter point). If we were to follow his thinking, we'd ask instead: Is it okay to do wrong things in video games for fun? I'm making my question a bit more basic.

25. Johan Huizinga, *Homo Ludens: A Study of the Play-Element in Culture*, trans. R. F. C. Hull (London: Routledge and Kegan Paul, 1949).

26. Bernard Suits, *The Grasshopper: Games, Life and Utopia* (Toronto: University of Toronto Press, 1978).

27. Ibid., 41.

28. For an interesting take on this, see Greg Lastowka, "Rules of Play," *Games and Culture* 4, no. 4 (October 2009): 379–95. This is a serious argument with real legal repercussions: he takes the position that we can't regulate games and bring lawsuits about in-game actions on the same grounds as other legal situations.

29. "A game gives us the possibility of engaging without risk in ethical decision making in which we would otherwise never engage. From this point of view, the choices the designer creates in the game do not suppose any kind of moral risk for the player, as they are only relevant in the game world." Miguel Sicart, *The Ethics of Computer Games* (Cambridge, MA: MIT Press, 2009), 44.

30. Marcus Schulzke, "Moral Decision Making in Fallout," *Game Studies: The International Journal of Computer Game Research* 9, no. 2 (November 2009): http://gamestudies.org/0902/articles/schulzke; Sicart, *The Ethics of Computer Games*. On p. 49, Sicart says: "What makes both *Carmageddonn* and *Grand Theft Auto* ethically interesting is that the rules afford player behavior that is violent, and player behavior that is not violent."

31. David W. Simkins and Constance Steinkuehler, "Critical Ethical Reasoning and Role-Play," *Games and Culture* 3, no. 3–4 (July 2008): 333–55. It is fair, by the way, to question what *kind* of ethics video games model. The mechanistic, systematic bias of the medium means video games tend to favor consequentialist ethics. That is, we define right and wrong behavior in video games based on the results actions have. This is in contrast with Aristotelian ethics, wherein virtue is the middle path between two extremes, or Kant's categorical imperative, the idea that what we should do in one situation we should do in all situations. In *Dragon Age*, I may think that turning in Jowan for practicing blood magic is cowardly or I may think it brave, but in the end, what I choose has results, and it is those results that matter to the rest of the gameplay. I'm subtly pushed toward a rather mechanistic variety of ethics.

32. Mia Consalvo, "There Is No Magic Circle," *Games and Culture* 4, no. 4 (October 2009): 408–17; Vili Lehdonvirta, "Virtual Worlds Don't Exist: Questioning the Dichotomous Approach in MMO Studies," *Game Studies: The International Journal of Computer Game Research* 10, no. 1 (2010): http://gamestudies.org/1001/articles/lehdonvirta; Thomas M. Malaby, "Beyond Play," *Games and Culture* 2, no. 2 (April 1, 2007): 95–113.

33. Lehdonvirta, "Virtual Worlds."

34. Consalvo, "There Is No Magic Circle."

35. Thaddeus Griebel, "Self-Portrayal in a Simulated Life: Projecting Personality and Values in *The Sims 2*," *Game Studies: The International Journal of Computer Game Research* 6, no. 1 (2006), http://gamestudies.org/0601/articles/griebel. Also see Robert Andrew Dunn and Rosanna E. Guadagno, "My Avatar and Me—Gender and Personality Predictors of Avatar-Self Discrepancy," *Computers in Human Behavior* 28, no. 1 (2012): 97–106. This study is more nuanced, but it shows that at least some people choose avatars that are similar to themselves.

36. Griebel, "Self-Portrayal." Again, also see Dunn and Guadagno, "My Avatar and Me."

37. Yasmin B. Kafai, Deborah A. Fields, and Melissa S. Cook, "Your Second Selves," *Games and Culture* 5, no. 1 (January 2010): 23–42.

38. Ben DeVane and Kurt D. Squire, "The Meaning of Race and Violence in *Grand Theft Auto*," *Games and Culture* 3, no. 3–4 (July 2008): 264–85.

39. Gary Alan Fine, *Shared Fantasy: Role-Playing Games as Social Worlds* (Chicago: University of Chicago Press, 1983), 181–204. Similarly, Gordon Calleja has identified six different "modes of involvement" in playing games, such as "spatial involvement" or "narrative involvement," each of which operates differently in the short term and long term: "Digital Game Involvement," *Games and Culture* 2, no. 3 (July 2007): 236–60.

40. Sicart, *The Ethics of Computer Games*, 34–35.

41. 1 Cor. 10:23–33.

Chapter 5 Escape!

1. Amanda Chan, "Man Dies after Three-Day Video Game Binge," *Fox News*, February 22, 2011, http://www.foxnews.com/scitech/2011/02/22/chinese-man-dies-day-gaming-binge/.

2. "Helen's All Thumbs," *Martha Speaks*, season 1, episode 30, produced by Sarah Wall (Boston: WGBH Boston, Studio B Productions, 2009), television. The vocabulary words for the day were: *addict, obsessed, preoccupied, monitor, restraint, hooked, quit, level, rid,* and *break*.

3. Mike Fahey, "I Kept Playing—The Costs of My Gaming Addiction," *Kotaku,* October 19, 2009, http://kotaku.com/5384643/i-kept-playing--the-costs-of-my-gaming-addiction. Also see Elizabeth Marsh, "Gaming Addictions: Adverse Interaction," *The Escapist Magazine*, March 24, 2009, 3, http://www.escapistmagazine.com/articles/view/issues/issue_194/5886-Adverse-Interaction.

4. On-Line Gamers Anonymous is at http://olganon.org/ and WoW Detox is at http://www.wowdetox.com/.

5. Josh Lowensohn, "Virtual Farm Games Absorb Real Money, Real Lives," *CNET*, August 27, 2010, http://news.cnet.com/8301-27076_3-20014817-248.html?tag=topTechContentWrap;editor Picks#ixzz0yInTONQU.

6. Liana B. Baker, "Zynga Draws Fewer Paid Players Than Expected," *Reuters*, August 11, 2011, http://www.reuters.com/article/2011/08/11/us-zynga-idUSTRE77A6RL20110811.

7. Chris Morrison, "Super Whales: Top Social Game Spenders Pay More than $10,000 Apiece for Virtual Goods," *Inside Social Games*, June 10, 2010, http://www.insidesocialgames.com/2010/06/10/super-whales-spend-money-virtual-goods/. Also see Knowlton Thomas, "The Art of Social Gaming Monetization: It's All about Fostering the Whales," *Techvibes*, July 25, 2011, http://www.techvibes.com/blog/the-art-of-social-gaming-monetization-its-all-about-fostering-the-whales-2011-07-25.

8. John Hopson, "Behavioral Game Design," *Gamasutra*, April 27, 2001, http://www.gamasutra.com/view/feature/3085/behavioral_game_design.php?page=1; Nick Yee, "The Virtual Skinner Box," accessed September 20, 2011, http://www.nickyee.com/eqt/skinner.html.

9. Chris Birke, "Ethos before Analytics," *Gamasutra*, September 15, 2011, http://www.gamasutra.com/view/feature/6487/ethos_before_analytics.php; Hopson, "Behavioral Game Design."

10. See Mihály Csíkszentmihályi, *Flow: The Psychology of Optimal Experience* (New York: HarperCollins, 1991).

11. Katie Salen and Eric Zimmerman, *Rules of Play: Game Design Fundamentals* (Cambridge, MA: MIT Press, 2004), 350–52. Jenova Chen did his MFA thesis on flow ("Flow in Games" [University of Southern California, 2006], http://www.jenovachen.com/flowingames/thesis.htm) and turned it into a popular indie game called (naturally) *flOw* (available online at http://www.xgenstudios.com/play/flow). His wonderful PlayStation 3 game *Flower* employs many of the same design principles.

12. Nick Yee, "Attraction Factors," accessed September 20, 2011, http://www.nickyee.com/hub/addiction/attraction.html.

13. Daniel L. King, Paul H. Delfabbro, and Mark D. Griffiths, "Recent Innovations in Video Game Addiction Research and Theory," *Global Media Journal: Australian Edition* 4, no. 1 (June 2010): 4; Richard T. A. Wood, "Problems with the Concept of Video Game 'Addiction': Some Case Study Examples," *International Journal of Mental Health and Addiction* 6, no. 2 (2008): 170.

14. When writing this sentence, I was unconsciously echoing a line from Tolkien I had just read: "They have become like the things which once attracted us by their glitter, or their colour, or their shape, and we laid hands on them, and then locked them in our hoard, acquired them, and acquiring ceased to look at them." J. R. R. Tolkien, "On Fairy-Stories," in *The Monsters and the Critics and Other Essays*, ed. Christopher Tolkien (London: George Allen & Unwin, 1983), 146. He was not talking about hoarding *things*, but experiences—we'll get to these arguments in just a few pages.

15. Kris Graft, "Analysis: The Psychology Behind Item Collecting and Achievement Hoarding," *Gamasutra*, May 29, 2009, http://www.gamasutra.com/php-bin/news_index.php?story=23724.

16. Fahey, "I Kept Playing"; Yee, "Attraction Factors."

17. Wood, "Problems with the Concept"; Nigel E. Turner, "A Comment on 'Problems with the Concept of Video Game "Addiction": Some Case Study Examples,'" *International Journal of Mental Health and Addiction* 6, no. 2 (2008): 186–90; Alex Blaszczynski, "Commentary: A Response to 'Problems with the Concept of Video Game "Addiction": Some Case Study Examples,'" *International Journal of Mental Health and Addiction* 6, no. 2 (2008): 179–81; Mark D. Griffiths, "Videogame Addiction: Further Thoughts and Observations," *International Journal of Mental Health and Addiction* 6, no. 2 (2008): 182–85; Richard T. A. Wood, "A Response to Blaszczynski, Griffiths and Turners' Comments on the Paper 'Problems with the Concept of Video Game "Addiction": Some Case Study Examples' (This Issue)," *International Journal of Mental Health and Addiction* 6, no. 2 (2008): 191–93.

18. Doug Hyun Han, Jun Won Hwang, and Perry F. Renshaw, "Bupropion Sustained Release Treatment Decreases Craving for Video Games and Cue-Induced Brain Activity in Patients with Internet Video Game Addiction," *Psychology of Popular Media Culture* 1 (August 2011): 108–17.

19. Lowensohn, "Virtual Farm Games."

20. Also see Mark Griffiths, "The Role of Context in Online Gaming Excess and Addiction: Some Case Study Evidence," *International Journal of Mental Health and Addiction* 8, no. 1 (January 2010): 119–25.

21. King, Delfabbro, and Griffiths, "Recent Innovations."

22. Fahey, "I Kept Playing."

23. Rob Cover, "Digital Addiction: The Cultural Production of Online and Video Game Junkies," *Media International Australia Incorporating Culture & Policy*, no. 113 (November 2004): 110–23.

24. Erin Hoffman, "Life, Addictive Game Mechanics, and the Truth Hiding in *Bejeweled*," *Gamasutra*, September 16, 2009, http://www.gamasutra.com/blogs/ErinHoffman/20090916/3065/Life_Addictive_Game_Mechanics_And_The_Truth_Hiding_In_Bejeweled.php.

25. Sabine M. Grüsser, Ralf Thalemann, and Mark D. Griffiths, "Excessive Computer Game Playing: Evidence for Addiction and Aggression?," *CyberPsychology & Behavior* 10, no. 2 (April 2007): 290–92; Naomi J. Thomas and Frances Heritage Martin, "Video-Arcade Game, Computer Game and Internet Activities of Australian Students: Participation Habits and Prevalence of Addiction," *Australian Journal of Psychology* 62, no. 2 (July 2010): 59–66.

26. Salen and Zimmerman, *Rules of Play*, 355–56.

27. Belinda Luscombe, "*FarmVille* Social Game Maker Zynga Faces Trouble," *Time*, November 30, 2009, http://www.time.com/time/magazine/article/0,9171,1940668,00.html.

28. Tolkien, "On Fairy-Stories," 140–42; C. S. Lewis, "On Stories," in *C. S. Lewis: Essay Collection and Other Short Pieces*, ed. L. Walmsley (London: HarperCollins, 2000), 493.

29. Turning to a random page in my copy of the book, King Theoden confronts the wicked Saruman: "Even if your war on me was just—as it was not, for were you ten times as wise you would have no right to rule me and mine for your own profit as you desired—even so, what will you say of your torches in Westfold and the children that lie dead there?" Try reading *that* out loud. J. R. R. Tolkien, *The Lord of the Rings* (London: HarperCollins, 1991), 603.

30. Andrew Rilstone, "How to Misread *The Lord of the Rings*," accessed December 9, 2011, http://www.rilstone.talktalk.net/misreading-LOTR.htm.

31. Tolkien, "On Fairy-Stories," 145.

32. Rilstone, "How to Misread"; Tolkien, "On Fairy-Stories." For his discussion of primary and secondary worlds, see 132. For the bit about the importance of internal consistency in fantasy worlds, see 138–39.

33. Tolkien, "On Fairy-Stores," 153.

34. C. S. Lewis, "Tolkien's *The Lord of the Rings*," in Walmsley, *Lewis*, 519–25.

35. Tolkien, "On Fairy-Stories," 147.

36. Ibid., 144.

37. Ibid., 148.

38. Lewis, "On Stories," 493.

39. Tolkien, "On Fairy-Stories," 141–42.

40. Henry Jenkins, "Game Design as Narrative Architecture," in *First Person: New Media as Story, Performance, and Game*, ed. Noah Wardrip-Fruin and Pat Harrigan (Cambridge, MA: MIT Press, 2004), 118–30.

41. Lewis, "On Stories," 491–504.

42. Jenkins, "Game Design."

43. Note that this is not as much a limitation of books in general, as encyclopedias and almanacs are all text but well suited to jumping around.

44. Alex Wainer, "The Discarding Image: The Diminishing of the Mythic in the Cinematic Adaptation of *The Fellowship of the Ring*" (paper presented at the National Communication Association convention, New Orleans, LA, November 2002).

45. C. S. Lewis, "Learning in War-Time," in Walmsley, *Lewis*, 579.

46. Ibid., 582.

47. Ibid., 580.

Chapter 6 Real Men, Real Women, Unreal Games

1. And they participate in other ways too. At a big gaming convention such as the massive PAX (see chap. 9), many women now attend, and not just as "booth-babe" models hired to attract attention to specific products.

2. A book with a good explanation *and* critique of the distinction is Mary Stewart Van Leeuwen, *Gender & Grace: Love, Work & Parenting in a Changing World* (Downers Grove, IL: InterVarsity, 1990), 53–54.

3. Michael Kimmel, *Manhood in America: A Cultural History* (New York: Free Press, 1996). This book spends a significant amount of time discussing Robert Bly's *Iron John: A Book about Men* (New York: Vintage Books, 1990), a popular book that sought to recapture the essential masculinity Bly believes men have lost today. While such literature does pretty good business, and some people clearly spend a lot of time with it, most people don't spend that much time engaging gender topics so bluntly.

4. Gail Bederman, *Manliness and Civilization: A Cultural History of Gender and Race in the United States, 1880–1917* (Chicago: University of Chicago Press, 1995); Susan Douglas, *Listening In: Radio and the Imagination, from Amos 'n Andy and Edward R. Murrow to Wolfman Jack and Howard Stern* (New York: Times Books, 1999).

5. Woody Register, *The Kid of Coney Island: Fred Thompson and the Rise of American Amusements* (Oxford: Oxford University Press, 2001); Woody Register, "Everyday Peter Pans: Work, Manhood, and Consumption in Urban America, 1900–1930," in *Boys and Their Toys? Masculinity, Technology, and Class in America*, ed. Roger Horowitz (New York: Routledge, 2001), 199–228.

6. It's important to realize that the ideals just listed are simply one set of terms used to describe and organize things that aren't so neat in real life. Nobody ever says "if you want to be a roughly masculine man, act like so-and-so." What this means is that someone else could look at exactly the same stuff (movies, husband/wife conversations, or purchasing patterns—whatever it is we're studying) and come up with different descriptions. A good example would be Michael Kimmel's excellent *Manhood in America*, which develops the ideal of the

"self-made man," something of a hybrid of the respectable and rough men described here. Using such admittedly subjective terms is still helpful because it gives us language to talk about social and cultural stuff that most of us experience or are familiar with but rarely articulate.

7. Douglas, *Listening In*.

8. Roos Vonk and Richard D. Ashmore produce a very interesting list of common gender stereotypes, including variations of the ones I just listed, in "Thinking about Gender Types: Cognitive Organization of Female and Male Types," *British Journal of Social Psychology* 42, no. 2 (June 2003): 257.

9. See, for example, the commentary from this online mini-documentary on *Metroid*: "The *Metroid* Retrospective—Part 1," *GameTrailers*, accessed July 6, 2010, http://www.gametrail ers.com/video/part-1-the-metroid/22771 (the most relevant discussion comes at around 4:30).

10. We don't have space to discuss at any length *why* this was the case. The short version: the game industry was born in the midst of cultures that were overwhelmingly male, such as 1960s and '70s hacker/enthusiast groups and computer-research facilities (largely funded by the military and big academic organizations). With a few very notable exceptions, the *vast* majority of early game makers were men, and while the numbers have shifted a little, women are still underrepresented, especially in the core parts of the game production process (see Adam Gourdin, *Game Developer Demographics: An Exploration of Workforce Diversity*, report for the International Game Developer's Association [2005], http://archives.igda.org/diversity/ IGDA_DeveloperDemographics_Oct05.pdf).

11. This is my rewrite of a widely used T-shirt/bumper sticker slogan parodying Army recruitment taglines.

12. Henry Jenkins, "'Complete Freedom of Movement': Video Games as Gendered Play Spaces," in *From Barbie to Mortal Kombat: Gender and Computer Games*, ed. Justine Cassell and Henry Jenkins (Cambridge, MA: MIT Press, 1998), 262–97.

13. Take, for example, a widely quoted passage from Aristotle: "Woman is more compassionate than man, more easily moved to tears, at the same time is more jealous, more querulous, more apt to scold and to strike. She is, furthermore, more prone to despondency and less hopeful than the man, more void of shame or self-respect, more false of speech, more deceptive, and of more retentive memory. She is also more wakeful, more shrinking, more difficult to rouse to action." *The History of Animals*, trans. D'Arcy Wentworth Thompson, Book IX, Part 1, http:// classics.mit.edu/Aristotle/history_anim.9.ix.html.

14. Dmitri Williams et al., "The Virtual Census: Representations of Gender, Race and Age in Video Games," *New Media & Society* 11, no. 5 (August 2009): 815–34.

15. Nicole Martins et al., "A Content Analysis of Female Body Imagery in Video Games," *Sex Roles* 61, no. 11 (December 2009): 824–36.

16. A good illustration of the masculine culture of the game industry is that the princess, Daphne, was modeled after *Playboy* centerfolds. See: "*Dragon's Lair*—Videogame by Cinematronics," *Killer List of Video Games*, accessed July 28, 2010, http://www.arcade-museum .com/game_detail.php?game_id=7647.

17. Essay copyright by Janelle Weibelzahl, 2013. Used with permission.

18. This was already the case over a decade ago. See Henry Jenkins, ed., "Voices from the Combat Zone: Game Grrlz Talk Back," in *From Barbie to Mortal Kombat*, 329–41. Current women gaming groups include an interesting blend of stereotypically masculine and feminine language: the PMS Clan (http://www.pmsclan.com/), the Gamer Grrlz blog (http://www.gamer grrlz.net/), and the semi-professional Frag Doll team (http://www.fragdolls.com/).

19. And Eowyn of *The Lord of the Rings*. And the original Valkyrie of Viking legends. Or the Amazons of Greek myth. This trope has been around the block. But it wasn't a *standard* part of mainstream gaming culture until *Tomb Raider*, I'd argue.

20. Some claim that super-hot characters are a healthy expression of women taking charge of their sexuality and sexual power. One commentator, for example, argues that the over-the-top sex appeal of the title character in *Bayonetta* is an empowering thing. See Leigh Alexander, "Bayonetta: Empowering or Exploitative?," *Gamepro*, January 6, 2010, http://web .archive.org/web/20110607152912/http://www.gamepro.com/article/features/213466/bayonetta -empowering-or-exploitative/.

21. There is a truly astonishing list of Barbie games published over the years at game-history database MobyGames: http://www.mobygames.com/game-group/barbie-licensees.

22. Isabel Reynolds, "Japan Picks Schoolgirl among Cute Ambassadors," *Reuters*, March 12, 2009, http://uk.reuters.com/article/idUKTRE52B4JC20090312.

23. Yes, Sims *can* get in fights, but we really don't see it (it's represented by a cartoony cloud), and it takes some work to make it happen. And our Sims can die if we neglect them. But there's no murdering, conquering, beating, etc.

24. For those who are heavy gamers, yes, we can find plenty of the jagged, ripped aesthetic I identify as traditional. And the clean cute look has always been around—especially in Japanese games. We've always been able to find this if we wanted. I'm simply arguing that the mainstream has shifted.

25. There are a few games that still use fixed gender—the 2005 version of *Sid Meier's Pirates!* is notable for insisting that the main character is a man even though he is somewhat customizable and not a well-developed franchise character like Kratos of the *God of War* games.

26. All of these reasons were mentioned by participants in a recent study on gender swapping in MMOGs: Zaheer Hussain and Mark D. Griffiths, "Gender Swapping and Socializing in Cyberspace: An Exploratory Study," *CyberPsychology & Behavior* 11, no. 1 (February 2008): 47–53. Interestingly, over half of the people in the study had played characters of the other gender, a number confirmed by an earlier study: Mark D. Griffiths, Mark N. O. Davies, and Darren Chappell, "Demographic Factors and Playing Variables in Online Computer Gaming," *CyberPsychology & Behavior* 7, no. 4 (August 2004): 479–87.

27. This is originally from a cartoon by Peter Steiner published in the *New Yorker* magazine on July 5, 1993.

28. See, for example, Daniel M. Doriani, *Women and Ministry: What the Bible Teaches* (Wheaton: Crossway, 2003); John MacArthur, *Different by Design* (Wheaton: Victor Books, 1994).

29. See Lev. 20:10 and Deut. 22:22. Note that actually both the adulterers are to be killed, but by Jesus's day, it is unremarkable that only a woman would be brought forward to be killed (John 7:53–8:11), as happens today in places like Iran. A more clearly one-sided rule is found earlier in Deuteronomy 22, wherein if a husband of a supposed virgin can prove that she was not a virgin on their marriage night, she will be stoned to death—and here it's only the woman who pays the price (vv. 13–21). Of course, in the name of forgiveness, Jesus disapproves of the stoning of the adulteress, and some might cite this as clear proof that the older standards no longer apply. I would certainly agree with this argument, but the point is that these troubling passages are clearly part of the biblical tradition on appropriate gender standards. We can't *simply* observe biblical traditions when it comes to gender.

30. On silence in church, see 1 Tim. 2:11–12 (but read the whole chapter for some context). On head coverings, see 1 Cor. 11:2–16.

31. Judg. 4.

32. For example, see John 20:10–18. N. T. Wright makes this argument in *The Resurrection of the Son of God* (Minneapolis: Fortress, 2003).

33. Barbara Ehrenreich, *The Hearts of Men: American Dreams and the Flight from Commitment* (New York: Anchor Books, 1983).

34. One could argue that this is a description of video games in general and not just limited to male game characters. Certainly this is true, but I believe the consequence-free action style is typically more pronounced for male characters, if only because there are so many more men than women in video-game worlds.

35. Yes, we can find exceptions for female characters. But I think it's a fair rule in traditional video games. Not so much for the newer mass-appeal games.

36. As they should be, of course, in other media, such as magazines, film, and television.

Chapter 7 The School of Mario

1. Mark Driscoll, "The Cost of Discipleship" (Seattle: Mars Hill Church, February 20, 2011), http://marshill.com/media/luke/the-cost-of-discipleship, online video of sermon.

2. Blake Snow, "Why Most People Don't Finish Video Games," *CNN*, August 17, 2011, http://articles.cnn.com/2011-08-17/tech/finishing.videogames.snow_1_red-dead-redemption -entertainment-software-association-avid-gamers?_s=PM:TECH.

3. Mark Bauerlein, *The Dumbest Generation: How the Digital Age Stupefies Young Americans and Jeopardizes our Future (Or, Don't Trust Anyone Under 30)* (New York: Jeremy P. Tarcher/Penguin, 2008), 10.

4. Susan D. Jacoby, *The Age of American Unreason* (New York: Pantheon Books, 2008).

5. Bauerlein, *The Dumbest Generation*, 17–26.

6. Jacoby, *The Age of American Unreason*, 247.

7. They're hardly alone in this. Another very prominent praise of print culture is Neil Postman's *Amusing Ourselves to Death* (New York: Elizabeth Sifton Books, 1985).

8. Mark Warschauer and Tina Matuchniak, "New Technology and Digital Worlds: Analyzing Evidence of Equity in Access, Use, and Outcomes," *Review of Research in Education* 34, no. 1 (March 2010): 179–225.

9. Kathy Ann Mills, "A Review of the 'Digital Turn' in the New Literacy Studies," *Review of Educational Research* 80, no. 2 (June 1, 2010): 246–71.

10. C. Scott Rigby and Andrew K. Przybylski, "Virtual Worlds and the Learner Hero," *Theory and Research in Education* 7, no. 2 (July 2009): 214–23.

11. James P. Gee, *What Video Games Have to Teach Us about Learning and Literacy*, 2nd ed. (New York: Palgrave Macmillan, 2007); Sasha A. Barab, Melissa Gresalfi, and Adam Ingram-Goble, "Transformational Play," *Educational Researcher* 39, no. 7 (October 1, 2010): 525–36.

12. Will Wright, "Dream Machines: Will Wright Explains How Games Are Unleashing the Human Imagination," *Wired*, April 2006, 110. Also see Steven Johnson, *Everything Bad Is Good for You: How Today's Popular Culture Is Actually Making Us Smarter* (New York: Riverhead Books, 2005).

13. Gee, *What Video Games*, 59.

14. Johnson, *Everything Bad Is Good*; Jane McGonigal, *Reality Is Broken: Why Games Make Us Better and How They Can Change the World* (New York: Penguin, 2011); Katie Salen and Eric Zimmerman, *Rules of Play: Game Design Fundamentals* (Cambridge, MA: MIT Press, 2004).

15. Gee, *What Video Games*.

16. McGonigal, *Reality Is Broken*, 125.

17. Ibid., 98.

18. Ibid., 133–42.

19. Leslie Horn, "Gamers Unlock Protein Mystery That Baffled AIDS Researchers For Years," *PCMag*, September 19, 2011, http://www.pcmag.com/article2/0,2817,2393200,00.asp. Also see: John Timmer, "Crowd-sourced biotech: gamers tweak protein, give it big activity boost,"

Ars Technica, January 24, 2012, http://arstechnica.com/science/news/2012/01/crowdsourced
-biotechnology-foldit-gamers-make-a-custom-protein.ars.

20. Johnson, *Everything Bad Is Good*.

21. Jacoby, *The Age of American Unreason*, 252.

22. Bauerlein, *The Dumbest Generation*, 93–94.

23. Gen. 4:20–22 talks about the creators of certain technologies, and multiple passages in Joshua and Judges mention the challenge of facing cultures with iron chariots (e.g., Josh. 17:12–18). Clearly these passages are historically significant, since they demonstrate an awareness of what tools can do for humans, but their theological significance is much less clear. Notably, the prophets don't criticize the Israelites for adopting the technologies of their neighbors (agricultural practices, iron tools, and so on) but for taking up their religions.

24. A popular and accessible Christian book on the ideas of media ecology is Shane A. Hipps, *The Hidden Power of Electronic Culture: How Media Shapes Faith, the Gospel, and Church* (Grand Rapids: Zondervan, 2005). Neil Postman also does a good job of explaining media ecology in accessible language in both *Technopoly: The Surrender of Culture to Technology* (New York: Vintage Books, 1993) and *Amusing Ourselves to Death*. A more scholarly but still readable and fascinating book that is less techno-pessimistic is Joshua Meyrowitz, *No Sense of Place: The Impact of Electronic Media on Social Behavior* (Oxford: Oxford University Press, 1985).

25. The most accessible examples I know are: Postman, *Technopoly* and *Amusing Ourselves to Death*. One of the more profound critiques of technology that I know (although not directly about media and very hard to read) is Jacques Ellul, *The Presence of the Kingdom*, trans. Olive Wyon (New York: Seabury, 1967).

26. Postman, *Amusing Ourselves to Death*, 29.

27. See ibid., 25–26, for a far more eloquent and in-depth consideration of this.

28. See, for example, Steve Lohr, "Slow Down, Brave Multitasker, and Don't Read This in Traffic," *New York Times*, March 25, 2007, http://www.nytimes.com/2007/03/25/business/25multi .html?ex=1332475200&en=f2; Michael L. Waterston, "The Techno-Brain," *Generations* 35, no. 2 (Summer 2011): 77–82; Theodore S. Smith et al., "Effects of Cell-Phone and Text-Message Distractions on True and False Recognition," *CyberPsychology, Behavior & Social Networking* 14, no. 6 (June 2011): 351–58.

29. Gee, *What Video Games*.

30. Marshall McLuhan's *The Gutenberg Galaxy* (Toronto, Canada: University of Toronto Press, 1962) often addresses this topic. McLuhan is often cryptic and hard to understand, but here's one sample quote from the book that is critical of print culture: "The print-made split between head and heart is the trauma which affects Europe from Machiavelli till the present" (170).

31. The writer of Ecclesiastes warns "Do not say, 'Why were the old days better than these?'" (7:10 NIV), which would seem to indicate people were complaining about decline thousands of years ago! Also, see notes 15 and 16 from chap. 1.

32. Janet H. Murray, *Hamlet on the Holodeck: The Future of Narrative in Cyberspace* (Cambridge, MA: MIT Press, 1997).

33. This is not to say that oral communication or storytelling is completely unsystematic. Even improvisational storytelling or theater relies on our cultural knowledge and our language skills, which means we don't create *ex nihilo*. But the restrictions of culture and language are present in the creation of video games, in addition to the other restrictions of game rules and programming requirements.

34. See, for example, Wiebe Bijker, "Sociohistorical Technology Studies," in *Handbook of Science and Technology Studies*, ed. S. Jasanoff et al. (London: Sage, 1995), 229–56; Bruno Latour, *Aramis, Or the Love of Technology* (Cambridge, MA: Harvard University Press, 1996).

Chapter 8 Making a Different World

1. This event is legendary, so it's easy to find an account. Here's just one of many: Steven L. Kent, *The Ultimate History of Video Games: From Pong to Pokemon and Beyond—The Story Behind the Craze That Touched Our Lives and Changed the World* (Roseville, CA: Prima, 2001), 237–40.

2. David Kushner, *Masters of Doom: How Two Guys Created an Empire and Transformed Pop Culture* (New York: Random House, 2003).

3. ea_spouse, "EA: The Human Story," *Livejournal* (blog), November 10, 2004, http://ea-spouse.livejournal.com/274.html; David Jenkins, "Programmers Win EA Overtime Settlement, EA_Spouse Revealed," *Gamasutra*, April 26, 2006, http://www.gamasutra.com/php-bin/news_index.php?story=9051. As proof that these issues aren't going away, see a more recent example of exactly the same thing: Chris Remo, "Controversy Erupts Over Rockstar San Diego Employee Allegations," *Gamasutra*, January 13, 2010, http://www.gamasutra.com/view/news/26803/Controversy_Erupts_Over_Rockstar_San_Diego_Employee_Allegations.php.

4. Nolan Bushnell and Ted Dabney both put in $250 to found Atari in 1972. In 1976, they sold it to Warner for $28 million. By 1980, sales of Atari's home console (the VCS, later called the 2600) were almost $2 billion per year. The American video-game market cratered in 1983 and Atari lost almost a half billion dollars in the second quarter of 1984. Warner sold off most of the company that year, and within a few more years Atari had ceased to be a truly functioning company. Again, see Kent, *The Ultimate History*.

5. David Sheff, *Game Over: How Nintendo Zapped an American Industry, Captured Your Dollars, and Enslaved Your Children* (New York: Random House, 1993), 213–16.

6. Frank Cifaldi, "World of Warcraft Loses Another 800K Subs In Three Months," *Gamasutra*, November 8, 2011, http://www.gamasutra.com/view/news/38460/World_of_Warcraft_Loses_Another_800K_Subs_In_Three_Months.php.

7. It's also worth noting that shareware models were very popular in the 1980s and '90s: customers got the game for free but the maker asked for a donation if they liked it, or they got the game for free but they needed to pay to unlock advanced content.

8. Greg Tito, "Angry Birds Downloaded Half a Billion Times," *The Escapist Magazine*, November 2, 2011, http://www.escapistmagazine.com/news/view/113996-Angry-Birds-Downloaded-Half-a-Billion-Times.

9. See, for example, the very entertaining and informative video "Working Conditions," *Extra Credits*, season 3, episode 15, created by James Portnow, Daniel Floyd, and Etienne Vanier (Penny Arcade TV, 2011), http://penny-arcade.com/patv/episode/working-conditions, online video. It's inspired by the people at Nine Dots studio: Guillaume Boucher-Vidal, "Extra Credits Episode on Working Conditions Is Out!," *Nine Dots* (blog), November 2, 2011, http://ninedots studio.com/2011/11/02/extra-credits-episode-on-working-conditions-is-out/. The developers I interviewed said many of the same things.

10. Webcomic *The Trenches* (http://trenchescomic.com/) has two anonymous posts per week about the idiosyncrasies of working in the industry, and I think they're a fantastic view inside. Keep in mind, however, that it tends to be a gripe box, and as one poster mentioned, the industry is not *all* doom and gloom!

11. I should clarify that in this chapter, I'm focusing only on game makers themselves, because that's who I interviewed. The manufacturing of consoles and other computer equipment, however, is also important. A great deal of gaming hardware is made in the developing world, and many of the factories have terrible working conditions featuring long hours, abusive managers, and unsafe work environments. These issues deserve more attention—another topic for a future book. For now, here are a couple of good starting points: Päivi Pöyhönen and Debby Chan Sze Wan, *Game Console and Music Player Production in China: A Follow-Up Report on*

Four Suppliers, report for Finnwatch, SACOM and SOMO (February 11, 2011), http://makeitfair
.org/the-facts/reports/game-console-and-music-player-production-in-china; Charles Kernaghan,
*China's Youth Meet Microsoft: KYE Factory in China Produces for Microsoft and Other U.S.
Companies*, report for National Labor Committee (Pittsburgh, PA, April 2010), http://www
.globallabourrights.org/admin/reports/files/Chinas_Youth_Meet_Micro.pdf.

12. Of course, "*can* promote properly" is not the same thing as "*will* promote properly." For
a wide variety of reasons, major publishers sometimes do a poor job of promoting even games
they have made! See, for example, Greg Costikyan, "Death to the Games Industry, Part I," *The
Escapist Magazine,* August 30, 2005, http://www.escapistmagazine.com/articles/view/issues/
issue_8/50-Death-to-the-Games-Industry-Part-I.

13. EA put some quality-of-life policies into place following the public shaming by ea_spouse;
see Paul Hyman, "'EA_Spouse' Hoffman: Quality Of Life Still Issue, Despite EA Improvement,"
Gamasutra, May 13, 2008, http://www.gamasutra.com/view/news/18621/EASpouse_Hoffman
_Quality_Of_Life_Still_Issue_Despite_EA_Improvement.php. The Rockstar complaints of
2010, however, demonstrate that big companies don't *have* to treat their employees well; see
Remo, "Controversy Erupts."

14. This was pretty much what Brock Henderson said to me in our interview, bits of which
we'll discuss in the subsequent parts of the chapter.

15. This is true of Christian bookstores just as much as of mainline retailers.

16. To be clear, in no way is he suggesting that games are an appropriate substitute for
the Bible.

17. In this part of our discussion, Priebe cited *VeggieTales* creator Phil Vischer's *Me, Myself,
and Bob: A True Story about Dreams, God, and Talking Vegetables* (Nashville: Thomas Nelson,
2006) as an inspiration.

Chapter 9 Plays Well with Others

1. A small part of me is still irked that we PC gamers have lost that terminological battle.

2. There are lots of places to find information on this—just go to the websites (and especially
forums) of the major games like *WoW* or *Aion* or *RuneScape* to see it firsthand. For an interesting
read about MMOs, see the interesting, albeit dangerously utopian, Edward Castronova, *Exodus to
the Virtual World: How Online Fun Is Changing Reality* (New York: Palgrave MacMillan, 2007).

3. Big MMOs such as *WoW* may have millions of subscribers, but they have many different
servers, so we never have literally millions of people playing together.

4. Although this is not invariably the case, many game makers encourage modding. Some
even release editing programs that make modding very easy, such as the *Elder Scrolls Construction Set* for *Elder Scrolls: Oblivion.*

5. Kyle Orland, "Protests Over Ending of *Mass Effect 3* Show Fan Investment in Story
Control," *Ars Technica,* March 12, 2012, http://arstechnica.com/gaming/news/2012/03/protests
-over-ending-of-mass-effect-3-show-fan-investment-in-story-control.ars; Kyle Orland, "Bio-
Ware Responds to Mass Effect Ending Complaints as Protest Continues to Grow," *Ars Technica,* March 19, 2012, http://arstechnica.com/gaming/news/2012/03/bioware-responds-to
-mass-effect-ending-complaints-as-protest-continues-to-grow.ars; Ben Kuchera, "Mass Effect
Retaken: Bioware Described Extra Ending Content at Surprisingly Positive PAX East Panel,"
Penny Arcade Report, April 11, 2012, http://penny-arcade.com/report/editorial-article/mass
-effect-retaken-bioware-described-extra-ending-content-at-surprisingly-.

6. See, for example, 3 Day Respawn (http://www.3dayrespawn.com/), Everyday Gamers
(http://everydaygamers.com/), Gamechurch (http://gamechurch.com, discussed in more detail
later), Hardcore Christian Gamer (http://www.christian-gaming.com), and Christ and Pop
Culture (http://www.christandpopculture.com).

7. "Welcome to the Forgiven—New Members Package," *The Forgiven* (website), (2010), http://files1.guildlaunch.net/guild/library/126831/Welcome%20to%20The%20Forgiven.pdf.

8. Drew Dixon, "Videogames, Bibles, and Beer: An Interview with Gamechurch," *Christ and Pop Culture*, October 24, 2011, http://www.christandpopculture.com/featured/videogames-bibles-and-beer-an-interview-with-game-church/.

9. Ibid.

10. Kevin Schut, "Evangelicals and Video Games," in *Evangelicals and Popular Culture*, ed. Robert H. Woods (Santa Barbara, CA: Praeger, 2012); Kevin Schut, "Evangelicals' Quest to Find God's Place in Games," in *Understanding Evangelical Media: The Changing Face of Christian Communication*, ed. Quentin J. Schultze and Robert H. Woods (Downers Grove, IL: IVP Academic, 2007), 198–209.

11. It almost goes without saying that there are a lot of gamers under the age of sixteen. But either they are not part of these communities (which is likely since children tend to play different kinds of games, especially online) or they didn't take the survey (which is also likely, as the survey indicates that participants under eighteen need parental approval).

12. "The Cross-Platform Report," *Nielsen*, 2012, http://nielsen.com/us/en/insights/reports-downloads/2012/the-cross-platform-report-q4-2011.html.

13. The classic work on this is Ferdinand Tönniës, *Community and Society (Gemeinschaft Und Gesellschaft)*, trans. Charles P. Loomis (London: Transaction, 1988). Tönniës, writing in German, uses the word *Gesellschaft* (typically translated as "society") to denote the loose modern bonds of classical liberal society, bonds based on self-interested social contracts. He uses the word *Gemeinschaft* (usually translated "community") to describe the blood bonds of kinship in the medieval village.

14. Any name in this chapter is a "screen name" (the name they choose in games or on game forums), and I am using it with permission. All quotations are also used with permission.

15. A classic example of this is the now-legendary (in game culture, anyway) clip of Leeroy Jenkins, an over-eager *WoW* warrior who decides to charge headfirst into combat before the raid leader finishes detailing the strategy. Even if it's a faked setup, it's pretty amusing: "Leeroy Jenkins," YouTube video, posted by pj007101, August 6, 2006, http://www.youtube.com/watch?v=LkCNJRfSZBU.

16. More precisely, the game had the player take the role of an undercover antiterrorist agent who had to do awful things to convince a terrorist organization that he was with them.

17. For a thorough and thought-provoking analysis of the challenges of developing community online, see, Quentin J. Schultze, *Habits of the High-Tech Heart: Living Virtuously in the Information Age* (Grand Rapids: Baker Books, 2002), 165–88.

18. This was very clearly illustrated by a posting on the webcomic site Penny Arcade, where the writer Tycho, who is hardly a paragon of genteel language and mild manners himself ("I offend people more or less for a living," he explained in the post), complained about the rank horror of the conversation that goes on in *Modern Warfare* games. Tycho, "Thank You, Edgar," *Penny Arcade* (blog), November 11, 2011, http://penny-arcade.com/2011/11/11.

Chapter 10 Do You Want to Continue Playing?

1. "Gamechurch Co-Op: Episode 5, E3 Special," *Gamechurch* (2011), http://gamechurch.com/co-op/episode-5-e3-special/, online video.

2. Isa. 43:5 (NKJV).

3. Steven L. Kent, *The Ultimate History of Video Games: From Pong to Pokemon and Beyond—The Story Behind the Craze That Touched Our Lives and Changed the World* (Roseville, CA: Prima, 2001); Brad King and John Borland, *Dungeons and Dreamers: The Rise of*

Computer Game Culture from Geek to Chic (New York: McGraw-Hill/Osborne, 2003); David Kushner, *Masters of Doom: How Two Guys Created an Empire and Transformed Pop Culture* (New York: Random House, 2003); Harold Goldberg, *All Your Base Are Belong to Us: How Fifty Years of Videogames Conquered Pop Culture* (New York: Three Rivers, 2011); Tristan Donovan, *Replay: The History of Video Games* (Lewes, UK: Yellow Ant, 2010); Rusel DeMaria and Johnny L. Wilson, *High Score! The Illustrated History of Electronic Games*, 2nd ed. (New York: McGraw-Hill/Osborne, 2004).

Glossary

adventure games—A very old genre of video games that has the player explore another world, find items, and solve puzzles. In its purest form it has no combat, but there are many hybrids. Prominent examples: the *Monkey Island* games.

anime— Japanese animation, whether for television or movies. Famous examples would include the TV series *Dragonball Z* or Miyazaki's famous *My Neighbor Totoro*. Done in the same artistic style as "manga" (see entry below).

casual games—Any game not aimed at hardcore markets. Typically, this means games that are easy to learn, easy to play, and easy to put down again: the kind of game played while commuting to work or for a study break. Prominent examples: *Angry Birds*, *Bejeweled*, *FreeCell*.

console—A device made for playing video games and marketed as such. Typically, this means full-size devices hooked up to TVs, such as the Xbox 360, but some people include handheld gaming systems such as the Nintendo DS.

cut scene—A noninteractive mini-movie within a video game sandwiched between pieces of gaming action. Typically cut scenes are used to develop a game's story.

developers—People or companies that make video games. This includes designers, artists, programmers, and more.

fighting games—While fighting is part of many games, the fighting *genre* typically features time-limited one-on-one combat, although it may occasionally denote group combat games as well. Prominent examples: the *Street Fighter* games, the *SoulCalibur* games.

first-person shooters—A genre of games where the player visually takes the role of a person moving through an environment and shooting enemies. Typically all we see of the main character is hands and/or a gun, which suggests the player is *in* the game. Prominent examples: the *Doom* series, the *Halo* games, the *Call of Duty* series.

hardcore—This is a flexible term that can describe gamers or games. It connotes challenge, violence, dedication to gaming, aggressiveness, or some combination of all the above.

mages (aka wizards, magic users)—Game characters that use magic.

nanga— Japanese comics, known the world over for their unique artwork and storytelling style. Most Japanese video games use the artistic style of manga (and anime—see entry above).

nedium (plural, media)—Anything that we can use to communicate. That includes tools like phones or televisions, but it can also include institutions (e.g., a production company) and cultural practices (e.g., language).

MMOs (aka Massively Multiplayer Online games)—A genre of games that consist of permanent online worlds that gamers can log onto and play with thousands of other gamers at the same time. Sometimes called MMOGs or MMORPGs. Prominent examples: *World of Warcraft* (aka *WoW*), *Second Life*.

open-world games—A genre of games that creates worlds and then let the player go and do whatever he or she is capable of doing. Many big-budget action games limit where the player can go in order to develop a rather linear story. Open-world games sacrifice the linear story but give the player a great deal of freedom. Prominent examples: *The Elder Scrolls* games, the *Grand Theft Auto* series.

power-ups—Anything a player can pick up in a game that gives special abilities. For example, in the Mario games, certain mushrooms make Mario very large.

publishers—Companies that typically don't *make* games but handle all the support activities necessary to make games such as funding production, managing printing and distribution, and doing the marketing. Game publishers tend to be very large corporations, like EA, Activision, or Nintendo (which is *also* a console designer and manufacturer).

puzzle games—A genre of games that focuses on solving puzzles. They may be action oriented, like *Tetris*, or longer form, like Sudoku puzzles. They are typically relatively simple to learn and don't involve many different screens. The term is sometimes synonymous with "casual games."

RPGs (aka role-playing games)—A genre that gives the player control of a character or a group of characters, which the player uses to complete quests, which then increases the power of the characters. Most RPGs have story lines for the player to complete. A prominent subgenre is Fantasy RPGs, which feature magic and monsters. Prominent examples: the *Fallout* games, the *Dragon Age* series.

sandbox games—Games that don't typically have a win or loss condition—they simply let the player play around. Sometimes described as "toys" rather than games. Prominent examples: the *SimCity* games and other Sim-themed games by Will Wright.

social games—Games played on social networks like Facebook. To this point in time, most of these games are quite simple. Prominent examples: Zynga games (e.g., *FarmVille*, *CityVille*), *The Sims Social*.

sports games—Video-game versions of sports. Prominent examples: EA's *Madden* football series, the *Tony Hawk* skateboarding games.

strategy games—Games that focus on the strategic management of resources and typically focus on military or economic struggle. Turn-based strategy games let the player take as long as necessary, while real-time strategy (RTS) games are more action oriented. Prominent examples: the *Civilization* games (turn-based), the *StarCraft* games (RTS).

worlds—The alternate realities created by games.

Index